WHAT DOES IT MEAN TO BE KAZAKHSTANI?

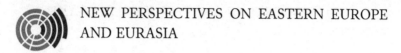# NEW PERSPECTIVES ON EASTERN EUROPE AND EURASIA

The states of Eastern Europe and Eurasia are once again at the centre of global attention, particularly following Russia's 2022 full-scale invasion of Ukraine. But media coverage can only do so much in providing the necessary context to make sense of fast-moving developments. The books in this series provide original, engaging and timely perspectives on Eastern Europe and Eurasia for a general readership. Written by experts on—and from—these states, the books in the series cover an eclectic range of cutting-edge topics relating to politics, history, culture, economics and society. The series is originated by Hurst, with titles co-published or distributed in North America by Oxford University Press, New York.

Series editor: Dr Ben Noble—Associate Professor of Russian Politics at University College London and Associate Fellow at Chatham House

DIANA T. KUDAIBERGEN

What Does It Mean to Be Kazakhstani?

Power, Identity and Nation-Building

OXFORD
UNIVERSITY PRESS

Oxford University Press is a department of the
University of Oxford. It furthers the University's objective
of excellence in research, scholarship, and education
by publishing worldwide.

Oxford New York
Auckland   Cape Town   Dar es Salaam   Hong Kong   Karachi
Kuala Lumpur   Madrid   Melbourne   Mexico City   Nairobi
New Delhi   Shanghai   Taipei   Toronto

With offices in
Argentina   Austria   Brazil   Chile   Czech Republic   France   Greece
Guatemala   Hungary   Italy   Japan   Poland   Portugal   Singapore
South Korea   Switzerland   Thailand   Turkey   Ukraine   Vietnam

Oxford is a registered trade mark of Oxford University Press
in the UK and certain other countries.

Published in the United States of America by
Oxford University Press
198 Madison Avenue, New York, NY 10016

Copyright © Diana T. Kudaibergen, 2025

All rights reserved. No part of this publication may be reproduced,
stored in a retrieval system, or transmitted, in any form or by any means,
without the prior permission in writing of Oxford University Press,
or as expressly permitted by law, by license, or under terms agreed with
the appropriate reproduction rights organization. Inquiries concerning
reproduction outside the scope of the above should be sent to the
Rights Department, Oxford University Press, at the address above.

You must not circulate this work in any other form
and you must impose this same condition on any acquirer.
Library of Congress Cataloging-in-Publication Data is available

ISBN: 9780197820704

Printed in the United Kingdom
by Bell & Bain Ltd, Glasgow

CONTENTS

List of Figures and Tables	vii
Note on Transliteration and Translation	ix
Preface	xi
Introduction	1
1. Kazakhstan: Its History and Its Vocabulary	19
2. The December 1986 Protests in Alma-Ata	59
3. Who are the Fourth *Zhuz*?: On Russians and Kazakhstani Multiculturalism	87
4. *Mankurts* versus *Mambets* (The 'M'-Word): On Divisions and Hybrid Identities	119
5. 'We are the Ordinary People': The January 2022 Protests in Kazakhstan	143
6. The Long Post-January: Forming Civicness	163
Afterword: Decolonising Kazakhstan Starts with De-Nazarbayefication	181
Notes	199
Bibliography	231
Index	241

LIST OF FIGURES AND TABLES

Figures

5.1	Jar with Qantar 2022 donations in an Almaty bar	156
6.1	Lenin statue in Sary-Arka park, Almaty, pro-Ukraine march, 6 March 2022	176
7.1	Saule Suleimenova's *Qandy Qantar* (Bloody January) exhibit	191
7.2	Askhat Akhmediyarov (right) with his *Qandy Qantar* installation	192

Table

2.1	Ethnicity of higher education students in the Kazakh SSR	69

NOTE ON TRANSLITERATION AND TRANSLATION

I use the Library of Congress transliteration for all Russian words and the transliteration provided by the Kazakhstani government in its ongoing efforts to transfer the Qazaq language from the Cyrillic to Latin script for most Kazakh/Qazaq words. Many Russian words are italicised and provided in parentheses after their translation into English in the text. However, for most Qazaq words, I follow the practice of other decolonial scholars in not using italicisation in order to avoid 'exotifying' the language. For Kazakh/Qazaq transliteration, I use 'Kazakh' when citing English- and Russian-language sources, following spelling conventions in both these languages; but I use 'Qazaq' for all sources originally in Qazaq, according to the new and more accurate form of transliteration now used across Kazakhstan/Qazaqstan. As I explain in more detail in Chapter 1, 'Qazaq' and 'Qazaqstan' are also commonly employed by decolonial scholars and activists as an affirmation of Qazaq identity and a rejection of the Russified, colonial past. Readers will therefore note both spellings throughout the text.

All translations from Russian, Qazaq or any other language, including the secondary literature and interview transcriptions and fieldnotes—which I usually keep in several languages—are my own. In the quotes, I sometimes include short words in the original in brackets to note the original sound and pronunciation of specific concepts, words and colloquialisms.

PREFACE

This book is the result of a decade of research into nation-building and the political sociology of power in the independent states of Eurasia,[1] the no-longer-postsoviet states. As I aged and matured, my own field of research and the states where I conducted my fieldwork matured too. My initial question of whether these states can still be considered 'new' was soon followed by another one: Why do we still know so little about these places?

Kazakhstan rarely made headlines in the UK before the January 2022 mass protests known locally as Bloody January or 'Qandy Qantar'. In the numerous interviews I gave during the protests, editors and journalists asked me to give them a 'crash course' on Kazakhstan's history while also explaining the protests' underlying causes. Although the country is as big as the whole of Western Europe, with major oil and gas reserves, has been an independent state for thirty years, with a very long history outside of Russian colonisation, it remained unknown to so many people. I was asked when Kazakhstan gained independence, whether ethnic Russians still outnumbered ethnic Kazakhs and whether there was a chance of an ethnic conflict breaking out.

But above all, I was asked to help make sense of what Kazakhstan is and how to deal with the sudden news emerging out of there, this unknown land with burning cars and dead civilians on the streets. As a scholar who has engaged with the question of nationalism, contentious politics and ethnicity for years, I was at a loss—how could I even begin to simplify the complex social, historical and political relations that had led to the protests? Trying to answer this question served as a learning experience that has hopefully helped me write more clearly and accessibly. But as a citizen, as a Kazakhstani, I also had to deal with my own emotions, which I often felt forced to suppress at the time. Speaking to the press, often not knowing how my own family was doing in Kazakhstan and receiving requests to speak live on air when my country was entering an official day of mourning for the victims, I was visibly nervous and on edge. Was I even the right person to speak up? But my phone was restless, and the questions pouring in ever more demanding. So, I diverted interview requests to the many Kazakhstani activists I was in contact with, having just finished writing a manuscript on protest culture and social movements in Kazakhstan two months prior to the 2022 Bloody January protests.

Still, a lot of interviews and questions landed in my mailbox. Sleepless, anxious and constantly on the phone, I sometimes found answering these questions cathartic—it took my mind off the rather difficult question of whether I'd find some of my friends on the list of Qandy Qantar's victims as soon as this information became available.

Scrolling through my social media feed after the January protests, I could still see people commenting on the Central Asian states who were unable to view the region outside the Russian gaze or outside of terms like 'Russia's backyard' or 'Russia's underbelly'.[2] In these reports, Central Asia, let alone the countries of Central Asia—Kazakhstan, Turkmenistan, Uzbekistan, Kyrgyzstan and Tajikistan—has no agency. The region only seems to exist when understood as part of Russia's sphere of influence. Many commentators still do not see anything beyond Central Asia's corrupt dictatorships and disregard the lives and feelings of these states' citizens.

Finding myself in the situation inwardly, while looking and analysing outwardly, I felt a constant need to tell anyone not familiar with Kazakhstan the story of the country's socio-political transformation, which may have gone unnoticed outside but meant so much to those inside the country. And one of the biggest questions haunting Kazakhstan's independence years is the question of identity and belonging, and how to unravel the country's difficult history in order to make sense of its no less challenging present. Identity is also one of the most ubiquitous frames of analysis when discussing Kazakhstan in academic circles. Will Northern Kazakhstan, with its large ethnic Russian population, secede to Russia? Will Kazakhstan's Russian-speaking communities—a term that has long required a critical rethinking—revolt against the 'ethnonationalists'?

Away from these questions, I often found that Kazakh nationalism was one of the most popular topics of discussion among people who come from Kazakhstan. At one point, I stopped counting how many emails were landing in my mailbox from my fellow Kazakhs asking me to read their policy memos and documents on how a 'solid' national identity could be constructed in Kazakhstan. What they meant by a 'solid' national identity was the type of identity that no longer posed questions of 'who are we?' and 'what does it mean to be Kazakhstani?' Many people in Kazakhstan believe that resolving these painful questions, which were often posed publicly by former president Nursultan Nazarbayev, will allow society to overcome its historical trauma, enabling people to start building their lives away from the ambiguities and confusion that the regime's top-down efforts to establish a national identity have created.

However, even in post-Nazarbayev Kazakhstan, the question 'What does it mean to be Kazakhstani?' prevails. My interlocutors in numerous fieldworks at home believed and continue to believe that the power to define what Kazakhstani means belongs to the people rather than the politicians, who try to monopolise the right to define the type of nation Kazakhstan's citizens are building.[3] Controlling how Kazakhstan is defined is about claiming power and carving out space for selfhood in a state that has been infected by dictatorial politics.

It is hard to write a complete history of one place in one book. Some have tried, and I applaud them. Mine is a more modest, reflective exploration of complex events and the life of identity, an invitation to ask similar questions without hoping to find definitive answers, an attempt to mediate what the long independence period means for us and what awaits us at the turn of the next decade. I admit that it is also an experiment for me to write in ways I have never written before, to put myself on the page, even if it is the

PREFACE

most challenging thing to do, and to share my personal journey of investigating lost archives, burnt pages and silenced witnesses of violence while asking myself questions about the trauma we have all experienced since 2022, and some since long before that.

The war

In 2021, just days before Kazakhstan entered its thirtieth year of independence, I expected monuments to be erected in the country's public spaces, as well as speeches, spectacular events and banners celebrating the anniversary of its independence. I thought that little would change the mundane process of proclaiming our independence. But Russia's full-scale invasion of Ukraine in late February 2022 changed all that. The war changed political subjectivities in every Central Asian country and made people in high places visibly anxious about the possibility of their country's independence being brought into question.

For many people on the ground, Russia's invasion[4] came as a shock and posed complex questions that continue to divide communities, neighbourhoods and families today. In Kazakhstan, pro-Putin supporters can often live in close proximity to those who actively participate in gathering humanitarian aid for Ukrainians; people in coffee shops debate the pros and cons of NATO involvement; and people openly share their anxieties about Russia's potential invasion of Northern Kazakhstan and the continuation of its imperialist project in Central Asia, should it ultimately fail in Ukraine. Kazakhstani artists and activists, still traumatised by the violent suppression of the mass protests of January 2022, cried their eyes out for Ukrainians sheltering in subways from the Russian bombing, for residents of Mariupol attacked by the same Russian soldiers who were in Kazakhstan just a month earlier to crack down on our protests. One of my friends who attended an exhibition in support of Ukrainians said he felt shattered inside as he looked at Saule Suleimenova's painting reflecting on her feelings about the Ukrainians sheltering in Mariupol. The hundreds of people who came to the pro-Ukraine rally in Almaty in March 2022 and sang Ukrainian songs and cursed Putin shared similar feelings of solidarity but also a hope that the

PREFACE

Ukrainians' will to victory would pave the way to a future without Russian domination. This happened in a country where many people still openly speak of Putin as a 'saviour' who can make 'order' in any country (*navedet poryadok*); some even refer to him as Uncle Vova (*dyadya Vova*).[5]

The Bloody January protests, only a month before the Russian invasion, were still fresh in the minds of Kazakhstanis as they watched the Russian tanks roll into Mariupol and the Ukrainian army unveiling the atrocities of Russian imperialism in Bucha. State repression of the mass anti-government protests claimed the lives of more than 230 citizens in Kazakhstan and unleashed an unprecedented level of state torture and harassment of the political opposition. The early days of Russia's invasion of Ukraine were filled with sorrow, anxiety, horror. Violence was everywhere. In February 2022, people in Kazakhstan mourned with the people of Ukraine, who had in turn mourned with us the previous month after the Bloody January protests.

Bloody January, Qandy Qantar or, simply, Qantar became an important part of the everyday vocabulary in Kazakhstan. Qantar is the horror of a complete shutdown of all independent media and online sources; the sounds of a war, explosions outside residential areas, the pain of tear gas suffocating peaceful protestors in Almaty on the night of 4–5 January. Qantar is a long moment of the most death-intense days of the clashes, shootouts and unbelievable conspiracies spreading around Kazakhstani cities; the long moment of just a few days when it was completely unclear who had the monopoly over violence. Every year without access to a transparent investigation haunts my compatriots, my friends and acquaintances, the families of victims, the families of people who were sent to prisons on falsified evidence and the survivors of the torture chambers. Qantar is timeless pain. 'Qantar!' is a slogan that an independent journalist in deep depression screams at the top of his lungs to remind people around him that we still live amid the horrors of that violence. Qantar is the deep feeling of insecurity my interlocutors share as I finalise this manuscript in late 2024.

Qantar is the news about the deployment of Russian soldiers to Kazakhstan via the Collective Security Treaty Organization—CSTO, a postsoviet copy of NATO—which sent shock waves around the country as it mourned its own dead. When the deployment happened, many people openly spoke about what a potential Russian invasion would feel like. Suddenly, you would see Russian soldiers, the invaders, walking up the streets of your city with their guns in their hands or on their backs. When the news about Russia's full-scale invasion of Ukraine broke out a month later, Kazakhstanis were stunned. The category of the 'postsoviet', long used to unite or group together the fifteen independent states that emerged out of the former Soviet Union,[6] came crashing down—there was no longer anything that could unite this vast region. A sense of utter horror in the face of Russian neo-imperialism and fascism filled that void. And even the most fervent pro-Putin supporters among the local Russian population started turning against the war when their families in Russia began receiving closed coffins with the dead bodies or pieces of the bodies of their loved ones, the bodies of those who had invaded Ukraine. The war suddenly felt very close, with its tragedies and despair even for those who had gladly welcomed it while living in a completely different state, neither Russia nor Ukraine.

In this book, I take a step back from state and elite narratives to ask what it means to be Kazakhstani outside of the country's presidential palaces, ministerial offices and state cortèges. What does it mean to be Kazakhstani on the streets, in coffee shops, at opposition rallies and at family dinner tables? What are the stories, feelings and anxieties people share about their personal identities and about their country's future?

Although the regime in Astana continues to dictate the frames of the state identity discussion, in reality Kazakhstan's identity is fragmented, fiercely debated and can sometimes be incredibly ambiguous on the ground. Citizens believe they have an equal right to be at the decision table even if their fight for further political engagement lies through the difficult path of bloodied struggle and underground resistance. To be Kazakhstani is to struggle with the difficult questions of the Soviet past, with the remaining and unresolved 'national question' the Soviet elites believed could be solved quickly by creating a new, 'Soviet people'. But when the Soviet empire crashed into numerous broken pieces, it opened the way to the difficult and thorny questions of 'who are we?' and 'where are we going from here?'

For Kazakhstanis, as much as for many other citizens of now 'no-longer-postsoviet' states, the imperial collapse is constant. We saw it in our most recent history in the 1980s, then 1991, then the long 1990s when Yeltsin was battling with Chechen separatism, the Communists, rival elite groups and his own people. The Putin era has been a long collapse as well, a collapse into the totalitarian system that Russia represents today, as I finalise this manuscript in late 2024. Looking at it from Almaty, Pavlodar, Astana, Karaganda, Taraz, Taldyqorgan and even the tiniest village where Russia's criminal propaganda finds a way to propagate Moscow's views, it is clear that Russia's imperial revanchism and annexation of even more territory is the statement of a failing empire. Russia's dysfunctional state, uninhabitable postsoviet villages and towns way out of Moscow's focus are evidence of the empire's collapse. This imperial collapse will be different from the Soviet collapse. But both serve as an important backstory to the main narrative of this book, since creating 'Kazakhstanis' is a question of battling with what 'postsoviet' meant in the 1990s and establishing an identity that reflects the country's multilingual and multi-ethnic nature. Both require asking incredibly difficult and painful questions about our traumatic past. Thus, the pages of this book alternate with the narration of that past and the responses people have to it in the present.

Why do my respondents refuse to be postsoviet?

In 2018, decolonial scholar Madina Tlostanova wrote a book with the intriguing title *What Does It Mean to be Post-Soviet?* The book reminds us that 'decolonization of collective and personal memory is an extremely difficult task' and that 'it is painful asking for ruthless self-criticism'.[7] I certainly share this feeling both when doing fieldwork and when writing about it. This book is no exception. But I also feel the pressing need to keep on asking 'for ruthless self-criticism' and for self-reflections, for questioning the frames of the colonial, for collectively trying to make sense of what sovietness is.[8] The same goes for 'Kazakhstani' as a label, category or concept that many associate with the thirty-year dictatorship of Nazarbayev, who tried to control the nation-building process to gain more power but did so without critically reflecting on the coloniality of which he himself was a product. I address this issue of Nazarbayevite coloniality throughout the pages of this book. However, in the book, and based on the research findings, on the voices of my respondents, I propose that we can think of what it means to be Kazakhstani beyond Nazarbayev and the postsoviet, away from it being a 'meaningless term', because, as it turns out, it brings a lot of meaning and empowerment to our compatriots who claim Kazakhstan or Qazaqstan alike as their only homeland.

Is it at all useful to call a whole region postsoviet or post-Soviet or ex-Soviet to clarify its borders and space-ness to foreigners while locals of that same region long stopped applying this term to their everyday realities? Opinions differ. 'I refuse to be post-soviet, to be the fraction of the shattered empire [*byt oskolkom raspavsheisya imperii*]', said Anuar Dyussenbinov, a well-known Kazakh decolonial poet at an open discussion on postsovietness in Almaty in July 2023.[9] People who went to the same Qazaq Indie concerts in Almaty as him agreed: they too are not simply the shattered fragments of the collapsed empire even if their passports still state they are Russian citizens,[10] now fashioned in the new concept of 'relocates'—those who went into exile in Kazakhstan after Russia, their own country, invaded Ukraine. Many of them, desperately seeking a new identity, prefer no longer to be defined as Russian.

Could Kazakhstan be home for them too? One of the female relocates, a recent migrant I met in Almaty in the summer of 2023, told me just that: 'I feel *homed* here, in Kazakhstan.' Her friend sitting nearby anxiously looked around and murmured, 'we felt like we were/are welcomed here'. Can this concept of Kazakhstani surpass its past competition with the Soviet person and postsoviet subjects to welcome anyone willing to make this country their own home, a site of refuge, a space of reflection?

The term 'postsoviet' was always ambiguous. On the one hand, it declared the end of the Soviet Union but not the end of sovietness and the habits, values and mindset (*mirovozzrenie*) that lived on with its final generation. On the other hand, the term was supposed to bring some sort of cohesion to the space that was once the 'Soviet Union'—from Riga to Vladivostok—despite the realities of life in Russia's capital city, Moscow, differing markedly from Vladivostok, in Russia's Far East, as early as 1991. I find the term 'postsoviet'—without the hyphen and with a lowercase s in 'soviet'—more useful as it decentralises and historicises the 'Soviet Union': a state, a political reality and a specific experience that many in my generation of Kazakhstani, Latvian, Uzbek, Kyrgyz and even Russian citizens never experienced and that many in the generation after us consider even more alien and distant. In turn, sovietness (*sovetskost'*) is the continuation of the Soviet Union's colonial projects, and this is what we are still experiencing today in one of the most significant forms of imperial difference and hierarchy—through the Sovietised institution of ethnicity.

'Postsoviet' as a historical term allows us to deal with its complexities from a temporal perspective, while in the present we can attune more to the new vocabularies and new frames that emerge out of the field and the societies that have long stopped being 'postsoviet'. In other words, letting go of this label and only using it for a time and with people who openly associate with it will give more space to the pluriversal—and not unilateral, one-dimensional, universal—understanding of the complex experiences of the no-longer-postsoviet states and their societies and subjectivities. In the narratives that follow, I use 'postsoviet' as a historicised term and in some quotations of texts or in interviews where my interlocutors openly talk about their affinity to the postsoviet category even though it often translates as 'sovietness', for example when people say 'I am a soviet person' or when people say 'this was part of the postsoviet development'. I am fully on board with continuing the theorisation of what postsoviet and sovietness mean as concepts and as forms of historical meaning-production but not as a label externally applied to the complexities of spaces, experiences and subjectivities in places and by people that do not use this word in their everyday encounters or to identify their contemporary lived experiences.

I owe my narrative in this book to my respondents and its conclusions to all those who were willing to take this journey with me and read it through. Readers should feel free to skip some chapters to get to the ones that are of most interest. This might be the historical narration of the December 1986 protests in Chapter 2 or the discussion of the Bloody January protests of 2022 in Chapter 5 and their difficult and traumatic aftermath in Chapter 6. Or you might be more interested in the book's discussion of hybrid identities, of Kazakh Russians in Chapter 3, the marginalised co-nationals lost in the colonial language and colonial legacies explored in Chapter 4 or the political discussion of the rise of the Nazarbayev regime—parts of Chapters 1 and 2—and his crushing fall in the Afterword. I wrote Chapter 1 for those who need a mind map to understand what Kazakhstan is and what contemporary Kazakh culture represents. This book, ultimately, is intended for everyone interested in the complex hybrid identities of the post-colonial, postsoviet, post-socialist, post-imperial condition.

In states like Kazakhstan, regimes play an important role in controlling the nation-building process. So, part of the story will be built through the elitist imagination of the nation 'they' were building. At the same time, the citizens and their everyday approach to ethnicity—often in very hybrid and complex terms—and identity matter a lot too. The everyday practice of (non)ethnicity and even national identity plays an important role in conceptualising what these identities mean for the citizens and for the state and how these meanings shape the past, the present and the future of the state and the individual lives of its citizens. This is the other part of the story I attempt to tell in this book—the stories of aspirations, disappointments, discrimination and fears that surround people's understandings and lived experiences of identity-making and their contribution to making the Kazakhstani identity more inclusive and open. This book is an invitation to delve into these complex stories and narratives of a political subjectivity that is no longer postsoviet and one that aspires, one day, to be post-dictatorial.

* * *

Writing this book was a journey that started long before the first words were typed on a blank computer screen in August 2020. I want to thank my family and friends who supported me while writing this book. My brother Kuanysh was always eager to discuss

PREFACE

my ethnographies of the protests or simply check how I felt in between the dinners he cooked for us. Olive oil and rosemary sticks, large grains of salt and freshly ground mixed pepper; all the smells of his cosy kitchen, the openness of his home and the wide embrace of his T-shirts provided much-needed emotional support on days that sometimes felt grey, cold and pessimistic—thank you so much for your endless love and for not being grumpy at me for spending so much of my time at home working. Marzhan, Karima, Kaisar, Mansour and Luna made my fieldwork unforgettable. Thank you for the endless support I felt in every word of 'when are you coming back home?'

The sound of my sister's laugh and her jokes and caring messages on my social media remain music to my ears. Malika is my biggest cheerleader of my writings in Kazakhstan and beyond. She is also a source of endless inspiration. I am grateful to Aunt Roza, my second mother, Aunt Maskhuda and my whole family for all the support throughout my fieldwork at home.

Oksana, Tleuzhan, Aigerim, Assem, Zarina, Suinbike, Medina, Saule and KUBA, Zhar, Askhat, Jama, Alima, Adiya, Zhenya, Kamilla, Aldiyar, Olga, Anya, Madina, Anuar, Dima, Sofya, Anel, Aizada, Aiganym and many more friends taught me so much and provided a helping hand at each stage of this process. I owe my perseverance to Botakoz, Darya, Assel and Asel, Erica, Gulzat and Nodira. Each of your examples set a guiding light in my own work; I will forever be grateful for your advice and friendship over the years. I also want to thank all of the people I met at workshops and in online discussions. Thank you to colleagues and friends in Ukraine who inspire me every day and set a great example to follow. Thank you to Kuanysh Bazargaliev for your incredible talent, open heart, friendship and ability to lift my spirits and put a smile on my face; thank you for your words of wisdom, which accompanied me in some of the most challenging situations. And thank you for allowing us to use your superb artwork for the cover of this book. Your incredible art speaks volumes to the questions I've had here and beyond. You and your reflections on canvas, on paper and in our conversations remain one of the biggest inspirations in my own writing.

PREFACE

I am very grateful to Ben Noble, Michael Dwyer and Alice Clarke for believing in this project, guiding me in my outlines, editing and providing suggestions on the earlier manuscript, supporting me through the writing up. I want to thank Michael for his many inspiring words, which shaped how I thought of this project before the manuscript was finished, and the whole Hurst team for making the process so smooth. I cannot thank enough the two anonymous readers for their superb suggestions and encouragement. Thanks to Lara Gisborne, who cheered this project on with me every day in our old office at 16 Mill Lane, where I spent many late evenings writing. My colleagues and students at the Department of Sociology in Cambridge helped at every step, and our thought-provoking discussions and seminars fed back into many pages of my writing and thinking. I am grateful to my mentors for reminding me of how to be a 'student of life' and write as if I'm 'playing music'. Our Talking History workshops in Cambridge Sociology taught me a lot in the three years we've been running them. I am grateful to each participant and to Prof. Hazem Kandil, who has been irreplaceable in guiding me and others on this journey. Days spent with a PhD colloquium at Cambridge Sociology, where I taught 'how to do fieldwork', offered great inspiration and reminders of how exciting research and writing really is. Thank you to my group of scholars who work on 'writing from *home*' when writing about and *with* Central Asia. A big thank you goes to my co-fellows at Homerton College in Cambridge, where every lunch and every candlelight dinner was filled with laughter, support and cheering. Thanks to Marta for encouraging me to enhance my ethnographies and for improving my writing; to Robin for the sparkling sense of style, excellent playlist suggestions, rebooting our writing Thursdays (and Fridays with Una) and for being such an inspiration; to Roberto for the inspiring quotes of the day and reminding me to smile; to Sofia for inspiring me to think of things as monuments; and to Fernanda for everything really—from boosting my confidence, walking me through the editing process and brainstorming the titles of my future books.

I don't write my texts alone. My tireless co-authors, co-writers and co-editors are always with me. I owe this book to my respondents, to fellow archivists, to people who are always willing to share, to discuss and to open new, uncharted spaces for my thinking. I've consulted with several great minds while writing some of the most challenging pages of this book. Thank you for being there for me. Thanks to Tleu and Bota, who managed to cheer me up during some of the most intense days of writing and for forcing me to take walks on the beach to recharge. Thanks to Assel, who always wisely reflected on my presentation of ideas in our monthly phone calls and discussions and co-writings. Thanks to Olga for teaching and inspiring me so much through our writing and *jeonging* together.[11]

My mother Raushan Ibragimova-Kudaibergenova and my father Turarbek Kudaibergenov have done so much to make this and many of my other texts happen. Without their unconditional support—even though I stand fully responsible for my errors and doubts—I don't know where I would've landed. You hold my hand close and far; you travel with me to every fieldtrip and count the hours before my plane lands; you keep up with my messy working table and long hours of work almost up to New Year's Eve. The quiet summer days in Malinovka/Terekti auly, the cosy evenings spent reading, the long conversations on the phone, you carefully keeping all my old books and 'ideas' notebooks and the jars of my favourite cherry jam at home, so many countless memories and experiences make home ever closer. Thank you for everything. And thank you for allowing me to write about our memories and our experiences in the pages of this book.

Diana T. Kudaibergen
Cambridge–Almaty–Malinovka–Barcelona–Almaty,
and back to Cambridge, 2023–4

INTRODUCTION

Multi-ethnic Kazakhstan

My grandma's house, where I spent a lot of time growing up, was located on a small street in one of Kazakhstan's towns, in a quiet residential neighbourhood where everyone took extra care to create a micro-space of harmonious relations. Growing up, my cousins and I rarely questioned issues of identity at home or outside our courtyard. We played with kids from the neighbourhood, spoke a mix of Russian and Kazakh and shared homemade food and stories of our beloved dogs. Our childhood was shielded from the horrors of the early postsoviet period, when economies were crashing, leaving families with no savings, their money having disappeared overnight when the Soviet rouble collapsed, and the difficult dilemmas of building a new state with a distinct national identity. In the winter, we had snowball fights; in the spring, we picked flowers and played badminton; and in the summer and autumn, we picked cherries from the orchard an old Russian lady kept in the neighbourhood and made cherry jam and homemade cakes.

In our games and daily conversations, we rarely bothered with questions of ethnicity or identity. Somehow it was taken for granted that the Mashas were probably Russian, that our friends from the three families living in three houses neatly connected were Korean even if their names were Russian—Tolya, Anya and Maksim. And it was only when the famous singer Zemfira became popular in Russia that we learned that our neighbour, a quiet girl also called

Zemfira, was probably Tatar. When my aunt asked a man who lived in a house right next door to help with our dog, we found out he was Ukrainian because they joked in Ukrainian. Little did we know that his wife was half-Chinese, as she and her children spoke perfect Russian, and they too never spoke of their ethnicity or ethnicities. Other neighbours were Kazakh, half-Tatar and half-Kazakh or mixed Russian and Ukrainian, while our old neighbours whom my grandma considered family were ethnic Germans. In 1994, they collected all their belongings and moved to Germany after spending their whole life living in our small neighbourhood. They often sent letters back that made my grandma cry, but we were very happy as every parcel they sent contained a great selection of German candy.

The whole neighbourhood celebrated weddings and other happy occasions together and mourned their dead together. Collectively, we spoke a mix of Russian and Kazakh with some additions of Korean, German, Uzbek and Tatar, occasionally using Dungan and Uyghur words for food, celebrations or nicknames. These words only acquired their 'ethnic' connotations when someone specifically referred to them. But when a hungry child reached out for a bowl of soup, she rarely cared if it was an 'Uyghur' manpar or a 'Ukrainian' borsch. Soup was soup, and a delicious soup was even better. Friends were friends, so long as ethnicity remained the always fleeting secondary issue to more important things. In the tough years of the mid-1990s economic crisis, neighbours shared food, matches and salt and candles during the frequent electricity outages. Every neighbour offered their helping hand for free, like the man who lived in a big house down the street and fixed refrigerators. He had hoped that his two teenage sons would learn from him and would also become handymen, but in the late 1990s they followed their mother who had migrated to Israel searching for a better life while he stayed behind in a big empty house full of broken Soviet refrigerators. There was also an old Greek lady, baba Katya, with a Kazakh husband and her numerous children with big wide smiles and Kazakh names. My childhood memory of seeing her make an open fire in the tiny courtyard squeezed in between apartment buildings to cook some food outdoors because there was no gas, electricity or means to make food at home remains one of my strongest and most vivid memories of the hardships of the early 1990s.

All these ethnic details were recounted to me years later once I announced that I intended to write a doctoral dissertation in sociology with a focus on national identity. Bits and pieces that went unnoticed before suddenly spoke of ethnicity and ethnic distinctions because neighbours and friends thought I would find those details valuable in my work. Things that did not interfere and that were not made visible in our interactions before were suddenly highlighted to help me along the way in my analysis, an analysis of the 'multi-ethnic Kazakhstan' that had managed to remain peaceful for three decades despite the potential dangers of an interethnic conflict that were often discussed in President Nazarbayev's circles.

If anything, the workings of ethnic identifications perplexed me even more because I grew up with a grandmother who refused to identify with any ethnicity assigned to her by the Soviets, who engaged in 'the pervasive shaping and structuring of national identities'.[1] Strictly codified and highly divisive, this pervasive vision of ethnic division—and colonial hierarchy—only worked out contextually and whenever ethnicity had to be enacted, when someone had to announce their ethnicity. For example, some of my ethnic minority respondents mentioned that they were only allowed to occupy certain positions in Soviet institutions if there was a quota for their ethnic group. For some, this even applied to party membership—the status that opened many doors and provided numerous institutional opportunities in Soviet times. Ethnicity as hard currency was part of the toolbox used by politicians to identify, divide and rule over communities in the political language that suited a given regime.

The lived experience of ethnicity that I saw in my daily interactions was only used in specific contexts, and as I was growing up, the question 'Kto ty po natsii?', which used to send me into a state of confusion, quickly became a form of rudeness and incivility. In the more colloquial reading, it translated from Russian as 'what's your ethnicity?', but in a grammatical sense it meant 'what nation do you identify or side with?' With that second connotation, where does one even begin? Did my neighbour, baba Katya, identify with Greece because she was ethnically Greek? Would my grandma identify with

WHAT DOES IT MEAN TO BE KAZAKHSTANI?

China if Xingjian or East Turkestan, and more importantly Kashgar, where a significant part of her lineage originates, were part of China? I do not think she thought of China when she listened to the tapes with music from Kashgar that a relative brought her in the early 2000s, and when she teared up while listening to the music, was it even appropriate to ask her what nation she associated her memories and emotions with? The Soviet regime made the question of ethnicity and national identity incredibly difficult and often painful for many people[2] as it imposed divisive and strictly codified systems and coerced people to identify with them. It made kids of ethnically mixed families de jure identify only with the ethnic group of their father when they were documenting their nationality in their national ID cards and passports. But de facto, it left them with the complexity of their family tree. Many never bothered about it, but for many the questions that often required a firm identification, which nation to side with, made them ever more confused. Does it matter? Aren't we all Kazakhstani? I thought to myself when faced with these questions in my undergraduate studies.

The Soviet question of 'Kto ty po natsii?' hammered on the heads of people who did not want to identify with one ethnicity or any ethnicity at all. But this same question drew strict boundaries between different ethnic groups no one in the Soviet Union was able to escape because it was written down in their passport in the notorious 'fifth paragraph' (*pyataya grafa*). The fifth paragraph identified your ethnicity but also your chances of building a career or even finding a partner.[3] The Soviet Union's demise left an even messier context for an array of ethnic, national and other identifications, feelings and enactments.[4] For many of the people who were either invited out of their comfortable categories of belonging or, on the contrary, violently pushed into the spaces of an obligatory ethnicity, the whole process of national identity became arduous, dangerous, self-limiting and, in times of interethnic conflict, often even deadly. The imperial collapse continuously and violently influenced our sense of selfhood by forcing us to choose ethnicities even when the fifth paragraph, the obligatory legal ethnic identification in official documents, was gradually abandoned in independent Kazakhstan. The fixation on the ethnically defined frames of political belonging remains one the biggest and most challenging legacies of the Soviet empire.[5] This fixation does not matter in most everyday contexts, but it still divides people at a political level and remains a dangerous instrument in dictatorial hands.

When thinking about the processes and temporalities of postsovietness—here defined as the specific temporal moment of the immediate collapse of the Soviet Union—I often come back to my childhood memories, where ethnic questions did not matter as much in the everyday lives of my fellow citizens, as illustrated in this vignette of my childhood neighbourhood. Right after the collapse of the Soviet Union, people cared more about the economic hardship they had to endure. The happy moments of my childhood with German candy, big family dinners on a Saturday night with all my uncles and aunts and the Soviet 'champagne' popping on New Year's Eve long after the Soviet Union ceased to exist coincided with the most challenging economic and political period my country had ever faced.

Many formerly Soviet citizens felt like they had lost a promised future of stability and dignified retirement. People started quickly adapting to the 'wild capitalism' of the early 1990s—known locally as *dikiy kapitalizm*—to make a living.[6] Many younger women engaged in the shuttle trade to China and Turkey and quickly filled the open markets with clothes and cheap footwear.[7] Old Russian ladies started trading chewing gum, sunflower seeds[8] and cigarettes on the corners of their apartment buildings to top up their minuscule pensions.[9] Cultural elites also entered the new market and started offering relatively affordable piano and ballet classes; others sold their libraries, literally spreading their books out on the streets that led to the local markets. One of my schoolteachers, a middle-aged Kazakh woman who spoke inspiringly of the Kazakh language (Qazaq tili), once came to the class crying out of shame. She briefly explained that she could not pay her bills and had decided to sell homemade pastries in the school's hallway during breaks to make some additional income to survive.[10]

In these stories of hardship and anxiety about the future, ethnicity slipped through the cracks of something more significant—economic survival, community and everyday resilience. While state officials were battling over the highly politicised issue of whether Kazakh or Russian should be the main state language,[11] the country's citizens fought hard to make ends meet. The lives of the political elites and Kazakhstan's ordinary citizens rarely coincided. As one of the higher-up politicians once told me, in the early 1990s they were more preoccupied with the literal process of state-building than the concerns of everyday matters—whether public transport arrived on schedule or teachers were paid enough and on time. I often wondered why it was that *they* had the power to decide our lives for *us*.

Kazakhstan and Nazarbayev after independence

In 1991, Nazarbayev, once the chairman of the Communist Party of Kazakhstan (CPK) and then the president of Soviet Kazakhstan, was playing a wait-and-see game with the situation in the Soviet Union. Although only barely fifty, he was a seasoned apparatchik who knew the importance of taking his time to calculate the political mood in Moscow. Would Gorbachev stay or fall from power? Would the Soviet Union survive? Nazarbayev declared independence from the Soviet Union on 16 December 1991, the last leader to officially do so, at a time when the Soviet Union had practically ceased to exist. But as soon as it happened, Nazarbayev did not hesitate to consolidate power in the hands of his own regime—his closest allies in the Communist institutions and some young and ambitious entrepreneurs, economists and managers eagerly helped him build his own version of authoritarian neoliberalism.[12]

Thus the Nazarbayev regime swiftly took over from the Moscow-based Politburo when the right time came. Nazarbayev did so as soon as it was clear that the Politburo and the Soviet Union were dead. After consolidating his rule, he denigrated ideology as an anachronism and instead promoted his vision of what he described as the Kazakh Dream.[13] Occasionally sensing society's mood, he also spoke of the Soviet Union as an 'empire' and promised the population that the now-independent Kazakhstan was entering a bright new future where the free market would solve all the country's problems all at once.[14] His promises often materialised in written state programmes and ambitious pamphlets but took a long time to transfer to everyday life.

Did he publish those pamphlets because he felt the urge to give something to a nation that was accustomed to reading (Kazakhstan had one of the highest levels of readership and literacy in the Soviet Union)? Or was he simply doing things the only way he knew how, the Soviet way, when every party decree had to be proclaimed, then printed, disseminated and discussed widely in public circles? Either way, he was obsessed with printing his state vision, owning it and boasting of the new terminology he had learned.[15] He spoke to the citizens through pamphlets, newspaper articles printed in state media and occasional presidential speeches until these were made into an annual and obligatory presidential address in 1997.[16] Quotes from these addresses proclaiming a 'multi-ethnic', happy Kazakhstan were then printed on posters and billboards that started occupying cities in the 2000s and later, with more state spending, even major highways and villages. Nazarbayev's regime was obsessed with littering our everyday reality with his images, books and meaningless words.

In 1993, Nazarbayev responded to the socio-economic crisis in an ideological pamphlet, 'Ideational Consolidation of the Society as the Condition for the Progress of Kazakhstan', which described the crisis with the Durkheimian term *anomie*.[17] Nazarbayev wrote that

> 'anomie' is a personal state of confusion when conditions dramatically change and established systems of values are rethought [and] life ideals change radically. It is a difficult challenge not only for each citizen but for the whole society. And although a majority of Kazakhstanis support the reform course, we [elites] need to understand that many [citizens] who understand the necessity of changes in their heart, so to speak, still do not perceive the nature [of these reforms] with their conscious mind, [and] experience insecurity; [citizens] are not able to imagine their own future.[18]

This patronising language remained part of Nazarbayev's rhetoric throughout his thirty-year dictatorship, in which he and those around him saw him as the ultimate visionary, taking Kazakhstan forwards on its new path to development and sovereignty. Yet the prosperous future he painted for all only worked out for the few, particularly his family members and closest allies.[19]

Looking back at this quote from 1993 and comparing it to the experiences of those 'ordinary' but extremely smart Kazakhstanis that Nazarbayev pushed into the camp of the helpless, insecure subjects of his rule who were 'not able to imagine their own future', these same people, the citizens, had little to no place in his grand narratives about the new Kazakhstan of the 1990s or 2000s. I wonder how aware President Nazarbayev and his elites were of the real situation on the ground. Did they visit the courtyards of the apartment buildings where people burnt wood and cooked food in large cauldrons (*kazans*) on open fires because their homes had no electricity, gas, hot water or heating?[20] Did he know the story of my Kazakh schoolteacher who sold her homemade pastries in the school halls and cried herself to sleep because she was so ashamed of her own poverty?

In the 1990s, we were the nation of the incredibly resilient 'ordinary people'[21] to whom ethnicity did not play a particularly important role in the immediacy of everyday life and the nation constructed by the small group of people comprising the elite who were busy building a regime that turned into Nazarbayev's dictatorship. What follows is an attempt to read the history of post-independence Kazakhstan through ordinary people's eyes and experiences and to theorise how citizens can reshape and reimagine the process of building a national identity. In doing so, I turn to one of the most debated terms of the postsoviet period—the conceptual tool of 'civic identity' and the empirical category of 'Kazakhstani' (Qazaqstandy).

In this book, I argue that 'Kazakhstani' is not a monolith or nationalistic project; rather, it is a complex condition, a relation of an identity-in-the-making riddled with contradictions, opposing views and anxieties. At the same time, it is a project of searching for one's true political subjectivity away from the imperialist, colonial and authoritarian legacies of the Soviet period. Some readers may claim that Kazakhstani is a form of civic national identity, an identity that 'means that people identify strongly with their country not because it represents any specific ethnic, linguistic, or religious group but because it represents an inclusive vision of the citizenry as a whole'.[22]

However, this form of civic national identity could not develop under the tight control of a dictatorial regime. Nazarbayev's search for a compromise led only to further ambiguity over what Kazakhstani means and was largely stuck in the old Soviet ways of dealing with the 'national question'.[23] Nazarbayev exacerbated and politicised ethnicity instead of critically re-evaluating this colonial category and made a Soviet-era fixation on ethnic divisions key to his own rule. This happened because he viewed the population as divided into two dominant and antagonistic groups of 'Russians' and 'Kazakhs' in the same way as the Moscow elites saw Kazakhstani society on the eve of the mass protests of December 1986 (discussed in Chapter 2). Put simply, civicness cannot come from dictators, but it can form in the resistance politics their policies generate. Dictators produce different forms of political cultures no less significant or important to the people,[24] but dictators cannot produce an understanding of civic identity. Because they constantly circumvent wider society's participation in these projects and instead claim their dictatorial authority over them, the meaning of civicness is lost. Civic culture or civic ideas and values come from citizens and cannot be harboured by a presidential administration, no matter how the dictatorial bureaucrats try to abuse the language of supposed civicness and liberalism.

Nazarbayev never intended to construct a civic identity, but he skilfully played into the ambiguity that surrounded that concept. He knew that the civic–ethnic divide stuck neatly to the so-called 'postsoviet nation-building' of the new states where ethnic meant the backward, exclusionary and 'bad' type of nationalism based on divisions and the dominance of one strictly defined ethnic group, whereas civic nationalism was seen as the 'good' type of nationalism—liberal, tolerant, based on state identity and liberal values, where ethnicity did not matter.[25] To quote Rogers Brubaker, Nazarbayev used the language of civic nationhood to portray his country as a state 'of and for all ... citizens, rather than ... of and for a single ethnocultural group'.[26] But, in Nazarbayev's case, this typology and division into civic–ethnic was a type of zero-sum game imbued with the unanswered questions of settler colonialism, mass and forceful Russification and the denigration of specific socio-lingual and non-urban groups—mostly rural Kazakhs—as 'backward' and 'uncivilised'. Was there a clear-cut distinction that could distinguish all Kazakhs from all Russians or all Russians from all Slavs? Where did Russified Kazakhs or Uzbeks or Tatars belong on this grid? Where were the trilingual Germans in this categorisation, and what was the place of the Koreans? Who was the 'dominant ethnic group' with the sole right to define the ethnocultural makeup of the nation when Kazakh-speaking communities felt like state-language policies were insufficient to free them from everyday linguistic discrimination in predominantly Russified urban spaces and employment contracts that demanded the grammatically correct use of Russian (which even many Russian speakers don't always have)? An even more difficult question to answer today is who are the Russians of Kazakhstan?

This ambiguity allowed Nazarbayev to stay in power without needing to commit himself to civic, post-ethnic or any other form of nation-building and to instead build on the hybrid identities defined by the postcolonial condition and act as an arbiter in potentially conflictual situations. Because of this policy, Kazakhstani people can still decide what language their children are educated in,[27] including minority languages schools, and the types of identities they can adopt. But what mattered most to Nazarbayev was loyalty to his rule and his personalist dictatorship and control over meaning-making, leading him to adopt the old Soviet ways of categorising people into ethnicities via strict and hierarchical divisions.

The project of creating a Kazakhstani identity cannot be understood away from the socio-political challenges caused by the post-1991 or even post-1986 condition, when the Soviet view on ethnicity and ethnic difference ruled society and the polity, and where political elites attempted to dominate this project with their own views of what national identity was supposed to look like. I dedicated much of my earlier work to the discussion of these power dynamics and the constant rivalry over the power to define the boundaries of national imagining at the state level. At the same time, I also stressed that 'what the domination of the nationalizing regime as a power structure brings to the social dynamics is actually further dispersion of the meaning of "Kazakh" or "Qazaq" and divisions into urban and rural Kazakhs, *mankurts* and *mambets*, Russophone and Kazakh-speaking, and many other distinct identities'.[28]

In this book, I want to highlight these complex meanings and provide a space for the multiple voices of the Kazakhstani people. In what follows, I discuss *Kazakhstani* as a relational space widely discussed and negotiated at a societal level and as the lived experience of the ordinary people who take an active part in reshaping and re-imagining it.

These ordinary people, my grandma's neighbours, my classmates in a bilingual, multicultural educational setting, their parents and everyone who constitutes Kazakhstani society, are not just simple consumers of elitist projects but active players who shape the process of making state identity and imbue it with meaning in their everyday encounters. It is their active role in rethinking the old categories of citizenship, ethnicity and nation that constitutes Kazakhstani as a project of political subjectivity. In other words, while the political elite might think they are the ones making the final decisions about nation-building, it is up to the citizens to decide how this will play out on the ground. The state, after all, is not a singular entity that rules over everyone from above and decides how and when and what to nationalise. On the contrary, the state has a plural nature and is made up of thousands of important components and competing authorities.

Kazakhstan's and Kazakhstani contributions to the field

Why choose Kazakhstan as a case study for the analysis of these processes? The second-largest country, after Russia, in what used to be the Soviet Union and known to most of the wider public because of the oil boom of the 2000s and the fictional humour of Sacha Baron Cohen's 'Kazakh journalist' Borat Sagdiyev, Kazakhstan is a lot more than simply a dictatorship and a story of failed democratisation.

Subjected to numerous Soviet experiments—including Stalinist projects to exile whole ethnic groups, voluntary waves of migration (for the construction of major Soviet infrastructure and colonial projects like the Virgin Lands campaign, the Soviet project of converting the Northern Kazakh steppe into land suitable for agricultural production), Russification, modernisation and forced sedentarisation of the nomadic societies, which destroyed their culture and livelihoods—Kazakhstan is a unique case for those seeking to study ethnicity and nationalism. We can study why and how the Kazakh ruling elites who positioned themselves as global players chose to recycle old Soviet paradigms of 'divide and rule' and why Nazarbayev remained loyal to the totalitarian Communist style of governing but masked it under his idea of civic identity, 'the principle of the formal recognition and celebration of ethnic differences'.[29] This is one part of the story this book tells in unravelling what I call regime–society relations—the conditions under which citizens are forced to normalise authoritarian rule and depend on the regime instead of seeking to intervene directly in political decision-making.

The way people protest and contest regime–society relations over such delicate questions as national or ethnic identity is the second part of the book's narrative. I weave these two ideas together by demonstrating how the regime's control of some of the main narratives about what it means to be Kazakhstani are directly contested, re-imagined and critiqued by the country's citizens.[30] And it is perhaps this aspect of the story that is the more interesting one, as the citizens' response to the idea of codified ethnicity and the contextual practice of socio-ethnic, linguistic and other categories is often distinct from the regime's rigid framing of these same categories.

The book combines findings from archival data, interviews, observations and fieldnotes collected during a prolonged 'fieldwork at home' that started in the spring of 2011 and ended in the summer of 2023 with some occasional digital ethnography on the case of former economics minister Kuandyk Bishimbayev (discussed in the Afterword) in the first part of 2024. For the narratives of ordinary citizens, the Kazakhstanis, I mostly use unpublished data, and in historical narratives, I follow the available archival and secondary data to compile a consistent and comprehensive narrative. The book is based on the many voices of my respondents, who have varied over the years from political elites—presidential advisors, former ministers, MPs, political 'middlemen'—to actors in Kazakhstan's thriving civic sphere—activists, protestors, members of various social movements, protest artists, NGO workers—to ordinary people (among others, my sample includes ethnic Kazakh returnees from Mongolia and China and ethnic Russians residing in Kazakhstan). The book often moves from people and their subjectivities to events and legacies—the devastating famine of 1933 known as Asharshylyq, the 2011 Zhanaozen protests that claimed civilian lives, the nuclear weapons testing site, the 'Polygon', near Semey city—which I try to balance out with the narratives of personal stories. I do so because I believe that one of the more meaningful ways to answer the question of 'What does it mean to be Kazakhstani?' is through the complexity of the experiences, histories and personal readings of these contexts.

Kazakhstan has a lot to offer to the study of nationalism, authoritarianism and power because its history reveals how autocratic regimes manipulate meaning-production and limit the official frames of nation-building policies. I have written about these strategies before,[31] and this study is a continuation of that search to investigate why these categories stick and become routinised, normalised in everyday life. This book is a study of categories that have survived major economic crises, shifts in oppositional forces and the emergence of social movements and even unprecedented and unexpected changes within the regime itself with the nominal departure of President Nazarbayev in March 2019.

A note on positionality

I am Kazakhstani. Some might say I am a 'foreign' Kazakhstani because I divide my professional life between Britain and Kazakhstan and wider Central Asia, which I consider 'home'.[32] I grew up in a multilingual family where my maternal grandmother viewed the Soviet institution of ethnicity as a foreign tool of external policing, which explains why I often found it hard to discuss my own ethnic background without noting how fluid and flexible it is, even though I knew that it was important for many of my respondents in Central Asia, where I lived and conducted fieldwork from 2011. I grew up in post-independence Kazakhstan and spent the first years of school in a fully Qazaq-language school, one of the many that mushroomed in my home city after 1991. This explains why I often find it easier to think or comprehend things in Qazaq, especially when reading, and hopefully this translates well to my texts, almost all of which are now written in English.[33]

My friends and colleagues who, like me, divide their time between Kazakhstan and a foreign state (or states) that we make our secondary homes often ask what it means to be a foreign Kazakhstani. When I participate in rallies in London in favour of democracy or opposing domestic violence in Kazakhstan, I cannot help but ask that question too. At these rallies, my multilingual compatriots continue to unite under the blue and yellow flag and often use three or more languages on their placards—Qazaq, Russian and English but also French, German, Italian, Turkish, Korean, the languages of places and states where they live outside Kazakhstan. When we chant slogans, no one has any trouble pronouncing them in Qazaq. A blonde girl next to me who holds the other end of the big Kazakhstani flag I brought to the rally in London tells everyone 'I'm from Atyrau, and I am Kazakhstani' quite naturally. 'I live in London, but I am Kazakhstani' says another who stands at my other side and listens to the latest news I just brought from Almaty, having recently returned from a spring break there.

In this crowd, far from home on Trafalgar Square, we feel at ease speaking a common language, with my interlocutors quickly switching from Russian to Qazaq and back, without feeling a need to translate anything. It turns out that we all watched the scandalous court hearing of the ex-minister Bishimbayev, who, in May 2024, was found guilty of the aggravated murder of his wife, thirty-one-year-old Saltanat Nukenova from Pavlodar. We all happily accepted the offering of salty *qurt*, dried milk, that one of the participants brought, and discussed the floods that had devastated many parts of Kazakhstan in April 2024. At the end of the rally, groups of people in the crowd discuss where to have lunch—preferably plov, the traditional rice and meat dish from Central Asia—and hot tea (another Central Asian tradition). But what really makes us Kazakhstani? Surely, it is not just the flag that many brought to the rally so that more people from Kazakhstan would be able to identify where the rally was taking place. Maybe it is our shared experience that slips through the familiar words and conversation starters. Is it the vernacular language we use with identifiable words and accents? Even our Russian is different from the Russian spoken in Moscow or some other far-away place in Russia. Does it mean that our sense of Kazakhstani can travel far and wide, even if other identities and experiences layer up on top or in between our Kazakhstani-ness?

Kazakhstanis unite in times of crisis, such as the Zhanaozen protests of 2011 and the protests of 2014 and 2019–24, all of which were met with police brutality. We united during Bloody January and its long aftermath, when people were actively fundraising and donating to support the affected families, for those who lost their breadwinners, for those who needed the help of lawyers in the never-ending court hearings, for those who were affected by the floods. Our sense of Kazakhstani-ness is activated at times when we need to act as a civically minded group of people, and in these cases, ethnicity remains the least important part of our practice and self-identification. I write this book partly out of that feeling that drives me and my compatriots to rallies all over the world to stand with Saltanat Nukenova and other victims of domestic violence, to stand for the implementation of a law criminalising domestic violence. And to affirm our collectively shared experience of being Kazakhstani.

I am a multilingual Kazakhstani without a traceable ethnicity, with a family whose stories are divided by imperial borders and now nation-states that often separate communities that were previously united. I am a Kazakhstani in London (and, before that, for almost two decades in Cambridge); I am a Kazakhstani and a Central Asian; I am a Kazakhstani and a decolonial writer. And like a steppe tulip that travels far, I am always carrying 'home' with me, in my writing and praxis.

Structure of the book

So, what does it mean to be Kazakhstani? What sorts of identities were formed during these three decades of statehood in this vast post-postsoviet space? Why didn't the ethnic Russian majority revolt against the vision of the nation-state that the Kazakh ethno-nationalists proposed after the Soviet collapse? And how would the Russian invasion of Ukraine on 24 February 2022 influence Kazakhstan? These are the questions guiding this book, which spans the defining years of the 1980s and the early 1990s to the turbulent era of the 2010s, an era of protests and socio-economic inequality, and finally to the era that seemed impossible only a few years ago—the era after Nazarbayev.

The chapters that follow tell the story of the country seen through the archives of its highest political decision-makers and through the life-stories of ordinary Kazakhstanis and their everyday approach to ethnicity, their search for a singular national identity and their responses to the regime's authoritarian efforts to impose a national identity. The following chapter is intended as a map for those who may not be familiar with Kazakhstan and its complex history. My choice of keywords and events in this narration are not accidental. I carefully mapped out the discourses or events that dominated my data when people spoke of national identity. Some spoke of these discourses and events as 'traumas', while others believed it was impossible to understand historical and present-day Kazakhstan without being aware of this history.

The book's first chapter deals with the vocabulary of contemporary Kazakhstan and introduces Kazakhstan and Kazakhness (*Qazaqshylyq*) to readers who may not be familiar with the region. The book then weaves the story across various historical and thematic scenes. Chapter 2 looks at the December 1986 protests in Soviet Kazakhstan, also known as Zheltoqsan, which is how December translates into the Kazakh language. I pack together the bits and pieces of the burnt-down archives of the violent crackdown and tell the stories of the eyewitnesses who described the blood-soaked snow at the main square in Alma-Ata, as Almaty was known at that time. This event, a major national trauma, continues to haunt Kazakhstani society, not least because the numbers and names of the victims are still unknown, as are the names of those who tortured and butchered the peaceful crowds of protestors on the square and then beat and raped young female protestors in the police torture chambers. Local KGB officers were quick to get rid of thousands of detailed reports of the 'events' in 1988–9.

INTRODUCTION

Chapters 3 and 4 turn to the discussion of everyday identities—Russian, Kazakh, *shala* Kazakh, Soviet and postsoviet, and *mankurts*—and stress how these identities and views of the nation 'from below' are important to understand the country's development. I begin the discussion in Chapter 3 in the aftermath of Zheltoqsan and detail how Moscow approached interethnic relations in the republic. Moscow's policies divided Kazakhstan, separating Russian- and Kazakh-speaking groups into two parallel communities, which in turn dictated how the state approached these communities in the years after independence, from 1991 up to the present day, and remains one of the most challenging legacies of Soviet rule.

Ethnic divisions divide the Kazakh-speaking groups into those who predominantly speak Kazakh and those who don't—often termed as *shala* or mixed Kazakhs or *mankurts*, colonial subjects who have forgotten their true identity. I discuss this division in Chapter 4. The exclusionary and derogatory terms used in this chapter speak of the Soviet legacy of discrimination. This unfortunate ethnic colouring defined the waves of protests in the post-independence era—the protests in Zhanaozen in 2011 and the mass protests of Bloody January 2022.

In Chapter 5, I focus on the Bloody January 2022 protests and discuss how and why these important events shaped the regime's politics and the underlying identities of the citizens demanding further democratisation and better governance. The public response to the January protests has helped shape local understandings of civicness, with the provision of mutual help for the survivors, their families and other groups in Kazakhstan who find themselves in need of additional support, notably the people of the industrial town of Ekibastuz, who were left without heating after the mass breakdown of their heating infrastructure in December 2022, or the families who lost their breadwinners in Qandy Qantar. In Chapter 6, I demonstrate how civicness is built on the idea of helping fellow co-citizens regardless of their ethnicity.

In the Afterword, I briefly address the decolonial debates that continue to shape Kazakhstani discussions about the future of their country and its turbulent history. The chapter also discusses the complexities generated in Kazakhstan by Russia's colonial war in

Ukraine. While Nazarbayev's successor, President Kassym-Jomart Tokayev, and the political elite have taken a neutral stance towards the conflict and have refused to recognise the Donbas and Luhansk People's Republics as political subjects inside Russia, Kazakhstani society remains divided on the issue. Whereas many among the older generation, who continue to consume Russian propaganda about the war, often support Russia's actions, there is also a strong group of civic activists who condemn the war and side with Ukraine in its fight for independence. The war has also caused many to grow anxious over Kazakhstan's future as a sovereign state, fearing that Russia could make similar claims on Kazakhstan to those it has made on Ukraine. The chapter's reference to de-Nazarbayefication stems from a quote from political activist and independent journalist Assem Zhapisheva, who concludes that the end of Soviet imperialism must start with the complete rejection of the policies of the former Kazakh leader Nazarbayev, who, as she and many others believe, never stopped being Soviet in his mentality and tactics in governing the state. This chapter focuses on the new generation of bilingual and trilingual globalised Kazakhstani youth who no longer want to live in the shadow of the 'postsoviet' and actively claim its final burial.

1

KAZAKHSTAN

ITS HISTORY AND ITS VOCABULARY

Kazakhstan is the second biggest country of the former Soviet Union. Its territory stretches from the Siberian steppes in the north to the oases and densely occupied cities of the south. It is a country that has changed its capital three times—from Kyzyl Orda to Almaty to Astana—in a span of about 100 years (and Orynbor, a city that is currently part of the Russian Federation, before that). Astana was also briefly known as Nur-Sultan, in honour of Nazarbayev, from 2019 to 2022. Kazakh elites boast that the country is home to more than 140 ethnicities and one national identity—Kazakhstani.

The Russian empire occupied Kazakhstan from the eighteenth to the start of the twentieth century, and many of Kazakhstan's present-day cities grew out of the imperial fortresses that later became full-fledged Soviet cities.[1] Kazakhstan was one of the fifteen Soviet republics and had a long Soviet century until it declared its independence in December 1991, the last Soviet republic to do so. Many Kazakhstanis bitterly joke that, for a few days in December 1991, Kazakhstan was in fact the Soviet Union, the rest of the republics having already declared their independence. The Kazakh leader, Nazarbayev, took a long time to declare that an independent

Kazakhstan had been born. Many local commentators suspect that he waited to declare independence on 16 December in an effort to erase the memory of the peaceful protests that happened on 17 December 1986, which were violently crushed by the Soviet leadership. Rather than being the day the country gained its independence, many Kazakhstanis continue to consider 16–17 December a day of remembrance for the victims of the Soviet regime.[2]

This book will tell the perplexing story of diverse nationalisms, protest movements and developments in Kazakhstani society, which inherited late Soviet categories and institutions of ethnicity. Based on memories, feelings and realisations about different categories of state, nation, society and ethnicity, these discourses are crucial for understanding how Kazakhstani society transformed over this period of independent statehood. Thus, this chapter is full of vignettes from my fieldwork in Kazakhstan that highlight the working of everyday community-building and citizens' responses to the regime's efforts to construct a single national identity. In this chapter, I offer a brief discussion of the key historical periods and concepts necessary to understand the context in which Kazakhstani identity exists today.

This chapter focuses on key themes—the famine of 1932–3, Soviet collectivisation and the forceful sedentarisation of the nomads, the detrimental effects of the Semipalatinsk nuclear testing site and Nazarbayev's vision of post-independence Kazakhstan. I then weave in more contemporary themes and discourses, such as the 2011 Zhanaozen protests and ongoing debates about national identity—*kimdik* in the Qazaq language—at the end of the chapter. The aim of this introductory analysis is twofold. On the one hand, it seeks to give some historical context to the study of Kazakhstan by focusing on the key events that influence Kazakhstani identity. For example, many Kazakh national-patriots (*ultshyldar*) actively use the traumas of the Soviet period, like the Asharshylyq famine, to substantiate their claims that Kazakh nation-building should seek to remedy the trauma experienced by ethnic Kazakhs and give more space in national identity to ethnic Kazakh discourses and histories. On the other hand, exploring these key themes and events, coupled with an expanded discussion on major 'ruptures' in Kazakhstan's history—the December 1986 protests and the Bloody January protests of 2022—allows me to focus on the key narratives often used in discussions about national identity. For example, while the December 1986 protests discussed in the following chapter signalled the emergence of anti-Soviet sentiments, they also marked the beginnings of the Russo-Kazakh divide in society that local elites skilfully used as a challenge to civic nation-building. These events and traumas, like the famine and the situation surrounding the Semipalatinsk nuclear testing site, were used by the regime to frame the impossibility of building a unified vision of Kazakhstan while also being actively interrogated by the communities outside the regime—by the citizens of Kazakhstan.

Asharshylyq—famine of 1932–3

On a sunny spring day, a group of museum workers invited me and my academic colleagues to the Museum of the Golden Man (Altyn Adam),[3] the archaeological marvel of the dead Scythian warrior and *their*[4] armour all made of gold. The museum was in the picturesque village of Issyk just outside Almaty, where in 1969–70 a local team of archaeologists found the Scythian warrior and the golden armour when they inspected one of the area's numerous burial sites. Since then, the mysterious Scythian warrior has become an obsession for scientists and a source of pride for the Kazakhstani elite.

In 1996, then-President Nazarbayev opened a monument to independence on the main square in Almaty; it was a 91-metre stella topped by a statue of the Golden Man. The statue was so far away that it almost felt as if it was built for the birds and drones that occasionally flew around the area. At the bottom of the monument was an open book containing the Kazakh Constitution, and inside it, on the left-hand side, was an imprint of a human palm.[5] No one really understood what the palm in the open book represented, but it became a popular ritual to place your hand there and make a wish. In 2007, the book was stolen—rumour had it that someone had a lot of wishes to make, so they stole the book with the palm imprint to make wishes all day long.[6]

When I was travelling to the said Museum of the Golden Man in Issyk in the summer of 2015, the Scythian warrior had become a mundane symbol of the regime's obsession with making its version of the nation as ancient as possible. Some people liked the idea that Kazakhs had the ability to magically transform themselves and trace their history to any predecessor, be it a Scythian warrior, the contemporaries of Alexander the Great—a myth that is also popular in Turkmenistan—or the direct relatives of Genghis Khan. As long as these people had some sort of connection to the Kazakh lands, they were deemed local. I lost count of how many times I heard that the 'great Kazakh leader, Genghis Khan' was buried with several tons of gold in one of Kazakhstan's gorgeous valleys or in its endless magic steppe—we just had to find the grave.

My journey to Issyk in 2015 was not my first. I have previously been to the exact place where the Golden Man was found and to the numerous tourist attractions that have sprung up in the surrounding area. The village was thriving with vines, horse riding, fishing, lodges, local cafés and a giant statue of the Golden Man next to the spring where people flood to drink the sacred water and take pictures next to the statue. The addition of the museum was designed to boost tourism to the region. It was well built and curated by a team of local enthusiasts, who even put up a yurt outside the museum to host important (and foreign) guests. The museum's director took me and a group of archaeologists on a tour. Inside the museum, there were a lot of archaeological artefacts from the Issyk area found in mostly looted *kurgans*, the burial places. There were pieces of old pottery, some of which we were able to hold in our hands. What can be more exciting than holding a piece of broken pottery made hundreds of years ago?

I appreciated the museum's interactive exhibits and how it enthusiastically welcomed its visitors. However, the museum dedicated to the Golden Man only had copies of the actual golden armour and three small original golden artefacts found during the famous 1970 excavations. No one knew where the real Scythian warrior was kept. Perhaps it was in a hold inside the presidential palace, Ak Orda, or maybe even abroad. 'No one knows', the museum staff told me. But there were good copies made from the original, and these were on display in the National Museum in Almaty.[7] The museum workers glanced at me and told me in Kazakh that 'of course, everyone knows it is a copy', but there was no need to repeat that to the esteemed foreign guests. Some things that are an open secret in Kazakhstan—that we know little to nothing about what is going on in the presidential palace, that a lot of museum treasures are well-done copies and very few people know where the originals are—had to be kept hidden from foreigners. Everyone else had to be impressed with the golden arches that the National Museum in Almaty hosted. They were not made from real gold, but it was important to make a good impression. Isn't that what museums are for? Making impressions and creating a coherent historical narrative of the esteemed nation.

The Issyk museum hosted far more modest copies, posters and artefacts than the central museums. But this small museum's inviting atmosphere made it far more attractive than some of the halls of the National Museum in downtown Almaty that tried to impose the view that Kazakhstan's modern history started with Nazarbayev, literally with his birthday on 6 July 1940.[8] In the Issyk museum, the visitor was invited to create their own story without being constrained by grand historical frames. State slogans did not scream at you from the walls, and the cold breezy halls were inviting in the burning late spring sun.

Outside the museum stood two *balbals*, ancient stone figures that had been placed throughout the Kazakh steppe, which Kazakh elites later claimed as an ancient Kazakh tradition.[9] The same logic of local-ness applied here as well—everyone and every artefact found on the territory of Kazakhstan was immediately made Kazakh in the state narrative.[10] These *balbals* appear to have been used for various purposes, whether as gravestones, as some claim, or as direction points in the vast steppe.[11] In the imagination of contemporary Kazakhstanis, the *balbal* figure is a signifier of culture because they appear on the national currency, on the state television's cultural channel and on postcards and tourist brochures. The *balbal* is for the Kazakh steppe what Gaudi's lizard is for Barcelona—a symbol of tourist identification with the space.[12] The Issyk museum proudly hosted two of these figurines in their courtyard and considered them historical artefacts.

There is an interesting story about how these two *balbals* were acquired from the local people. One of the museum workers told me that Issyk is a sacred space that had always occupied a special role in nomadic geography and Tengri shamanistic rituals. But since the village was so close to the expanding megapolis of Almaty, it became a lucrative space for local businesses and was a popular destination for the recent migrants and repatriates, ethnic Kazakhs who had moved from Uzbekistan, Mongolia and China.[13] Plots of land were sold sporadically, and people often occupied archaeological sites with their kitchen gardens (*ogorod*), planting cucumbers, melons, tomatoes and salad plants on ancient graveyards. 'History means nothing to them', my interlocutor said in Kazakh. One of the *balbals* standing in front of us was found accidentally when a tractor was ploughing the fields to plant potatoes, and museum workers fought hard to acquire it as an artefact. 'These people [locals] wanted to display it in their garden!' my interlocutor exclaimed.

I just smiled. Life goes on even at the archaeological sites, and history *means* a lot to these people even if sometimes they have no artefacts with which to commemorate it, as I found out on my ride back to Almaty. An elderly man sitting next to me on a minibus, *marshrutka*, stared at the long stretch of the road we were passing by. After a moment of silence, he connected the palms of his hands close to his chest, murmured a prayer and raised his hands to his face, covering it for a moment in a gesture to the local Muslim ritual. Then he whispered to me and a middle-aged woman sitting next to me: 'On this road, in 1933 hundreds of people passed by dying from hunger. Those were the days of Asharshylyq [the Great Famine] and there is no single monument to indicate their existence and death here', he said in Kazakh. The woman next to me sighed, and we both indicated that we wanted him to continue the story. The elderly man said that when he was a little boy, no one in the family spoke of those who perished, even though everyone knew about the famine. Then, when he was growing up, he heard stories of his older sister dying during the famine. 'It was the tragedy that touched every Kazakh family at the time', he said, still whispering, and pointed his right finger to the long stretch of road. 'Everything here was covered with dead bodies as far as you could see!' And yet there was not a single monument in the area to remember this history. Not a single *balbal* to mourn the dead.

Asharshylyq, the famine of 1932–3 when 'about one and a half million people died', amounting to 'more than a third of all Kazakhs, or a fourth of Kazakhstan's entire population',[14] remains a national tragedy. Asharshylyq was a result of the Soviet Union's efforts to 'modernise' Kazakhstan by sedentarising the nomads, mostly Kazakhs the Soviet regime deemed 'backward' and who, according to the Soviet vision, required modernisation. 'What the people perceived as a sequence of dramatic trepidations, the men around Stalin saw as an efficient strategy to rule the country. Incessant escalation was their mode of rule. Crises were both the method and aim', writes German historian Robert Kindler.[15] There was a similar famine in Ukraine, which also became a national trauma—the Holodomor—as well as the North Caucasus and the Volga region in Russia, which is why many Russian propagandists still insist that the period's famines were a 'common tragedy' in which everyone suffered. Yet in Kazakhstan, not Russia, the human loss from 'Sovietisation by hunger' led to the greatest losses 'in proportion to its total population'.[16] The famine was a man-made catastrophe resulting from ambitious colonial policies designed to enable the Soviet Union to conquer, civilise and control local populations along with their lands and resources that ultimately led to mass death, touching 'every Kazakh family' at the time, as my interlocutor in Issyk whispered, and forcing thousands to flee to neighbouring states—to East Turkestan in China, to Mongolia, Afghanistan and other states where large diasporas of Kazakhs were formed outside the Soviet Union.[17] Since my visit to Issyk, I kept wondering how the famine had affected other Kazakh families at the time.

When my father brought me to the stone commemorating the famine in his home village, he walked in silence around the site. It was a big gravestone with engravings in Kazakh that he and my brother— who was far from happy at being made to carry such a big stone—had brought from a far-away stone and marble factory located somewhere in the mountains of Tekeli, which they then placed in a picturesque field next to a tree in the village. The stone was surrounded by a little fence, like a place of burial in modern cemeteries. From the stone, one could either stare at the valley dotted with small hills, a picturesque site in the spring, when the valley is covered with red tulips and other steppe flowers, but a sunburnt grass in the summer and completely covered in snow in the winter, or walk to the left to a small bench next to the tree. I have known this bench since my early childhood. We often visited my father's friends in the village and always stopped by the bench where he would walk around, sometimes sitting in silence to gather his thoughts. Occasionally, he would pray, whispering some words in Kazakh and raising his hands over his glasses, his eyes full of sadness. Many more Kazakhstanis are accustomed to the same prayer ritual when remembering the dead. Sometimes I could hear him whisper the names of his own father (Kudaibergen) and grandfather (Oksikbai).

We never spoke about the site; it was only years later, when my brother remembered carrying the heavy stone on his back, or I participated in Holodomor discussions and conferences in Canada, that my father finally started talking. 'You don't know this story, *qyzym* [my daughter]. The Great Famine, Asharshylyq, claimed so many lives and almost destroyed my family.' For years of Soviet rule, no one spoke about it, but after 1991, my father gathered some strength and decided to place the commemorative stone in the place where his grandfather used to rest and overlook his herds in the valley, right in the place where we always stopped on the way to the village, or *aul*.[18]

'No one knows where my grandfather, our other family members and a lot of other villagers died during Asharshylyq. They just perished. No grave, no trace, no record in official documents', my father said. The word 'perished' acquired a completely different meaning to me that day. It entered my life like sudden thunder, an explosion. That no one knows where the graves are was another shock. Unable to grieve in the Soviet period, my grandfather, the surviving child of the family that perished, used to come to this same place, sit on the bench under the tree and remember his relatives. Their absences spoke loudly even in times of forced silence, trauma weeding deep into his body and eventually killing him before we could meet. Because it was still the Soviet period, he could not make or erect anything to commemorate the victims, but he passed on the stories to his children and to my father, his eldest son. The stone my brother never stopped complaining about was not really for the graveyard, because there was no graveyard. The stone was a last resort to keep alive the memory of the many victims of Asharshylyq who once used to live in the *aul* but then perished without a trace, my great-grandfather included.

In the chaos of those violent years, my grandfather, Kudaibergen, tried to escape to China with his mother but stopped just before the last mountainous frontier between them and East Turkestan. They stayed in the village nearby and somehow, miraculously, survived. When Kudaibergen married, he knew he could not pass on his family name to his children because his father was a *bai*, or *kulak*, someone the Soviets considered an enemy of the state. The sacred family line that Kazakhs cherished was kept on a piece of paper covered in pencil scribbles in one of the many books the family managed to acquire after the 1930s. It was kept in secret so that one day we would write the truthful genealogy, *shezhire*, either when the Soviet Union had ceased to exist or when the repression of those years had come to an end.

My grandfather died in 1983 and never lived to see the Soviet collapse. All of his children apart from my father adopted the name of a distant relative to avoid persecution as relatives of a *kulak*. But my father, the first son who survived after birth, took on the name of his father, Kudaibergen, with the obligatory Soviet gendered ending '-ov' to indicate he was male, and the no less obligatory fifth paragraph in the passport indicating his nationality—'Kazakh'. The family genealogy, *shezhire*, was safeguarded as well—it was printed in a fat book along with other people from our tribe (*ru*) and our Horde (*Zhuz*) in the late 1990s, finally recovering the name of my great-grandfather who had otherwise been almost completely erased from official documents during the Soviet era. Similar books of *shezhire* were proudly displayed in many houses in the *aul*; pages with good paper, Kazakh names printed in Cyrillic, the legacy of Stalinist language reforms.[19] But, as far as I could tell, in the nearby villages there were not many more other stones with the names of relatives who had perished in the famine. As Kindler explains:

Keeping silent and not speaking publicly about famine are among the consequences of a Stalinist communication strategy that tied large parts of the population not immediately affected by famine to the regime. It worked because the interests of the rulers and the ruled coincided more than it may at first seem. Where no one spoke of dying and suffering, no one asked about personal responsibility and guilt. Silence held people together. When no one spoke out, it was not only for fear of the regime, it also suppressed awareness of one's own involvement. Excluding the victims meant including everyone else and doing so far before the end of the famine itself.

Perhaps we find here an answer to the question of how Soviet society continued to function even in times of extreme crises such as years of famines or during the excesses of terror in 1937 and 1938. It did [not] come to a war of each against all, nor did state terror and violence atomize society. Refusing to mention the famine was an offer the dictator made to the people, and it was a threat. The populace understood that they basically had no other choice but to follow the lead of the regime.[20]

Despite studying the Asharshylyq for many years, I only heard people whisper about the famine. Kazakh national-patriots who proudly attacked any attempt to denigrate the Kazakh language or downplay Kazakh values on television, during rallies or on the pages of Kazakh-language opposition newspapers would only whisper things to me about Asharshylyq even in conversations that happened as late as 2013. When I went to the museums located on the territories of Stalin's numerous gulags, his 'gifts' to the Kazakh steppe, Asharshylyq was one among many tragedies of excruciating human trauma. People next to me cried looking at the pictures of famous Kazakh writers and politicians who looked unrecognisable in their final gulag pictures in 1937. These were the last memories they were leaving behind, their mass graves never recovered, their bones never identified by DNA test labs.

In Almaty, one of the central parks had a black square stone with the engraving 'On this place the monument to the victims of the 1931–3 famine will be placed.' It stood there for more than twenty-five years until the monument, a figure of a mother holding her starved child, was unveiled on 31 May 2017, the official Remembrance Day for the victims of the Stalinist terror. The monument features quotations from Nazarbayev's speech, 'Famine That Brought an Entire Nation to the Brink of Extinction Will Never Be Forgotten'.

But if it would never be forgotten, why did it take the whole nation more than two decades to commemorate its dead despite living in an independent state?[21] The country was not short of material for monument-making nor of talented sculptors. The news constantly reported on scandals surrounding various monuments, such as those to the founders of Kazakh statehood, the fifteenth-century rulers Zhanibek and Kerei.[22] Somehow, there was always money for monuments of Nazarbayev. The regime's narrative carefully promoted the idea that Asharshylyq, the man-made famine that claimed millions of lives, belonged in the category of 'Stalinist crimes' along with the 1937 repressions and the political murders of thousands of people and the gulagisation of Kazakhstan. This categorisation allowed the regime to divert the focus from the famine itself, which touched almost every Kazakh family, and to maintain good relations with Moscow, which carefully filtered any news about the 1930s famines in its near abroad even before the 2014 annexation of Crimea and the start of the war in Ukraine. The rhetoric attributing the famine to 'Stalinist crimes' also allowed those who were nostalgic about the Soviet period, or *sovki*, to continue to claim that 'Stalin was bad, but the Soviets were good.'

Perhaps Kindler is right, and the silence around Asharshylyq was a way to avoid opening up old cupboards and disturbing old skeletons. But breaking these silences and asking often uncomfortable and traumatic questions is also a way to deal with these traumatic silences and erasures.

In 2014, I was invited for a chat after a conference in Astana. Dozens of people who barely knew each other landed in a 'traditional Russian restaurant' that promised good borsch and dumplings. Unable to join my group of more familiar friends, I somehow found myself sitting in front of two Kazakh men savouring hot Russian drinks. They were loudly discussing one of the men's first name and 'legendary' last name. 'Do you know who you're sitting next to?', one of the men asked me. I didn't have a clue. 'This is the descendant of the great Soviet man, a Soviet revolutionary.' He then spelt the man's last name, which I knew well from archival documents. Indeed, a true 'Soviet man', someone who helped greatly to violently sedentarise the nomads and kill or drive off all those who disagreed with the new regime. 'The descendants of the greatest people walk among us!', exclaimed the man, who was introducing the grandson of the man who helped in the Soviet campaign to destroy the villagers along with my great-grandfather. I politely refused the offer of dumplings with vodka and made an excuse to leave, quickly called a cab and left.

Years later, I still question whether I made the right decision. Perhaps I should have stayed and told the two men the horror stories of broken families, children separated and sent to far-away orphanages, and the people kept in Stalin's concentration camps we politely call gulags, stories of people who were still scared to death to speak openly about the Stalinist atrocities. My grandfather had a sister, but she was given away to a Russian family who were able to feed her during the famine. Our family never found her after the famine, after the terror, after the war. 'She was too little to remember her roots to find her way back', my uncle once exclaimed and cried. She was long gone. 'She was probably signed up as Russian [by ethnicity]', my aunt said. Our Russian grandmother never came back to her native *aul*. My grandfather, Kudaibergen, passed the stories on to his children but died without ever recovering her or any other members of his family or their places of death. He mourned in silence; he prayed behind closed doors and kept his family line written on a piece of paper carefully tucked away and hidden from the secret police officers who continued to search for enemies of the state long after Stalin's death.[23]

Despite its obsession with certain aspects of Kazakh history, and especially the skeleton of the Golden Man, the regime seemed to care little about the bones scattered in the hungry steppe or of those who perished in mass graves, unaccounted for and many long forgotten. There is no howl, the traditional Kazakh song *zhoktau* commemorating the dead, sung over them, though some villagers do organise remembrance days with traditional food offerings, *as*, for them, and some mullahs or priests may occasionally mention them in the prayers people ask for. This is how Kazakhstanis commemorate their dead. Quietly, collectively, locally. They commemorate in a hybrid mix of different religious rituals away from the regime's pompous speeches by placing flowers on the graves or throwing a handful of soil (*topraq*) over the burial after the obligatory whispering of a prayer in Russian or Kazakh, or Polish and Korean, or German and Chechen, or Uyghur, Uzbek, Kazakh, Tatar mixed with Arabic, or Ukrainian, or Yiddish, or Kurdish.

Places that were once the burial sites of the dead bodies of starved nomads who failed to 'modernise' had now become roads from the picturesque village of Issyk to Almaty or isolated commemorative sites and stones, just like the one my brother had carried on his back, in some less visited villages and *auls* all around Kazakhstan. Unlike Ukraine, there is no museum to the victims of Asharshylyq in Kazakhstan, no quotations of the Soviet decrees that stripped local people of their source of food—grain in Ukraine and livestock for the nomads in Kazakhstan; there are no 'books of sorrow' in Kazakhstan with the names of the victims of the famine that many researchers in Ukraine are still recovering today. Unlike Ukraine's Holodomor, Asharshylyq has not yet become the cornerstone of the state's national commemoration in Kazakhstan.

However, it is very much remembered and whispered about in families, where parents and grandparents wait for the youngsters to grow old enough to be able to stomach the horrifying story that someone in their family also perished in the famine, that a sister had been given away or, worse, exchanged for food to feed the family's other starving children. The whispers mount into a generational trauma when someone occasionally remembers to mention the family at a commemoration dinner or in light of news about how Ukraine continues to commemorate the anniversary of Holodomor at the end of November, even during the war.

Collectivisation: ending nomadic life

Almagul Menlibayeva, a famous contemporary Kazakh artist who uses the steppe as one of the prime protagonists in her artistic and historical rethinking of the Soviet colonial trauma, spoke to me of her feeling of cultural amnesia.[24] We first met at the end of 2013, and she also agreed to be interviewed online. In 2015, I attended KARLAG, a group exhibition she had co-organised about the Karaganda gulag in Astana's National Museum. We bonded instantly. Only Almagul could bring a video installation about the torture chambers of the NKVD—Stalin's Commissariat for Internal Affairs—to the National Museum in Astana, the city that is the episteme, the heart of authoritarian bureaucracy, especially at that time, when Russia had annexed Crimea and then-President Nazarbayev was still cautious to remain friendly with Putin. Her video installation was being broadcast on the biggest screen they could find and was placed in the centre of the exposition directly facing a giant cradle covered in ropes, an installation by another Kazakh artist, Syrlybek Bekbotayev, who travelled with Almagul to Karaganda and visited a number of gulags on the field trips with her and the third artist who participated in the exhibition, Ainur Sadenova.

On the wall behind Bekbotayev's cradle were the portraits of Kazakh intellectuals, parts of their faces shifted and distorted to demonstrate that their legacy had also been distorted. Central to the portrait was the canonical picture of three fathers of the Alash movement, the pre-Soviet pro-independence movement leaders—Akhmet Baitursynov, Alikhan Bokeikhanov and Myrzhaqyp Dulatov.[25] The tops of their faces had been painted light blue like the colour of the Kazakh flag; according to Bekbotayev, it was there to represent the historical violence that had been done to their legacy, which continued even after independence.

Just across from the portraits was the video exhibit, which Menlibayeva had been working on for a long time. She filmed in a real gulag and visited numerous NKVD torture chambers where innocent people were tortured to death. It was a disturbing video in which the camera moved slowly from one cell or one chamber to another, with poor light revealing the tiny rooms, cells and walls, accompanied by dramatic music. Sometimes, the scenes featured interviews with museum workers, archivists and historians. Sometimes the figure of an actor, dressed and painted like Stalin and wearing a fake moustache, walked around the empty corridors of the gulag. Sometimes he stared right into the camera.

Everyone who passed by the fake Stalin was horrified. The exhibition was traumatic because it was about the traumas that many of us have buried deep down inside our bodies. The figure of the fake Stalin triggered many of these traumas. After five minutes in the hall and despite the opportunity to listen to the talks of these superb artists and curators—all of whom later became my close friends—the sight of this fake Stalin gave me a panic attack. As I searched for fresh air or at least a corner where I wouldn't hear or see this Stalin, I stumbled upon a dark corner and decided to hide there. It was hard to see anything, but I could feel there were objects stacked in the corner, giving me some sense of space and distance. Suddenly, the objects—barrels, as I later found out—started singing lullabies in different languages. It was momentarily soothing, until a curator found me in the corner. 'Ah, you're *enjoying* Sadenova's work. Have you read the description?' she asked. I had not.

This installation was dedicated to the babies and children who died in the gulag during the winter and could not be buried because the soil was too hard. So, their dead bodies were placed in barrels and disposed of at a later date. But their mourning mothers would often pass these barrels in the camp, further intensifying their trauma. 'Only children who died in the summer were buried at the children's cemetery. It is still there, near Karaganda, in Dolinka. It is a site of commemoration now', Sadenova, who had created the installation, explained to me. Her decision to have lullabies coming from the barrels was intended to point to the inhumane nature of the Soviet empire and to commemorate these lost souls. At this point, I was in tears; the people around me were hysterical.

The exhibition opened on 31 May, Remembrance Day, but as it was a Monday, the National Museum was officially closed. Many art enthusiasts nevertheless found their way to the opening event. We cried collectively and could not stop discussing the atrocities of what had happened. I only managed to get through the museum security after being given special instructions from someone higher up. I was convinced the exhibition would be cancelled the next day or as soon as someone in the presidential palace, Ak Orda, or in the presidential administration heard about it.[26] When I asked Menlibayeva what had inspired her to organise this exhibition and centre her artistic and curatorial work on rethinking the traumatic Soviet past, she responded that her personal experiences of colonisation left her no other choice:

> I was born and grew up in the Soviet city of Alma-Ata [Almaty] and I went to the Russian-language school, I was a Soviet child like many of the urban Kazakhs who don't speak their language, and they remain in between, in between Russians and Kazakhs. It is a type of a new formation. In some ways, I think it was [Russification], a continuation of a cultural exodus because Kazakhs are no longer nomads, it [sedentarisation] happened in a very violent and tragic way and really, what we are experiencing is cultural amnesia. ... The nomadic lifestyle is gone; it is no longer there. We are no longer nomads. All of these new attempts of national self-identification, it is an attempt to build a new nation because what happened in the 1920s and 1930s [violent sedentarisation, the famine], it was incredibly traumatic, it was horrific. And we are no longer nomads. ... I often go to the steppe, and I stare at it, and I try to imagine how they [nomads] lived here, how they could gallop for a thousand kilometres to chase something or someone. Steppe gives freedom.
>
> It is impossible to conquer the steppe. ... Sedentarised people could not go deep into the steppe, they had no knowledge, no technology [to survive there]. When I travel across the steppe, in Central Kazakhstan, I visit small villages and often see *as*, traditional commemoration lunches, and people invite me. I take pictures, I talk to them. I see that they strive to sustain this tradition, that knowledge, that nomads used to commemorate their dead just like that. [With collectivisation and sedentarisation], the nomadic way of life was violently crushed, and people who remained had to survive. This is why I constantly see how our people know how to survive; they are resilient. ... But I also feel this amnesia, the lost knowledge of the way of living like our ancestors used to live. But we are no longer nomads. We live in Soviet apartment buildings; the real nomads were killed. But maybe it is horrifying to understand, to conceive this trauma. When you feel pain, you try to push it out from your consciousness, you try to forget [all the traumatic events] that

happened. I spoke to my relatives, to my grandmother ... stories of horrifying details, of cannibalism [during the famine]. People say, 'yes, famine, collectivisation happened'. But it is shameful to speak about bad things. We forget the pain, the bad things. But it all comes back. Trauma cannot be erased.²⁷

Menlibayeva visited the steppe a dozen more times after our first interview and had engaged in extensive research long before that. She told me she went to the steppe because she felt it would help her piece together the knowledge she felt she had forgotten and overcome the cultural amnesia from which she was suffering. At the time, still in 2013, we were both searching for the pieces of the same puzzle.

On the one hand, we wanted to make sense of what Soviet 'modernisation' had really brought to our people. Starvation, violence, torture and exploitation. We looked at historical documents. I read letters in the archives sent from Kazakhstan to Moscow declaring a state of emergency because nomads were unable to live in strictly allocated spaces, helplessly watching their land being plotted, excavated and given over to collective farms. They died en masse during the famine, together with their livestock, and received no help from the government.²⁸

Sedentarisation meant the seizure of cattle, land and pastures that were shared by different tribes and the creation of collective farms (*kolkhozes*) in places deemed useful for agriculture, clearing up spaces for the colonial plans that the Soviets, spearheaded by Stalin himself, had for the vast Kazakh steppes.²⁹ What to a nomad was full of meaning and freedom was, to the Soviets, simply an 'empty' and 'barren' steppe ready to be conquered by modernisation. As Kindler writes:

> Much more important was the circumstance that sedentarization was an essential prerequisite for the large-scale relocation of special settlers, Gulag prisoners, and later also 'enemy nations' [Germans, Chechens, Crimean Tatars, Koreans and anyone Stalin decided to brand as an enemy] in the Kazakh steppe. Whenever the planners spoke of opening up gigantic areas of land for development following sedentarization [of Kazakh

nomads], they thought of the development as a task for the people they would deport from elsewhere. Nomads were in the way and had to leave to make room for the victims of Stalinist repression; it was they who were to live and work in the steppe. This was especially true of territories selected for Gulag camps. According to a resolution of May 1930 the OGPU [intelligence and state security service of the Soviet Union] wanted more than 110,000 hectares put at its disposal to accommodate 'the enormous politico-economic and cultural significance of the camp to be erected' (that was later to become Karlag).[30]

Meshed together with trauma, the words both Almagul and I could not yet find in 2013 but that we found together in 2015 when we met after my panic attack at the Karlag exhibition were that the Soviet Union was a colonial empire. Speaking to me two and a half years after our first interview, when she spoke of cultural amnesia, and after conducting extensive fieldwork in Karlag near Karaganda and in other gulags nearby, she knew exactly what she had to do: 'Even if I wasn't an artist, I would've still come to this realisation. But it is always more interesting to do so [speak of colonialism and its traumas] through art', she said as we sat down in a popular Almaty café.[31]

Why is it hard to speak of colonial trauma when history clearly tells us that Kazakhstan was colonised by the Soviets, Stalin, Filipp Goloshekin, by the Soviet Union; that nomads were dispossessed of their culture, land and knowledge to build gulags on the territories of their former pastures? As we sat in the café facing the Stalinist-era apartment buildings with high ceilings and four rooms, a luxury in the Soviet era, when most people had to live in small, cramped apartments, I remembered that a well-known Kazakh writer, Sabit Mukanov, used to live in one of these apartments. I had never liked his writing, and a month later, in a central state archive in Almaty, I found out why he was so canonised. In 1937, he chaired the Kazakh Writers' Union and openly attacked many famous (and far more talented) writers, accusing them of nationalism. He chaired a colonial institution that fed us stories of internationalism and happy tales of industrialisation while hundreds of his former colleagues and friends died in the gulag. He lived in one of these Stalin apartments in the so-called Golden Square (Zolotoi Kvadrat) raion of Alma-Ata, even receiving the Stalin Prize in the 1940s. Somehow, most Almaty dwellers preferred to forget the word *stalinki* that was used for these apartments in Soviet times. Mukanov was a *stalinnik*, a fervent Stalinist, loyal to his bones, a cannibal in the flesh who sold the idea of the Great Soviet Union and Uncle Stalin to a generation of Kazakhstani children while at the same time allowing dozens of his colleagues and friends to perish in the same gulags Menlibayeva and I were now studying. Meanwhile, she continued:

> After all my projects, I have no drop of nostalgia for the Soviet time; no desire to take something and find something positive in that past. There were no positive [aspects] there. Something positive came in the postsoviet time, in the time of stagnation, but after the Soviet Union [ceased to exist]. I have no nostalgia for that time. I don't think we should be fooled to believe there was something international or internationalist about it [the Soviet period]. From my fieldwork, there was no internationalism, there was only pseudo-internationalism [that the Soviets practised] where we were friends with someone against someone.[32] We need a major re-think of it all. I think if the young generation or people who experience difficulties with communicating with the world and who cannot integrate into the global world, they probably think, let's build a new cool empire. I think it is a huge disillusionment because your own problems in the global arena should not make you come here and build your empires here. It is not a solution at all. It will never bring them to anything good. I think we need to change totally [*nado total'no menyatsya*]. Because soon this [postsovietness] will fall down like pieces of dirt [off our structures] and as soon as we emancipate ourselves of it, the better.[33]

Her words sounded even more bitter than the black Americano I'd ordered but had completely forgotten about. As the cup sat there on the table, we were both in deep conversation about Soviet colonisation. I told her about things I found in the National Library and the archives, and she told me of her harrowing experiences of learning the truth from seeing the unbearable conditions of the gulags she had been visiting for years and that Nazarbayev failed to mention in his speeches boasting of Kazakhstan's multi-ethnic society.

Soviet 'ethnicity' policies allowed Stalin and his cronies to uproot whole villages, communities, the elderly, sick, children and breastfeeding women and send them away simply because they were Chechen, Meskhetian Turks, Koreans, Germans or any other ethnicity he viewed as a threat to his rule.[34] 'Enemy of the state'—what a dystopian term to justify the killing and torturing of masses of people. When those who oppose my view that the Soviet Union was an empire tell me there was no concept of 'race' and racism in the Soviet Union, I often want to remind them of the 'ethnicity' that substituted race and allowed Stalin and other Soviet leaders to kill, control and instil further violence by using a racialised understanding of ethnicity as a prerequisite for violence against people of a specific ethnic background.

Deconstructing the Soviet past and the violent project of modernisation that labelled people like the Kazakhs as 'backward' and in need of civilising requires a lot of challenging work. Not everyone in Kazakhstan can afford the journey Menlibayeva engaged in for years when she explored the Stalinist gulags. For many Kazakhstanis, a visit to Astana's shiny EXPO pavilions is an unaffordable luxury, let alone a trip to an old gulag or the gulag museum outside Astana or Karaganda. Yet, in recent years, I have found that more and more people are travelling to these sites in search of their families' lost histories.

Nevada-Semipalatinsk

On 29 August 1949, the Soviets conducted their first nuclear weapons test in the place now known as the Semipalatinsk Polygon in Eastern Kazakhstan. For forty years, it served as a secret testing ground for Soviet nuclear weapons, despite being in the vicinity of villages and *auls* and close to sites still considered important parts of Kazakhstan's cultural heritage. 'Soviet scientists and the military conducted more than seven hundred nuclear tests, with more than 450 of them at Semipalatinsk between 1949, when the Polygon was established, and 1989, when Kazakhstan's antinuclear protests stopped them', writes Togzhan Kassenova in her exhaustive study of the Polygon.[35] The tests left a significant amount of scarring on the land, in the steppe. The level of physical and emotional trauma the forty years of nuclear testing left on Kazakhstani citizens is still being evaluated. In her book, Kassenova carefully traces the programme's historical development and details the human and non-human losses—many animals were placed in the epicentre of the explosions to test the effects of the bombs—as well as the genetic and medical aftershocks these explosions left on the local population. Kassenova recounts the story of Kabden Essengarin,

> a local health official [who] lived in Sarzhal, a village in the vicinity of the Polygon known for livestock breeding. He had spent several days in evacuation after the test [in 1954] but was soon asked to return to Sarzhal to sort out the cattle of different households that had gotten mixed up after the residents evacuated. There he saw dogs and cats that had lost all their fur, and later on observed that returning villagers drank water from the open wells. 'Nobody warned them that the water could be radioactive,' Essengarin said.
>
> Families in the area would suffer the effects of radiation both immediately and for generations. Not atypical for these families, Essengarin's granddaughter Samantha, named after an American girl famous for her letter to the Soviet leader Yuri Andropov about a nuclear war, would be born with Down syndrome.[36]

Throughout most of my school years, the Semipalatinsk Nuclear Testing Polygon (or simply the Polygon) remained part of the background to our everyday lives. In school, there were special events with anti-nuclear weapons activists from the Semipalatinsk area; we attended exhibitions by artists from the Semipalatinsk area who painted with their feet because they had no other limbs; charity events were organised to help local children who were diagnosed with cancer. The Semipalatinsk Nuclear Testing Polygon was a lived trauma we grew up with because we lived in the period after Kazakhstan became independent, when information about the Polygon was no longer top secret but no less horrifying. We were growing up to understand that our country, our land, our people—and some of my friends who were from the Semipalatinsk area but had moved out of there in the 1990s—had been used as testing material for Soviet nuclear power. That realisation hits heavy even now, years after our parents found out and years after so many victims of the Semipalatinsk Polygon have passed away.

In the 1990s, there was still a great deal of anti-nuclear activism in Kazakhstan, even after Kazakhstani activists had fought for the closure of the Polygon in 1989–90 and although Kazakhstan gave up its nuclear arsenal in 1994. Local media widely discussed the anti-nuclear movement 'Nevada-Semipalatinsk' that emerged in 1989 and its charismatic leader, Kazakh poet and politician Olzhas Suleimenov. Beloved by the public for his literary writing, mostly poems but also some collections of essays, research and his *Az I Ya* book about the Turkic foundation of the Old East Slavic epic *Slovo o Polku Igoreve* (The tale of Igor's campaign), Suleimenov was a household name in Soviet Kazakhstan. Owning a book of his poems and *Az IYa*, which the Soviets censored after publication, was a sign of culture and patriotism.

In 1984, after becoming a deputy of the USSR Supreme Soviet (the top Soviet legislature), Suleimenov 'received desperate letters from people living near the Semipalatinsk Polygon, and other testing grounds in Kazakhstan, complaining about deteriorating health and hard living conditions'.[37] When a gas leak from one of the tests created a public outcry in February 1989, Suleimenov called for all citizens to join him in a rally in downtown Alma-Ata. On 28 February 1989, the Nevada-Semipalatinsk anti-nuclear movement was born. According to the prominent Kazakh thinker Murat Auezov, many commentators and activists saw the movement 'as redress not only for Moscow's brutal crackdown at the December 1986 protests but also for the Russian oppression of the Kazakh independence movement Alash Orda and for the execution of Kazakhstan's educated elite by Stalin in the 1930s'.[38]

A lot of the information about the Stalinist atrocities and the denouncement of the Kazakh intelligentsia as nationalists and their deaths in the Stalinist gulags slipped through the walls of the Writers' Union building where Suleimenov was one of the unofficial leaders. For decades, many Kazakh writers quietly discussed details of the prohibited literature during the Red Terror and whispered the names of the intellectuals who had perished. The union's archival documents record heated discussions in the 1950s about the possibility of rehabilitating some of the early Soviet Kazakh writers and their works.[39]

In the 1960s, Suleimenov and Auezov were part of the Sixtiers (*shestidesyatniki*) movement and the anti-Soviet Kazakh dissident intellectual movement Zhas Tulpar. Although Suleimenov wrote predominantly in Russian, his texts spoke of hybrid Russo-Kazakh culture and language, which made him incredibly popular not only in Kazakhstan but in other parts of the Soviet Union too. From the 1960s, Suleimenov involved himself in activist work that often bordered on dissidence. By the end of the 1980s, it was only logical for him to join the political field, where he became a voice of freedom. His leadership of the Nevada-Semipalatinsk anti-nuclear testing movement garnered him further political popularity, and many considered him a serious contender for political power in the now independent Kazakhstan. Suleimenov was charismatic, poetic, full of energy and ideas of freedom and liberation. By 1994, it was clear he was popular enough to stand against Nazarbayev himself in a presidential election; he also had the resources and the support behind him to power through an election, and it was the only time in the modern Kazakhstani history when a democratic election would be possible. But in the heat of the moment, with the democratic parliament falling apart and important political figures exiting the country to occupy diplomatic posts abroad, Suleimenov lost a key battle. It is still unclear why he decided to abandon the political party he was forming as well as his presidential ambitions, but in 1995 he swiftly left Kazakhstan for a diplomatic post in Paris, where he and his family remained for years.

Meanwhile, Nazarbayev used the period between 1994 and 1995 to consolidate his rule by dissolving parliament and then changing the constitution to give him more powers, creating a supra-presidential republic. In the absence of strong rivals, he turned Kazakhstan into an oil-rich dictatorship with a rubber-stamp parliament that solely hosts Nazarbayev loyalists, including Tokayev, who later became his successor. In the late 2000s, the elites around Nazarbayev campaigned for him to win the Noble Prize for Peace for 'his efforts to get rid of the Soviet nuclear arsenal Kazakhstan inherited upon independence and to close the Semipalatinsk test size'.[40] Nazarbayev wanted to assume a leading role in the anti-nuclear discourse and was allegedly sincere in his desire to win the Noble Prize for Peace for his anti-nuclear stance, but his two nominations and intense campaigns to get him the prize failed miserably. Suleimenov, on the other hand, remained the historic figure behind the Nevada-Semipalatinsk anti-nuclear movement and, upon his return to Kazakhstan, continued to savour his popularity but without actively engaging in politics, even in the post-Nazarbayev era.

Nazarbayev's futureless policy of the 'eternal nation'

On 15 June 1993, President Nazarbayev gathered together a group of politicians, writers and public intellectuals to form a new national committee for state politics under the president's direction. Opening the meeting, Nazarbayev stressed how the 'problem of strengthening the real sovereignty and independence of Kazakhstan' was the cornerstone of the first years of independence. Even though he was vague about the 'internal and external forces' that threatened Kazakhstan's interethnic stability or posed a danger of secessionism, it was clear he was acutely aware of the potential problems that interethnic conflict could create for Kazakhstan and that Russian imperialism was looming very large. He started off by saying that

> stability in our context is very important, in terms of Kazakhstan being a multinational [state], that international [*mezhnatsional'noe*] harmony—it is so to speak a very delicate thing; whether it exists [in Kazakhstan] or not, some of our political analysts and journalists have some doubts about it, and people outside Kazakhstan do so too. Anything can happen, and every state has different politicians and different approaches [to nation-building]. Right now, Ukraine thinks [*Ukraina schitaet*] that all Donbas movement is not theirs [*eto ne ih*], that it is imported from outside [*privneseno izvne*], that it is done on purpose [*special'no*

delayetsya]. I spoke to many ..., maybe it is like that, maybe not because all of it needs to be proven. In other words, there are many movements [*techeniya*] and we have to consider the interests of all groups of the population. It is not about [making] conditions for these people [*tomu narodu*][41] of this nationality or that nationality ... and just the whole society [*ves' narod*] needs to understand that the state of Kazakhstan [*gosudarstvo Kazakhstan*] is able and can offer some help given the state of the economy and finances that we have.[42]

Nazarbayev was very frank in his approach and asked the audience of this closed meeting 'Where are we leading our people? [*Kuda my vedem svoi narod?*]'—as if the people of Kazakhstan themselves had no say in deciding their destiny. This committee meeting was a rare moment when Nazarbayev was open for negotiations with the people outside his trusted circles within the political elite. He considered the committee useful for publicity purposes—the press mainly discussed the dates of the meetings and had no access to its deliberations—and as a basis to reconcile the competing political forces among the popular local writers and cultural intelligentsia, as well as some 'hot-headed' Kazakh nationalists. Left unchecked, Nazarbayev saw that the rise to power and popularity of these groups could create major problems for him.

At the time, on the wave of the rebellious 1960s and in the light of the December 1986 protests, the anti-nuclear movement Nevada-Semipalatinsk and the Kazakh poet Suleimenov and his unquestioned authority among many Kazakhstanis were a direct threat to Nazarbayev's ascent to power and his plans to build a personalistic dictatorship. On the other end of the table sat popular Kazakh ethnonationalists who spoke of the need to empower the Kazakh language now that independence had been achieved: they believed ethnic Kazakhs had to play a central role in nation-building and dealing with the legacies of Soviet colonisation. The national-patriotic agenda found a lot of support among Kazakh-speaking Kazakhs, who were tired of the Soviet Union's discriminatory policies and Russification under the banner of creating a 'Soviet people'. The echoes and traumas of the tragic repression of the December

1986 protests, discussed in the next chapter, were also very fresh, and national-patriots, among them an extremely popular poet, Mukhtar Shakhanov, formed another wing of potential opposition to Nazarbayev. Inviting these individuals to the decision-making table meant that Nazarbayev could gain support among various potentially troublesome groups, and it partly explains why Kazakh 'national-patriots' considered Nazarbayev 'to be one of them, rather than against them'.[43] They were at the negotiation table, and they believed the president was truly listening to what they had to say.[44]

Even though the committee's structure[45] changed over the years, and part of it became a tool of the Assembly of the People of Kazakhstan (ANK),[46] the formative years of the early 1990s were very important in positioning those actors who wanted to enter the field of nation-building. Over the years, Nazarbayev was successfully able to filter out any potential opponents, only accepting those intellectuals and national-patriots who openly pledged their obedience and loyalty to his regime.

Nazarbayev has superb managerial skills—he is a well-trained and experienced Soviet apparatchik and knows how to control the different institutions and people around him. This partly explains why he succeeded in building a stable authoritarian system despite the country's dire economic situation. Being president in a newly independent state did not come without its challenges, which he detailed in the meetings behind closed doors that the archives now give us access to. There, he cited potential separatists among ethnic Russians to the north of the country and spoke of unification with Russia, the miners in Karaganda who were constantly on strike and the pensioners in Almaty who had formed new social movements to put forward their demands. Nazarbayev felt like he had the remedy for it all—divide the groups based on strict socio-lingual divisions and keep on promising them what he thought they wanted. In Russian, he would vouch for interethnic stability and seek to soothe his audience's anxieties by claiming that no form of nationalism, whether ethno-Kazakh or pro-Russian, would be allowed. In Kazakh, on the other hand, he would speak of the dream of creating the Kazakh nation-state finally coming true.

The paradoxes in his speeches did not seem to bother him, as he planned to reconcile the 'national question' by not honouring any of his promises. For years, he and his regime failed to implement the proclaimed policies of strengthening the Kazakh language or making it more visible publicly, as the Kazakh national-patriots had demanded, but neither did he provide any assistance to non-Kazakh groups in their attempts to build a different type of multi-ethnic polity. For as long as he stayed in office, the regime's nation-building efforts centred on him and his abilities to negotiate with anyone, while at the same time he did little to solve the issue and instead duplicated state programmes, emptying them of any real meaning. Despite proclaiming that the concept of 'ideology' was a legacy of the past that we should all seek to forget, Nazarbayev was very skilful at publishing propaganda pamphlets, issuing decrees and formulating programmes that had little to no meaning but managed to create a sense that a lot was happening.

Kazakhstan's presidential administration issues new state programmes almost every year announcing a 'new era of the eternal nation' ('Mangilik El', 2012) or a 'burst of spiritual enlightenment' ('Rukhani Zhangyru', 2017). These programmes were generously bankrolled by the state but had little to no content in terms of defining what the national identity of Kazakhstan was supposed to be.

At the time, however, people still listened to what Nazarbayev had to say. To the 'hot-headed' leaders of the pro-Russian movements,[47] he offered well-paid positions in parliament, which obeyed any rule or decree he announced publicly or behind closed doors.[48] And he did the same to their ethnic Kazakh counterparts. He promoted some of the voices on both sides of the nationalist agenda and disempowered the rest, leaving little space for their institutionalisation and legally prohibiting any radical agenda based on 'inciting interethnic hatred' or upsetting the country's multi-ethnic stability. He did not neglect the political opposition, which mainly arose from the ranks of his own politicians—Prime Minister Akezhan Kazhegeldin in 1998 and, in the early 2000s, the Democratic Choice of Kazakhstan, which was formed of young technocrats, ministers and businessmen once loyal to Nazarbayev and instrumental in many of his political-economic strategies. Nazarbayev preferred to have the opposition forming within the regime itself, ideally by co-opting once dissident voices or persuading entire oppositional parties to become the most loyal members of the regime's parliament. This tactic allowed Nazarbayev to sustain a level of popular distrust towards those opposing the regime, almost making the word 'opposition' into a dirty word associated with politicians who would eagerly sell themselves out for the right price. This tendency for institutionalised opposition to come directly from the regime itself changed in the 2010s, when the economic crises and worsening socio-economic conditions led to mass grassroots protests like Zhanaozen 2011 (see the following section).

Nazarbayev assured himself that he was a popular leader. But while this might have been true amid the euphoria of the early independence era, it gradually ceased being the case in the face of a deteriorating economic situation and allegations of corruption. Nazarbayev was a brilliant bilingual public speaker, and he and his inner circle of elites convinced him that he had the same social capital in the 2000s and 2010s as he had in the early years of independence. When that popularity started to wane, he accelerated his crackdown on the opposition, rewrote the constitution to make it a super-presidential republic and eventually declared himself leader for life. In the late 2000s, an imprint of the palm of his hand was placed on almost everything in Kazakhstan—from the imprints on the national currency to the public monuments of himself—making it seem as though Kazakhstan was almost his personal property. In 2000, he declared himself the Father of the Nation (*elbasy*) and passed a law under the same name allowing him to stay in the office until his death. With many amendments to the law throughout the 2000s and 2010s, he declared himself, his public images, his own properties and those of his official family practically untouchable. The Father of the Nation was above the law. He was the one who made any law and any decree legitimate, as the constitution of 1995 declared him the final arbiter on any legislation, allowing him to veto any law proposed by the parliament or any other legislative entity.

Nazarbayev made the national question his own trump card, pulling it out of his sleeve whenever he needed it. The regime needed to appropriate the nation-building process in order to keep the country together, avoiding potential secessionism and providing a vision of the future that could compete with the nostalgia for the Soviet period. Control over nation-building also meant the regime's survival and strengthening Nazarbayev, who was still a popular figure in the early 1990s, as an authoritarian leader. Many of my respondents remembered the 'honeymoon' period of Nazarbayev's rule: he was young, ambitious, spoke interchangeably in Russian and Kazakh to different audiences who saw him both as the symbol of Kazakh nationalism and of the continuation of Soviet internationalism and interethnic harmony. He also positioned himself as a technocrat who was close to the people. His frequent visits to the regions to speak to striking miners and his attentive approach to the concerns of pensioners was something that qualified him as the 'people's leader'. He took pride in announcing himself as a political leader who always had his hand on society's pulse:

> I have never been on such a long work trip in one region [*oblast'*] before: three and a half days I travelled across all Eastern Kazakhstan region,[49] I met 10,000 people on plants, on all metallurgy factories, mining and processing plants, extractive industries and in rural areas where I never saw one person say that he didn't support [state] politics [meaning the direction of the regime in governing the state]. I told [them] directly that people say that there [was] separatism [in those regions], that some Cossacks formed here [*est' kakoe-to kazachestvo*]. [People there] said, 'don't trust anyone [about separatism talk], we will ourselves deal with them [separatists]. The politics that you are leading now and that's it, we don't need anything else' [*tu politiku, kotoruyu seichas vedeted, i vse bolshe nichego ot vas ne trebuetsya*].[50]

Nazarbayev used the first years of independence to cement his position as a politician protecting the rights of different ethnic groups. He used his work with the Russian communities in East Kazakhstan in the early 1990s to portray himself as a man who was in dialogue with different communities and who would be able to deal with the secessionist claims of certain Slavic organisations. Nazarbayev stressed the importance of dealing with the 'Russian question' in

Kazakhstan and took it under his own command. The role of Russian as the de facto second state language that was widely used in urban and industrial settings was something he cemented from the very start of his rule. Under Nazarbayev, the promotion of Kazakh as the second language and its teaching was largely ineffective. Numerous state programmes were launched stressing the need to create a fully bilingual society, but the programmes themselves did not achieve their proclaimed objectives—the number of Russians, for example, who had little proficiency in Kazakh remained quite high; at the same time, the number of Kazakh-language schools and bilingual Kazakhs increased.

Nazarbayev's nation-building policy aimed to keep the nationality question—a legacy of the Soviet Union—in balance by seeking to satisfy the non-Kazakh minorities and the Kazakh nationalists at the same time. So, he pursued what I have elsewhere called a 'compartmentalised ideology'—in Russian, he would say that the main priority was to build stability and interethnic harmony, while in Kazakh he would often launch into a lengthy historical discourse about the special role ethnic Kazakhs occupied in his vision of a Kazakhified nation-state. His presidential speeches became an important vehicle of the state's nation-building, and just like his Soviet predecessors, he actively engaged in speaking to the nation. This strategy only changed in 1997, when he introduced the state policy 'Kazakhstan 2030', which focused predominantly on economic development and modernisation, promising Kazakhstani citizens prosperity and an advanced economy in the distant future. Now that we are approaching the promised year of 2030, the economic situation in Kazakhstan, however, remains dire.

Zhanaozen 2011 as Nazarbayev's Zugzwang

As the country was preparing to celebrate the twentieth anniversary of its independence on 16 December 2011, violence broke out in Zhanaozen, a city in the western, oil- and gas-rich region of Kazakhstan. The violence started at the main square, where hundreds of oil workers had been protesting peacefully for seven months and crowds of people would ordinarily come for state celebrations like

Independence Day. Even though the square was full of protestors, local officials decided it was still important to celebrate the anniversary and went ahead with the preparations. In this section, I explain how a seven month-long standoff between impoverished workers and the local authorities turned this city into the centre of political and anti-regime resistance and why the 2011 protests and violence that unfolded led to what I call Nazarbayev's Zugzwang[51] and, ultimately, to his downfall.

The protesting oil workers in Western Kazakhstan developed into a strong political force after Kazakhstan became independent. Through years of labour disputes and strikes, the seven-month standoff in 2011 and the numerous arrests of activists, the underlying inequality in the oil-rich region helped opposition sentiment to grow faster than yeast in warm water. Workers in Zhanaozen had few options for employment other than working for foreign companies extracting oil and gas. Average salaries were higher than those in other regions, but living costs were much higher too. Ordinary workers could barely make ends meet.[52] Why else would hundreds of people strike for a pay increase and live with no income for months? Why else would they sit on the public square in large groups day after day for seven long months, from May until mid-December 2011, with the sun beating down or the cold air chilling them to their bones?

The 2011 Zhanaozen protests caused a deep crisis within the Nazarbayev regime and highlighted its inability to deliver good governance. The strikes began in mid-May 2011 with the workers of the Chinese–Kazakh oil company Karazhanbasmunai, who were joined by the workers of the gas company Ozenmunaigas on 26 May. Within a few weeks of the strikes breaking out, the local authorities arrested and then tried the Karazhanbasmunai labour union lawyer Natalya Sokolova, who was accused of 'inciting social discord' and sentenced to six years in prison. Another labour union activist, Akzhanat Aminov, was sentenced to one year on probation for organising unsanctioned rallies. Other protestors were harassed and intimidated. By August 2011, at least 416 workers in different local oil- and gas-related companies had been laid off due to the strike; many more joined the protests in Zhanaozen, which also spread to Aktau, a nearby city on the shore of the Caspian Sea.

Various opposition leaders visited the cities of Aktau and Zhanaozen during the first months of the standoff and even organised a fund to help the protestors' families, who had been left with nothing to live on, but Nazarbayev remained silent. The local authorities were also cautious in their response. In early September 2011, when the protesting oil workers (*neftyaniki*) failed to send their children to school due to a lack of money, they briefly managed to speak to the governor of Mangystau region, Krymbek Kusherbayev.[53] Kusherbayev, a heavyweight Soviet and postsoviet politician[54] who had previously served as minister of education, culture and health (1997–9) and ambassador to Russia (2003–6) and was a close ally of Nazarbayev, also failed to respond adequately to the protestors' demands. He promised they would receive some financial help to send their children to school but said that the labour disputes should be resolved with their employers.[55]

By that time, more than 1,000 striking oil workers had been sitting for months on the main square in Zhanaozen.[56] They had not been paid for four months or more when Nazarbayev's son-in-law and the then-chairman of the state's national welfare fund 'Samruk-Kazyna', billionaire Timur Kulibayev, generated more discontent with his public statements.[57] In an attempt to shift the blame on to the workers, he called the chief organisers of the protests 'repatriates',[58] by which he meant ethnic Kazakhs who had migrated to neighbouring West Kazakhstan from Turkmenistan and the Autonomous Republic of Karakalpakstan (in Uzbekistan). Many activists claimed that Kulibayev was dividing ethnic Kazakhs into first- and second-class citizens by referring to some of them as repatriates (back then known by the term *oralman*[59] and currently as *qandas*).[60] Kulibayev's comment fuelled further opposition from the workers, who were tired of the president's silence and the failure to establish dialogue with local or state officials. Many activists also reportedly tried to communicate via social media with then-Prime Minister Karim Massimov.[61] They wrote him collective letters, sending them as direct messages to his official accounts on Twitter and Facebook, but all to no avail.

President Nazarbayev's silence on the Zhanaozen workers' demands that they be paid the promised industrial coefficient and be given better working conditions, and for those who had lost their jobs during the strikes to be reinstated, cost him dearly. Just weeks before the bloodshed of 16 December 2011, the disputing parties—the protesting workers and their former employers—met in the office of the local municipality (the *akimat*) to discuss the striking workers' demands. But the meeting came to naught. The official line was that the standoff was illegal and that the protesting workers would not be reinstated or paid because they had been fired by their employers.[62] The protesting workers said they would continue to occupy the square day and night despite the cold.[63]

On 16 December 2011, the central stage was attacked. In the videos that emerged from Zhanaozen, the central square bore bright banners emblazoned in Kazakh with the words 'Blue Flag, Blue Skies, Great Kazakhstan!' First gunshots were heard, then the crowd started running, and women could be heard crying. Around the same time, several buildings—including the mayor's office and the headquarters of Ozenmunaigas—were set on fire. In the hours that followed, the city of Zhanaozen descended into total violence. By the end of the day, official media reported ten civilian deaths.

The country fell into a deep state of shock as more and more news emerged from Zhanaozen. Disturbing videos caught on ordinary citizens' cell phones showed people dressed like policemen firing at unarmed people. The death toll continued to rise, leading to an information blackout; many internet sources were also blocked. The road to Zhanaozen was closed to anyone but special forces. Within a few days, a veil of silence fell over the city, leaving citizens in the dark about the real number of victims and the identities of the real perpetrators and at a loss for real answers about what had happened.

The minister of internal affairs and the special committee investigating the 'riots' swiftly flew into the city, where officials had declared a state of emergency on the morning of 17 December 2011. Meanwhile, workers in the nearby city of Aktau gathered on the city centre's famous Yntymaq Square to demonstrate their solidarity with the workers of Zhanaozen and call for a halt to the violence.[64] Several groups of people, mainly from the local opposition, gathered on the central square in Almaty, where—on that day twenty-five years earlier, in 1986—the Zheltoqsan protests had taken place (see

Chapter 2). In the years that followed, this square would serve as a space for mass gatherings: every year on 16 December, people would bring flowers and banners to remember the victims of Zheltoqsan 1986 and Zhanaozen 2011.[65]

Elena Kostyuchenko, one of the few journalists who managed to get into Zhanaozen after the massacre, described it as a 'city of the dead' and claimed that reporting from Zhanaozen had been one of the most harrowing experiences of her life, even though she is an experienced war journalist. When she arrived in the besieged city, locals dressed her in their clothes and told her not to look into the policemen's eyes, because, as her local guide, a young Kazakh woman called Marzhan, told her, 'there are almost no Russians here, Russians have somewhere to escape'.[66] Marzhan's father had died from cancer after working at Ozenmunaigas for forty years. Just before his death, he gave his daughter 100,000 Kazakh tenge, roughly one-third of the monthly salary the local oil workers received before the strikes in 2011. He asked her to donate this money to the protesting oil workers in the hope 'they would break this bastard system as we didn't manage to' (*mozhet, govorit, oni slomayut etu ublyudochnuyu sistemu, raz u nas dukhu ne khvatilo*).[67] While the official death toll stood at sixteen dead in Zhanaozen and one more in nearby Shetpe, Kostyuchenko and other journalists, relying on eyewitness reports, reported higher figures. Eyewitnesses also reported seeing young children among the victims, as local schools and colleges had brought students to the central square to take part in the 'celebratory parade'. The official record never acknowledged this.

Taking students to obligatory celebrations for them to wave flags and await state officials for hours at any time of the year was a Soviet ritual that Kazakhstani officials and bureaucrats also adopted. University students, too, stood for hours waving flags in Astana's extreme winter temperatures. They were waiting for Nazarbayev, who was scheduled to open a new monument to mark the twentieth year of Kazakhstan's independence: the Mangilik El Triumphal Arch.[68]

Few Kazakhstanis remember the opening of the arch, and the term 'Mangilik El' has long since lost its importance, giving way to 'Zhana Qazaqstan' or 'New Kazakhstan', the title of Tokayev's nation-building programme after the mass protests of January 2022. But they do still remember the horrifying days after the Zhanaozen massacre in December 2011. Nazarbayev only made it to the city now known for tragedy on 23 December 2011, when he came to visit the victims' mourning families. In Zhanaozen, Nazarbayev claimed that rioters had been paid money and given alcohol to engage in violence. The same had been said about the protestors in December 1986, when Nazarbayev was a young and ambitious party apparatchik. In Zhanaozen in 2011, he admitted that 'he had lost his famous popular touch' and said he did not 'want our country to live through such a nightmare again'.[69]

Qantar

There is a rather sad tradition in Kazakhstan of remembering significant protests and tragic events with the names of the months when these occurred and naming them in the Kazakh language. The December 1986 protests, discussed in the next chapter, one of the biggest protests ever in Soviet Kazakhstan and in the Soviet Union itself, were known locally as Zheltoqsan—the Kazakh name for the month of December. When another protest happened on almost exactly the same day in 2011 in Zhanaozen, it was initially termed Zheltoqsan 2.0 before reverting back to the name of the city where it happened—Zhanaozen. Every one of these tragic events has its own history and commemorative practices. People lay flowers to the specific monuments in their cities or gather to commemorate the dead. Some commemorations are quiet and done in the presence of close family members, while some happen at cemeteries and others in mosques or public squares.

When the tragedy struck in January 2022 that claimed the lives of more than 230 people, the country was deeply shocked. Due to the lack of trusted information about what had happened and the reports of the war-like sounds of exploded grenades and scenes of burnt car carcasses reported on state television, it was hard for some Kazakhstani citizens to make up their minds about what had really happened. The number of victims among the civilians was only announced later in the year, and the official state investigation into the violence happened behind closed doors. The long and opaque investigation led to more protests, and even two years after the events and the publication of the official reports, many Kazakhstanis believe that questions still remain about what happened during the protests.

In the first days after the tragedy, when those living in the southern cities of Kazakhstan heard of the first civilian deaths among the protestors, local activists started campaigns to uncover the names of the dead as well as the torturers of those who had been arrested in the aftermath of the protest. The word 'Qantar' for January in Kazakh emerged as yet another tragic and horrifying label. Bakhytzhan Toregozhina was among the activists who searched for the names of the victims. The list was growing every day. On social media, anonymous volunteers and activists organised a group to share the names of the dead and collect funds to help their families and the families of the people who had been injured, arrested or tortured during Qandy Qantar. Meanwhile, activists were tried in courts. Qantar remains the biggest protest in Kazakhstan's post-independence history, and like many crises in the country, the trauma resulting from its repression unites communities on many political and apolitical levels while also sustaining important cleavages due to a lack of trusted information about what happened.

Kimdik (Identity)

The twentieth century has been the century of nation-states, where, in the words of Ronald Grigor Suny, 'if clearly defined and articulated nations do not exist within these states by the moment of independence, then the state elites busily set about creating national political communities to fill out the fledging state'.[70]

I identify nation here as a socio-political construct, an idea of the political community that 'mediates the relation between subjects and states (which are themselves social constructs too)'.[71] As Ernest Gellner points out, nations are only identified as such if people belonging to the nation 'recognize each other as belonging to the same nation'.[72] This definition also allows us to conceptualise multiple understandings of the national. But in the so-called postsoviet space, the idea of national identity was imbued with complex ethnic recognitions and diverse national belongings stemming from the legacies of Soviet nationality policy, when nation-building policies were always implemented from the top-down, from the powerful political elites at the centre down to the societal groups on the ground.

Soviet nationality policy assumed that the divisions between ethnic groups would disappear over time, opening the way to a post-national society united by communist ideology. Communism was supposed to win over the 'bourgeois' nationalist sentiments in the 'nearest future'; however, something went wrong, and this post-ethnic or post-national communist future never emerged. My generation of no-longer-postsoviets grew up in an atmosphere where few believed in the ideals of communism, and my respondents among the Kazakh national-patriots spoke openly and very critically of 'red propaganda', condemning its colonial nature.[73] The new generation of decolonial activists no longer needs to prove that Russian and Soviet rule was colonial, but they are preoccupied with the question of what to do with its legacy and how to navigate the local decolonial dialogue without falling into the trap of ethnonationalism.

To untangle this problem, they prefer to think with a pluriversality of voices, positions and narratives of what Kazakhstani means. For some, it could be the mixed *shala* Kazakh (mixed Russo-Kazakh speech) or quickly switching from one language to another, now also with the addition of English, Arabic, Turkish and other languages. For others, it could be the monolingual Kazakhophone identity without any additions from other languages or linguistic mixing. There are also proponents of spelling Kazakh with a 'Q'—Qazaq—to relate the English pronunciation more to the way it is pronounced in the Qazaq language, with a strong 'Q' (Қ) pronounced as a 'qkh' sound rather than the Cyrillic 'K'. There is also Q-pop—Qazaq pop, which is similar to K-pop but sung in Qazaq—as well as Qazaq indie and linguistic communities like Qazaq Grammar or Qazaqsha Zhaz (Write in Kazakh) and community-based spelling campaigns proposing their version of a new Latin script for the Qazaq language.

Kazakhstan's socio-linguistic and socio-cultural environment shifted dramatically over the 2010s. The new generation of Qazaq

Zoomers (Gen-Z), tech-savvy and often trilingual—Qazaq, Russian and English—dictate their own visions of how to be Kazakhstani. They are not stuck in the old ethnic- or even gender-based categorisations and accept the fluidity of their identities, which they often pronounce with the Kazakh word for 'identity'—*kimdik*. Collectively, they organise movements against gender-based violence and hold anti-war rallies and discussions on Qazaq queerness—pronounced with a Qazakhified 'qkh'—and contemporary Qazaq culture. The choice of language of communication does not come to them as a difficult choice but rather as something as fluid as the varieties of their *kimdik*. 'It is more important to be a good human being than being a jerk but a patriot', one of them once told me in a conversation about what Kazakhness means.

My own positionality as the first generation of no-longer-Soviet nor postsoviet children came into question once I started thinking of my own *kimdik* precisely in this new form of Qazaq language. The spaces where *kimdik* is practised are very different from the spaces of my youth, even if these are the same urban spaces and realities of globalised Almaty. With the difference of a mere ten to twelve years, Gen-Z no longer views the Kazakh language as a political issue but rather as a popular way of communicating. In popular Almaty nightclubs, people speak in a multilingual mix of languages where Kazakh words are pronounced with a sense of pride, and those who are able to speak only in Kazakh are highly respected. Kazakh is also used in the incredibly fluid and political art field. Kazakh speakers, writers and translators are now in high demand as cultural producers of all kinds are eager to translate their texts into Qazaq and only then into English or Russian.

The translations of Tlostanova's essays into Qazaq and the subsequent publication of her book in the same language were met with widespread popularity. By the summer of 2024, many IT professionals refused to communicate in any language other than Qazaq. The Kazakh language was no longer imposed as a claim to a singular view of Kazakhness—read through a rigid understanding of ethnicity—but opened up new spaces to claim one's identity. People who would otherwise be seen as non-Kazakh by ethnicity happily accepted this fluidity, mixing Kazakh words into their usual

Russo-English speech, and even the recent newcomers, the so-called reallocated people from Russia, eagerly assumed *kimdik* as a concept of homemaking in Kazakhstan.

Kimdik is also at the heart of this book and perhaps the key element in its vocabulary as it invites diverse, pluriversal views, experiences, feelings and embodiments of what it means to be Kazakhstani. The rest of the book weaves in the diverse understandings and diverse lives of *kimdik* from a historical, genealogical and contemporary perspective. I focus on protests and cleavages as the main sites where *kimdik* comes to the fore and where it creates a fruitful discussion. But at the same time, I believe there are other, different and more fruitful ways to study *kimdik*—through the everyday life of identity or everyday nationalism,[74] for example, or through a more detailed case-by-case study of Qazaq- or Russian-speaking communities[75] or through the state or regime's perspective.[76]

This chapter has sought to map out the key events, vocabulary and histories at play in the formation of a Kazakh identity. The Soviet imposition of ethnicity continues to play an important role in creating cleavages in Russian–Kazakh relations in Kazakhstan, yet the following two chapters will demonstrate that neither of these two dominant groups has a clear-cut group identity, meaning that their self-understanding of ethnicity remains in flux, often viciously debated within and outside the group. The December 1986 protests served as a nodal point for the crisis of identity but also for the unification processes in Kazakhstan on the eve of the Soviet collapse. People who believed in the first phases of perestroika[77] experienced significant trauma when their democratic protests were violently suppressed, which had a significant influence on their understandings of Kazakhstani as a civic-driven, societal identity.

The violence inevitably created cleavages among Kazakhs, who were the main target of the state's aggression, but as Chapters 3 and 4 will demonstrate, over the years, both ethnic groups of 'Kazakhstani Russians' and 'Kazakhstani Qazaqs' have experienced significant shifts in self-identification, which only further demonstrates how identity is not a monolithic or rigid category but a lived experience. In Chapter 3, I discuss how Russians in Kazakhstan have re-evaluated their identities, and in Chapter 4 I discuss how the long postcolonial moment often discriminates against Qazaq-speaking Kazakhs in Kazakhstan. I contend that these two experiences are one side of the same coin—the discriminatory and colonial Soviet nationality policy that left many people (minorities and those the Soviets labelled 'titular' ethnic groups) in a challenging and in-flux situation where they find it hard to identify either with colonial terms that are slowly dying (like 'titular' group) or with weak categories they no longer find useful (like compatriots abroad for ethnic Russians outside Russia).

The latter part of the book thematically focuses on a major protest—that of Qantar, or Bloody January 2022—and discusses how this new trauma unified Kazakhstani society. With the data that emerged after the protests, we can see how people created meaningful connections beyond ethnic cleavages and instead formed political and anti-regime identities. This process coincided with the flourishing of Kazakhstani decolonial thought and practice in the arts, literature, public activism and cultural life. The book ends with a discussion of these ideas and practices in light of another traumatic event—the killing of Nukenova and the televised trial of her husband, ex-minister Bishimbayev, who was once a loyal member of the Nazarbayev regime.

2

THE DECEMBER 1986 PROTESTS IN ALMA-ATA

On the 17th [December 1986] we went to the classes. Everything went haphazardly. Around midday, students from the theatrical institute came to our building with slogans 'Kazakhstan for Kazakhs'. That's unfortunate. Better said: 'Kazakhstan for Kazakhstanis' [Kazakhstan dlya kazakhstantsev]. We all rushed downstairs. ... They didn't let us go. Those students more senior than us moved them and we all escaped outside. I was in my suit [without a coat]. Protestors already went ahead of us. First, they went to ZhenPi,[1] students were not allowed to join the protest but managed to escape [the teachers]. Then [the protestors] went to the Medical [University], then to the Railways [Institute] ... We went to the square. From below[2] [the lower part of the city] the columns [of students] were coming and coming.

Protestor's account of the events of December 1986,
written down and saved by an eyewitness, V. Kaplin[3]

Dinmukhamed Kunayev served as the leader of Soviet Kazakhstan and as the first secretary of the CPK for over two decades. However, on 16 December 1986, the Moscow elites, spearheaded by the Soviet leader Mikhail Gorbachev, decided to replace the party leadership in Alma-Ata. Kunayev was ageing and needed to retire, and Gorbachev was not content with the situation in the southern union republics (the Central Asian states). There were allegations of nepotism, corruption and mismanagement,[4] which Gorbachev felt would be better dealt with by an 'alien'—from Russia proper—than a Kazakh. It was one of the first mistakes of many the Soviet leadership would make in the coming days.

The meeting discussing Kunayev's replacement lasted for just eighteen minutes—a fact that helped spur the protests that were about to happen and that would shake the very core of Soviet politics. The news was announced to the Kazakhstani public on the afternoon of 16 December 1986. A new leader, ethnic Russian Gennady Kolbin, who had no ties to Kazakhstan, was posted from Moscow,[5] disregarding the interests of the local elites, among them aspiring leader Nazarbayev, as well as the chairman of the Kazakh Council of Ministers and the head of the government, Zakash Kamalidenov. Groups of students started gathering in Alma-Ata dorms discussing the political changes on the evening of 16 December 1986. There was talk of organising a peaceful rally to oppose Kolbin's appointment. Many of the protestors felt that Moscow's decision was undemocratic, as no one in the Kazakhstani public sphere was aware of the changes that were being made, and there was no public vote or consultation about this major political appointment.

Numerous sources, including the official interviews with the prosecutor general and local police, point at the students at the theatrical institute as having instigated the protests, but people in all parts of Soviet Alma-Ata[6] and across the whole country were also discussing the decision. After the students formed in groups and met in their local dormitories on the evening of 16 December, Alma-Ata soon became a hotspot of the protests.[7]

Dormitories were the key points of growing discontent as they were home to many of the Kazakh students studying in the city, who had little chance of remaining Alma-Ata dwellers after their graduation due to the strict system of *propiska*—the residency registration system focused on balancing the ethnic divisions in the urban population by excluding ethnic Kazakhs from the largely Russified city.

THE DECEMBER 1986 PROTESTS IN ALMA-ATA

According to the 1979 census, Kazakhs made up only 13.6 per cent of the population in Alma-Ata, the country's biggest urban hub with more than 1 million residents. There were only two schools with Kazakh-language provision in the city; all the other schools were predominantly Russophone. Mikhail Solomentsev, the chairman of the Committee of Party Control under the Central Committee of the Communist Party of the USSR and the Politburo's official representative, quickly came to Alma-Ata to 'deal' with the riots and even scolded the local elites:

> There are perversions in policies, in the selection of students [among ethnic Kazakhs who study in central universities in Alma-Ata at the time]. Is this how you select cadres? I know there was a discussion here about opening schools with [the full] Kazakh-language instruction … Do the preschool institutions also organise according to the nationality principle in Alma-Ata? How, comrades, members of the Bureau [of the Central Committee of the Kazakh Communist Party]? [*Kak, tovarishi, chleny Byuro?*] And what's next? All education and upbringing … would be done in Kazakh language[?] [The situation] is very unfavourable in the educational work [*neblagopoluchno s vospitatel'noi rabotoi*], especially among the youth, [and] in general in the population, including in the sphere of internationalisation of training. [We] need to deal with the issue of the city's enlargement [urban migration to Alma-Ata]. Here is Alma-Ata. When I worked here,[8] I remember that [the ethnic] Kazakh population made up 8 per cent [of the total population of the city]. Am I right? And now it is 16 per cent. [The ethnic Kazakh population of Alma-Ata] increased twice [by 1986].[9]

Soviet Alma-Ata continued to be ruled by the centrally based elites in Moscow. The instalment of Kolbin, an unknown Russian party cadre, exhausted the last drop of the people's patience. In the early hours of 17 December 1986, columns of students started moving to Alma-Ata's centrally located Brezhnev Square. They had no weapons, only slogans citing Leninist self-determination policies, and were chanting Kazakh songs with the words 'Every country should have its own leader' (*Kazhdoi strane svoi vozhd'*).[10]

By 9.30–10.00 a.m., Brezhnev Square, in front of the official building of the CPK, was full of young protestors. Local KGB security forces reacted quickly and started telephoning the Moscow office. The police then besieged the square, and orders were given to close the city's airport and main train stations in fear of more protestors pouring in from cities across the country. Alma-Ata was closed off.

Due to a lack of communication and reliable information, Alma-Ata quickly filled with conspiracies and rumours, fuelling anxieties and creating further tensions. Misinformation was spread about those at the rally, leading some angry city dwellers to form groups of vigilantes (*druzhinniki*) to beat up the 'Kazakh nationalists'. These groups of *druzhinniki* would later play an important role in crushing the protests alongside the local law enforcement officers; later in the day, local factories were ordered to make heavy armour and chains to equip these groups of *druzhinniki* so that they could beat up young, unarmed people. The divisive Soviet nationality question fuelled some of these tensions further, as those who were targeted as 'nationalists' and 'hooligans' were Kazakhs, and those beating them up to re-establish order, the *druzhinniki*, were Russian. In the atmosphere of chaos and with an absence of reliable information, the city's streets were filled with fear and distrust. Any words about interethnic violence would cause more conflict and outrage. The party line would be prioritised over human life and human suffering.

But in the protest's early hours, with the chaos intensifying, local elites did not know which way to turn. Some of them would later say they had no involvement in the decision-making—Nazarbayev, for example, later claimed he had been with the protestors on the square leading their revolt against the unjust Soviet machine—while others would claim the protestors were not peaceful, although there is no evidence they had any weapons.

On the morning of 17 December 1986, the leaders of the Kazakh Communist Party gathered in the office of Kamalidenov,[11] a leading Kazakh Communist politician, because his office gave 'the best view' of the square and what was happening there. Eyewitnesses reported anything from 2,000 to 5,000 protestors taking over the square. Their rally was peaceful, with the protestors simply demanding an explanation for the decision to replace Kunayev with Kolbin. Politburo representative Solomentsev, who quickly arrived from Moscow, was furious: 'Do they [protestors] want us to reverse the plenum decision?!' he yelled at the local Communist leaders.[12] Everyone who was inside the main building, the top elites of the Kazakh Communist Party and their Moscow counterparts, considered the protestors enemies who had to be stopped at all costs.

From the testimonies given to the commission investigating the December 1986 'events' in 1989 and 1990, we know that the leaders of the Kazakh Communist Party were in disarray inside the building. Kolbin received his orders directly from Moscow and relayed them verbatim to his subordinates, perhaps to avoid leaving any trace of information. All official documents held by the local security forces—the office of the KGB, the Ministry of Internal Affairs and the local police—with information about the violent repression of the protests were destroyed soon after. Moscow responded swiftly by sending a group of high-ranking politicians and members of the Politburo to Alma-Ata to deal with the situation, among them Solomentsev, who served as a de facto leader—'his thoughts and evaluations were considered as political decisions and directives'.[13] An order was given to allocate special forces from eight Soviet cities—mostly in Soviet Russia but also from Uzbekistan (Tashkent) and Georgia (Tbilisi) and other union republics—to help clear the square and repress the protest.[14] Special operation Metelitsya (Blizzard) was in full swing.

At 11 a.m. the same day, 17 December 1986, a telephone rang in Kunayev's apartment. He was being invited to the Central Committee of the CPK in the central building on Brezhnev Square where all the party officials were discussing the ongoing situation. 'What is the reason for this [call]? I am retired now', Kunayev said, but the voice at the other end of the telephone line insisted: 'A large group of youth has gathered on the square and they demand an explanation of what happened at yesterday's plenum of the Central Committee [where Kolbin was installed as the leader of the republic] and discuss the point of it.'[15] Kunayev agreed to come to the building where he had spent most of his long career but did not forget to ask his interlocutor whether Kolbin had agreed to allow Kunayev to speak to the protestors. Oleg Miroshkhin, second secretary of the Central Committee of the CPK, to whom he was speaking on the phone, answered 'yes'.[16] Kunáyev arrived in the building and stayed in his old office, which was now occupied by Kolbin. The highest politicians of the local Communist Party were inside the room discussing what to do with the crowds of the protestors. 'Kolbin proposed that Kamalidenov [and Salamat Mukashev, the head of the Supreme Soviet (Verkhovny Sovet)][17] and Nazarbayev speak to the protestors', Kunayev remembered.[18] Both party officials went to the crowds and spoke in Russian and Kazakh to deliver the message that the protest was illegal, and everyone had to stop and go home. The crowd booed and threw snowballs at them.[19] This is how Nazarbayev remembered it:

> The members of the Bureau of the Central Committee [of the Communist Party of the Kazakh Soviet Socialist Republic (SSR)] and the chairman of the Presidium of the Verkhovny Sovet, S. Mukashev, were ordered to go to the square and speak to the people. No one [among the protestors] regretted that the ex-'first'[20] [leader] of the republic resigned from his post [*Nikto ne sozhalel, chto ushel so svoego posta byvshyi 'pervyi' respubliki*]. We were met with the slogans 'Every Nation [Should Have] Its Own Leader!' [*Kazhdomu narodu—svoego rukovoditelya*], 'We Need a Kazakh Leader!' [*Nam nuzhen rukovoditel' kazakh*], 'Enough of Dictating!' [*Khvatit diktovat'*], 'Perestroika Is Underway, Where Is Democracy?' [*Idet perestroika, gde demokratiya?*], 'We Are for the Leninist Nationality Policy!' [*My za leninskuyu natsional'nuyu politiku*]. There was nothing else that could have made a normal, thoughtful person protest or revolt against it. The protestors were peaceful. We were asked only one question: Why wasn't a local elected [for the position of the leader of the republic]? And we could not answer this question with anything intelligible. Then the protestors with their banners moved to the streets of Alma-Ata.[21]

Meanwhile, the situation inside the Kazakh Communist Party became increasingly acrimonious. Kunayev patiently waited for more than two hours to speak to the protestors, but Kolbin was busy 'speaking with Moscow'. Everyone but Second Secretary Miroshkhin left the room when Kolbin was on the phone. Then Kolbin invited all the members of the Bureau of the CPK inside the room and told Kunayev: 'You are free to go, rest. We will deal [with the situation] ourselves and will establish order [*navedem poryadok*].'[22] Kunayev remembered that before leaving he asked Miroshkhin why they had called him and made him come: 'We discussed it and decided that we should not allow you to the square, you should not speak [to the protestors]', Miroshkhin said.[23]

The situation inside and outside the building was highly unstable. Outside, the protestors started clashing with the police, who were refusing to allow new groups of protestors to reach the square. The protestors were looking for more people to join the rally and started walking around the city telling people about the situation, knocking on every dorm and demanding that Kazakhs 'speak up' in opposition to Moscow's colonial politics. Inside the party building, local elites were being screamed at by the Russian and Moscow-based authorities, including Kolbin, who accused Nazarbayev, Kamalidenov and Mukashev of organising the 'riot'. As Nazarbayev recalled in his memoirs several years later:

> In a fit of rage [they] threw words right into our faces that we organised the protest and we would deal with it [*my etu kashu zavarili, a znachit, my ee dolzhny i raskhlebyvat'*].[24] Much later, we found out that there was a transfer of major parts of internal army forces. [They, the party leaders in Moscow] resorted, so to speak, to the final argument [the violent crackdown of the protest].
>
> After some time, we managed to understand the character of the protests in a calmer way. At the 17th congress of the CPK and in the speeches, in the official documents adopted [to deal with the December 1986 protests], it was underlined that the December events were not the expression of nationalist resistance, were not directed at the Russian population and against people of any other nationality. Those who wanted to see only that colour in the [protest] proposed only one single argument—that Kolbin was Russian. This argument was insolvent. For example, when [the protestors] proposed to discuss other candidates for the post of the first secretary from the square, they named Demidenko, Morozov

and other comrades who were not [ethnic] Kazakhs but who knew Kazakhstan and its economy, its traditions and the specifics of the lifestyle better. It is possible to understand the more definite demands that a Kazakh should have been elected for the post. Because right now, for example, out of two good dozen leaders who ruled the republic [during the Soviet period], only three were [ethnic] Kazakhs. People were simply tired of temporary Vikings [*Narod prosto ustal ot zaezhih varyagov-vremenshikov*], of those who always looked down at people, be it Goloshekin, Mirzoyan, Belyaev, Ponomarev or Brezhnev [all of whom ruled the republic at different times during the Soviet period].[25]

There were indeed discussions among party officials on whether the protest had been organised. Announced at the end of 17 December, the official party line was that this was a riot instigated by a nationalist movement of ethnic Kazakhs against ethnic Russians, and that there were alcoholics and drug addicts among the protestors. Since the city was closed off and telephone communications had also been largely cut off, rumours started to swirl around the city, which fell into a state of mass anxiety. People spoke of 'trucks with free vodka' circling around the square and of students being given drugs like *anasha*[26] and claimed that most of them were under the influence during the protests. Though some of these claims were later disproved, in that moment of chaos they served to discredit the protest as a whole, allowing party officials to crack down on it with all repressive forces at hand.

The situation deteriorated further on the afternoon of 17 December when loud music was broadcast to the square—allegedly by the police—to silence the voices of the protestors. Eyewitnesses reported that many of those who were passing around the square rushed there thinking that some sort of celebration was taking place. Different cultural leaders, including Suleimenov, the prominent Kazakh poet and leader of the Nevada-Semipalatinsk anti-nuclear movement, were not allowed to speak to the protestors. Rumours started circulating that many people had been killed or arrested.[27] The city went into chaos. People in other Kazakh cities started forming protest groups in solidarity. Local KGB and militia forces were on high alert.

THE DECEMBER 1986 PROTESTS IN ALMA-ATA

The students revolt

On 17 and 18 December 1986, the Soviet city of Alma-Ata, together with Kazakhstan as a whole, witnessed the biggest ever protest within Soviet borders. Paradoxically, this defining moment in modern Soviet and postsoviet history remains little known and under-researched. An independent investigation into the protest was only launched in 1989, and the so-called December 1986 Commission chaired by the Kazakh poet Mukhtar Shakhanov experienced significant turbulence, being subject to criticisms,[28] harassment and hate mail[29] and facing numerous obstacles to its work. Most of the documents about the repression of the protest were quickly burnt by the prosecutor general's office, local police and the KGB as 'documents that had lost' their practical purpose[30] even before Shakhanov's commission could research them. The old administrative system tried to erase all traces of the violent repression and the 'fabrication' of criminal offences in court hearings that jailed more than ninety-nine protestors, at least three of whom died while in detention.

Two young women died in unexplained circumstances—sixteen-year-old Lyazzat Asanova,[31] who reportedly jumped from the roof of the KGB building after being subjected to a lengthy period of interrogation in Alma-Ata, and sixteen-year-old Sabira Mukhamedzhanova from the Ust-Kamenogorsk Pedagogical Institute, who fell from the fifth floor of her dormitory after meeting two men who were waiting for her on the top floor.[32] Another victim, eighteen-year-old Kairat Ryskulbekov, who was sentenced to death—later reduced to twenty years in prison—for killing a certain Savitsky, a middle-aged man working for a local telecoms company near the square—was found dead in his prison cell. The police claimed these deaths had been suicides, but suspicions mounted about the violent interrogation, torture and intimidation behind the closed doors of the security forces' torture chambers. It was an open secret that Soviet law enforcement officers viewed the protestors as direct enemies of the system they were so viciously defending. Violence was widespread.

The students who stood on the square demanded answers to their questions: Why had Kolbin been installed as the leader when there were so many more able people in the country itself? Why was Moscow single-handedly deciding the fate of the entire Soviet republic? But the party elites and Kolbin himself had no intention of speaking to the protestors and instead amassed more and more forces, including the local vigilantes (*narodnye druzhinniki*), who were quickly equipped with handmade steel sticks and cables to repress the protest. The protestors remained on the square for two days before being violently crushed by the security forces; the total number of dead and injured remains unknown.

Many students brought handmade banners reading 'Glory to Leninist Ideas of National Determination', 'Each Republic Should Have Its Leader' and 'No Preferences to One [Ethnic] Group, No Preferences to One Language'; some carried Lenin's books as a pointer to the Soviet nationality policy that promised every Soviet republic the right of self-determination, if only on paper. Those carrying these banners were later sentenced to three to five years in prison.

The protest was peaceful, and no one except the police was carrying weapons. Believing that glasnost—Gorbachev's policy of increased openness and transparency—was in full swing, the protestors came to speak their minds and wanted their voice to be heard during the deliberations over the country's leader and its future. They also proposed alternative candidates for the post: among the list were the names of local ethnic Russian politicians—the protestors wanted someone who was familiar with the local context to lead the country. But the official party line, ironically led by the reformist Gorbachev who had promised perestroika, was that the protests were 'nationalistic' and posed a threat to the country's interethnic balance—a statement that had a detrimental and long-lasting legacy for Kazakhstan's future nation-building.

Headed by the Russian Viktor Miroshnik, a key figure in the suppression of the protests, the Kazakh KGB office knew about the protestors on the morning of 17 December and quickly started amassing security forces to counter the protest. According to the commission's inquiry into the December 1986 protests, some 1,200 to 5,000 protestors were on the square on 17 December. Most of the protestors were Kazakh students and young workers.

Their chief demand was that the party remove Kolbin from his post. However, they also voiced socio-economic grievances. People were tired of waiting in lines for housing, as well as the limited provision in local stores and, more generally, the poor living conditions in the city. Kolbin's appointment was a symbol of Moscow's settler colonialism in Kazakhstan, with the local population having not even been consulted over who should lead the country. On the wave of perestroika's promises, the students felt they had the right to voice their concerns to the centre. Moscow heard them loud and clear but did not like the message.

The investigative commission reported that the protest had been peaceful, as confirmed by many eyewitness testimonies and the KGB's own photo and video surveillance. Young students came to the square singing folk songs and smiling.[33] The students stood on the main square in Alma-Ata for several hours before moving on to the city's streets looking for more people to join their rally; solidarity protests sprang up across the country. According to the eyewitnesses, protestors in Alma-Ata went to different dorms of the centrally located universities. Alma-Ata was a student-city at the time, hosting more than two dozen universities and institutes, and most of the dorms were closely connected to the central square. Although ethnic Kazakhs were a minority among the city's permanent residents (*korennoi almatinets*), Kazakh students made up most of the student population (see Table 2.1).[34]

Table 2.1. Ethnicity of higher education students in the Kazakh SSR[35]

Student ethnicity	1980–1 (%)	1984–5 (%)	1989–90 (%)
Kazakh	50	54	54
Russian	35	31	31
Ukrainian	4	4	4
Tatar	2	2	2
German	4	3	3
Other ethnicity	5	6	6

These students believed that the Moscow elites and Gorbachev himself, who portrayed himself as a democrat, would hear their concerns and change the plenum's decision. These were the first months following the announcement of perestroika in 1985, and students believed their rally was in line with the policies now being promoted by the state. Hundreds of people joined the rally when they heard the slogans referring to perestroika and Leninist values in nationality policy, and hence the protestors did not expect the violence awaiting them on the evening of 17 December. They decided to stand on the square until they were given explanations for the plenum's decision, and many believed the party would be open for dialogue.

'Bones were shattered'

After 2 p.m., the protestors returned to the Brezhnev Square and stood in front of the stage on the steps of the main building of the CPK. They were peaceful and unarmed. Small clashes occurred when further groups of young people attempted to join the square and the police tried to block them. By this point, the protestors amounted to 2,000 or 5,000 people, with some estimates suggesting there were more than 10,000 people.[36] Many of them were young women and girls, as well as people who had simply stopped by to see what was happening on the square. Kazakh Communist leaders Kamalidenov and Nazarbayev again spoke to the crowds, asking them to stop the rally and return to their homes. The local prosecutor general spoke to the protestors from the stage, calling their rally illegal and threatening them with severe consequences. But the protestors stood by their decision to remain on the square until their questions were answered.

One of the December 1986 protestors was part of the group sent from the square to discuss the issues with the political leaders. According to her, the people who formed a group of protestors to speak to the Communist political elites

> expressed their mental anguish: about the way of life [*byt*], social conditions, lack of housing, endless queues, needs [*o nuzhdah*],

about issues that we [Kazakhstan] produce meat, wool and see none [of it]. Nazarbayev started referring to economic statistics, and he did so in such a way that we understood nothing.[37]

Around 5 p.m., the police started clashing with the protestors. Eyewitnesses reported that some police officers had deliberately targeted young women and girls, beating them with batons. Further clashes started as soon as the crowds saw that blood had been spilled. At the same time, party officials knew that more cadets and policemen were coming to the city, and the KGB formed groups of local vigilantes, who were now armed. The police, reportedly, started storming local student dormitories and were particularly vicious towards young female Kazakh students, beating them while screaming 'You'll never bear children!' The dormitory of the local agricultural university came under police attack, and people started running away from the violence.[38]

While protestors were stood on the square, Kolbin and others in the party headquarters were anxiously telephoning Moscow calling for special forces to enter the city. One eyewitness described the situation:

> I was on the square around 8 p.m. Large groups of students were all over the square. In the middle [of the square] stood the burnt-out carcass of the bus. On both sides [of the square] there were burn-out cars. I went to one of the officers, probably a security police officer [*chekist*], and asked him why they didn't remove the burnt-out car. His response: there are other things aside from that. The youth was uncontrollable [*molodezh' neupravlyaema*].[39]

Violent clashes with the police spurred more discontent in the crowds; some protestors started throwing snowballs, as well as pieces of marble they had broken from monuments. The protestors were in a losing situation—they only had tree branches, snowballs and stones, if they could find them, whereas the riot police were specifically equipped to inflict injury. Soviet party officials and law enforcement later denied that the riot policemen and cadets had used sapper shovels (*sapernye lopatki*) to cause more injuries to the protestors, but the investigative commission confirmed this had in fact been the case based on the remaining documents and the reports of the cadets and policemen themselves.⁴⁰ The shovels could break bones; some of the soldiers deliberately aimed them at the protestors' backs.

The riot police that came from the Russian city of Novosibirsk 'were equipped with plastic shields and batons. Each punch of such baton equals 300 kilograms. Bones cracked', wrote eyewitness V. Kaplin.⁴¹ Following the initial clashes, the protest descended into chaos, leading to calls to remain calm and continue protesting peacefully. Then one of the eyewitnesses screamed 'Tanks are coming!'—from the left side of the square, armoured personnel carriers resembling tanks were coming from Lenin Avenue (now renamed Dostyk or 'friendship' in Kazakh). There was a bitter irony in the fact that the armed forces started coming from streets that had Russian names—'Lenin' and 'Mira' (Peace).

According to different sources, including Shakhanov's investigative commission, the number of police and special forces amounted to more than 8,000 people and the number of vigilantes to more than 10,000.⁴² As soon as the special forces arrived, the square started to be 'cleared up'. The authorities also ordered firefighters to suppress the protests, and the protestors were hosed in cold water in the freezing cold December temperatures. Five young women who managed to escape the riot police on the night of 17 December were attacked by police dogs in a nearby apartment building; reports later emerged that two police dogs had also been killed in the clashes.

Protestors were beaten with extreme violence. The square quickly started 'howling' with hundreds of wounded people. In the words of one of the riot police, they received 'the command to "drive out" [the protestors]'—'gnat!' in Russian:

> The attack on the crowd and mass beating began. The crowd started dispersing. Those who fell down were dragged into the police cars. Those [protestors] who were beaten up and injured were dragged by their hair and by their legs [*taskali za volosy, za nogi*]. After the beating, there was blood on the snow.⁴³

Special operation Blizzard, or bloodied snow

At 11 p.m. on 17 December, the soldiers and militia started 'clearing' the protestors from the square. They ran into the crowds in full armour and with sapper shovels. They were screaming 'hurray!'[44] and started beating the protestors regardless of their age. Unarmed people ran into the inner side of the square trying to escape the violence, but many got caught by the blows of the repressors. Young girls ran into the apartment building blocks around the square. According to N. Bereshev, the head of Alma-Ata's local police force:

> What the square looked like after the crowds were cleared, then it was a very gloomy picture [*mrachnaya kartina*]. Dozens and maybe hundreds of young people, among them many women, lay on the ground. All of them were covered in blood and had different types of injuries. [The police and soldiers] used sapper shovels when they dispersed the crowds ... In 10–15 minutes, many [of the protestors] stood up and attempted to leave the square, but they were detained by the police, brought into the police cars, and sent to the police stations for investigation.[45]

The city's police stations filled up so quickly that the remaining protestors were sent to the outskirts of the city and thrown on to the cold ground, some still wet from the water sprayed at them by the firefighters, some missing their coats and shoes. It was reported that people were ordered to lie on the ground in severe sub-zero temperatures for hours into the night.

The investigative commission found that the repression was organised as part of special operation Blizzard-1986 (Metel'-1986). The whole point of the operation was to repress the protests by ensuring that the armed security personnel outnumbered the protestors.

The investigative commission into the repression was only able to start its work after Kolbin's departure from Kazakhstan in the summer of 1989. He and other party officials denied requesting special forces and calling for special troops to be sent from eight Soviet cities to Alma-Ata.[46] Since these requests had been made verbally, the investigation into these issues met with many obstacles.

Nazarbayev, who replaced Kolbin as the head of the republic in 1989, also denied any involvement in the repression. The real number of victims was carefully covered up. The KGB intimidated families who received the dead bodies of their loved ones in closed coffins and who resided outside Alma-Ata into not investigating the causes of death. The investigative commission found that more than thirty people had been buried in the cemetery outside Alma-Ata. These burials were unaccounted for, and the bodies had been delivered in a secret operation by the local prosecutor general's office. There were claims that around 200 people died in operation Blizzard. But the numbers and names of the dead were never confirmed. Even the investigative commission, chaired by Mukhtar Shakhanov, could not determine the actual number of victims, with the authorities declaring that three people had died during the protests—a student from the local energy institute, a worker from a telecom company and a bus conductor. Those who allegedly committed suicide in detention—Lyazzat Asanova, Kairat Ryskylbekov, Sabira Mukhamedzhanova and others—were not accounted for as victims of the protest, but their names remain in the public memory as victims of the Zheltoqsan tragedy.

Figures vary on the number of those who were detained. According to data from the Ministry of Internal Affairs of Soviet Kazakhstan, 2,335 were detained, whereas the KGB security forces claim 2,212 and the prosecutor general's office claims there were at least 2,401.[47] Dozens of people, mostly injured policemen, started flooding local hospitals. Protestors who were tortured on the cold snow were less eager to consult local doctors as they feared further police detention, beating and legal prosecution. The prosecutor general's office did not hesitate to accuse people of committing criminal offences, with protestors even receiving prison sentences for carrying banners. The investigative report refers to the following sentences:

> Bekbosynov A. was walking down the street with the banner 'Glory to Lenin's Ideas!'—was sentenced to two years in prison. Auezov Zh. raised the banner 'To Each Country Its Own Leader!' [*Kazhdomu narodu svoego vozhdya*]—was sentenced to

five years in prison. Bisenbayev carried banner 'No Privileges to No Nationality' [*Nikakih privilegii ni odnoi natsii*]—was sentenced to seven years in prison.[48]

The Kazakh prosecutor general, Mr. G. Elemisov, found that the security services had not committed any violations of the law either during or after the protests. In his testimony to the investigative commission, he claimed that 'he was removed from his job' during the protests and described the protestors as nationalists and extremists,[49] in line with the official position.

In the chaotic aftermath of the protests, conspiracy theories started to spread among law enforcement officers. As one officer, Mr Volkov, stated to the investigative commission:

> When I got to the square [from the bunker on the evening of 17 December], there were 120–50 people [lying] on the ground. From the conversations from the radio set, I heard that protestors had killed cadets from the border guard institution [*demonstranty zabii nasmert' kursantov-pogranichnikov*] and then they [cadets] started chopping the protestors with shovels [*stali rubit' demonstrantov lopatami*] even though the order was to beat them using the flat side of the shovel. On 21 December in the morning [there was] a meeting in the department of internal [army] troops of Central Asia and Kazakhstan [on the conjunction of Gorky and Amangeldy streets], and the head of the operations department, Colonel Sherbatov, spoke about these numbers: 168 people dead, among them eight army soldiers, four cadets from border guard institute, one from the Alma-Ata militia [police].[50]

By the night of 17 December 1986, Brezhnev Square was a scene that few would ever forget. It was carnage. Eyewitnesses report that there was blood everywhere and injured people lying on the cold ground. In the vicinity, policemen with specially trained dogs searched for the protestors who had managed to escape, and there was a cacophony of barking, howling and beating. Young girls were screaming from the nearby apartment buildings as policemen caught and dragged them by their hair to the nearby police trucks. Tleuzhan

Imanbayev, a young conscript who was sent to clear the protestors from the square, remembered every detail:

> It is difficult to convey in words the level of cruelty and atrocity [of the Blizzard operation]. Of the [group] of fifteen-, sixteen- and seventeen-year-old teenagers who were beaten with iron sticks, no one could have stayed alive. The guys and girls [*parnei i devushek*] who fell down from the heavy blows were dragged like animals and loaded into [police] cars. At that point, it was impossible to determine whether they were alive or dead. After that [operation], when newspapers wrote that there were no mass deaths, I wanted to gouge out my eyes because [my eyes] were the witness of the killings.[51]

The eyewitness accounts are harrowing. The main site of the violence on 17 and 18 December 1986, Almaty's Brezhnev Square, is surrounded by official buildings and residential apartment blocks. People working in those buildings and living in those apartments reported numerous atrocities being committed against the unarmed protestors. Sagimbayeva G., an eyewitness who lived in one of the houses on Baiseitova Street right on the lower side of the square, gave the following account:

> When I went to the Bereke store [near the square] in the morning, I saw how young girls were dragged by their hands and legs across ditches [*po arykam volokli*] and how they screamed. Some of them were injured, they were thrown into the [police] cars. [The police] almost dragged away the shopkeeper because she wanted to protect one of the [detainees]. Some of the young women who came shopping for groceries were also caught up [by the police]. They were viciously beaten. When I came home [in one of the apartment blocks near the square], I saw another horrid picture: a policeman hit an old Kazakh woman who was walking on the street on her head from behind. She fell down. We were all shocked, [my] neighbour cried lying on the floor. We were all scared to leave [our apartments]. In those horrifying days, Russians showed their chauvinism. They took pleasure in beating up young women, beating up their organs, making them

sit on the cold ground, beating them below their stomachs and saying, 'so that Kazakhs won't be born'.[52]

Some eyewitnesses claimed that the riot police had specifically targeted young female protestors as an intimidation tactic to discourage other young people from joining the protests. Abdybayev Zarpen, chair of the Department of Mathematics of the Alma-Ata Architecture Institute, remembered witnessing the vicious beating of a young female student:

> Two policemen brought a young seventeen- to eighteen-year-old female student dressed in a coat and boots and high heels. They brought her to the bus that was parked near us and one of the policemen—a Russian—grabbed her hair and lifted her up trying to drag her to the bus. She started screaming and her screams continued inside the bus. I could not stand it. I entered the bus and saw how the policemen [still] held her by the hair and kicked her in the stomach. Only when I interrupted him, he let go of her, but she was already unconscious.[53]

Detained protestors later reported that people in the temporary prison cells lay there in their own blood, many with bone fractures unable to get any medical help.[54] Another eyewitness reported that

> after the beating by the soldiers, many [protestors] remained on the square unable to move or stand up by themselves. They were taken away by the emergency crews. Twenty soldiers circled around and started kicking one [of the protestors] who was barely alive or already dead. They kicked him in the stomach and on the head with their heels and then dragged him by his feet. The head of this poor man slid on the pavement and knocked every step when [they dragged him] down the stairs.[55]

It is still unclear why the riot police and the army were so aggressive in their operation to 'clear up' the square. One explanation is that the party officials and the KGB had described the protestors as nationalists who were opposed to Soviet internationalism and the presence of ethnic Russians in Kazakhstan. Framing the protest as reflecting antagonisms between ethnic Kazakhs who felt repressed in their own country and ethnic Russians who were part of Moscow's settler colonialism under the guise of Soviet internationalism undoubtedly exacerbated the tensions. Yet the groups of poorly organised protestors did not have a collective identity that would have enabled them to put forward a substantive and coherent nationalist agenda. Most of them were indeed Kazakhs, and most of them were students who had come to Soviet Alma-Ata—a fortress of Soviet settler colonial policies where ethnic Kazakhs were only allowed to be in a minority. But it is unlikely these students would have been able to form a significant nationalist force in just two days of protests, particularly as so many of them carried Lenin's portraits and quoted his nationality policy (inarguably also colonial in nature).

Party officials knew that emphasising interethnic antagonisms—portraying the protest not as a form of peaceful opposition to Gorbachev's decision to change a republican leader without consulting the local population but as Kazakh ethnonationalists assembling to bring down Kolbin—could kill two birds with one stone. On the one hand, the party quickly sought to discredit the protest among the city's residents, who saw it as setting a dangerous precedent, potentially opening the way to an interethnic conflict that would threaten the country's multi-ethnic unity. On the other hand, the party also organised and legitimated the riot police and vigilantes who might otherwise have considered the violent repression of citizens unnecessary.

Panic was widespread in Alma-Ata. People of all nationalities felt threatened—the ethnic Russians by the protestors and ethnic Kazakhs by the riot police and vigilantes. When a rumour spread that Kazakhs had killed children in a kindergarten—which was later completely disproved—parents started frantically calling the schools and looking for their children. One of my respondents recalled how she phoned her daughter at school and told her:

> You are ethnically mixed, and you have blue eyes. If you see Kazakhs, tell them your Kazakh-sounding last name and, if they ask about the colour of the eyes, say that some Kazakhs have blue eyes. If you see Russians and they think you're Kazakh, tell them that your name is Sveta, and your mom is Russian even though I am also ethnically mixed.[56]

THE DECEMBER 1986 PROTESTS IN ALMA-ATA

As one of the eyewitnesses recalled:

> On 17 December 1986, I worked from 8 a.m. to 8 p.m. [as a shop assistant in a Bereke shop]. In the evening I went to the bus stop on Mira–Satpayeva streets.[57] Two Russian soldiers took me away and brought me to the police car that stood near the stage on the square [*vozle tribuny*]. I and two more girls were brought to the [police] car and sent to the basement of the police station near Tselinniy cinema [in central Almaty]. There were more than thirty young Kazakh women there. We were all photographed. Then they brought us to the small room. My arms were covered with bruises in places where soldiers held me. Then they scolded us [with obscenities]. They said that 'we need to exterminate these Kazakhs' and so forth. In the prison cell, one girl had head injuries [and was bleeding], and another one had bruises all over her face. We spent twenty-four hours there.[58]

When the injured and dead were finally removed from the square and the party leaders had left the bunker on the same square following their secret meeting denouncing the protests as nationalistic, it was all eerily quiet. Just hours ago, people covered in blood had been dragged here. The final bodies were removed at 2 a.m. At 4 a.m. on 18 December, the square was washed with hot water to remove the blood stains, the ripped-off coats, pieces of clothing and the weapons left behind by the riot police. The screams continued in the interrogation rooms of the local police stations and KGB headquarters. Between sixty and 170 people died. As the square was washed of the physical reminders of the regime's crimes, the party apparatchiks quickly started erasing the traces of their own, individual crimes.

'Gorbachev, take back your Kolba!'[59]

At 2 a.m. on 18 December 1986, Kolbin gathered all the chairmen of different party *aktiv* (sub-groups) in a secret meeting that denounced the protests as nationalistic and extremist. The meeting passed a resolution calling the protestors alcoholics and drug addicts. The resolution also described the protest as having been meticulously organised, partly with the connivance of elements among the special forces, and claimed that there were trucks distributing free vodka and drugs. Among those who gave presentations at the meeting were the party's leaders—Kolbin himself, but also Kamalidenov, Mendybayev and possibly Nazarbayev too.[60]

The local press was immediately given orders to print stories describing the protestors as 'nationalistic elements' who threatened the country's internationalist policies and interethnic relations, a framing that further divided society. All of the official institutions and their chairmen were given orders to denounce the protestors in the explanatory meetings with their employees over the following days. Leading members of the local intelligentsia called the protestors alcoholics who threated the state. After 1991, many among the local Soviet elite publicly stated that they regretted agreeing to this statement but that they had been forced to do so by Soviet officials.

Operation Blizzard was carried out with the direct involvement of the Moscow elite. Some of them, like Solomentsev, were already on the ground giving orders and directions. Others, like Gorbachev and members of the Politburo, were in direct contact with Kolbin and gave him the orders via phone. Party officials refrained from using documented and written accounts of their orders. As Gorbachev had only recently announced perestroika and further democratisation, he wanted to distance himself from the violence in one of the Soviet 'peripheries'. The numbers of the deaths were kept a secret, but the highest officials knew there were more than just the three victims that had been officially declared.

After the protestors were cleared from the square, an intimidation campaign was launched. Injured students were tried, sentenced and imprisoned in large groups. Those who got away with administrative sentences for participating in 'unsanctioned rallies' were denounced, removed from the Komsomol (the All-Union Leninist Young Communist League) and the Communist Party, kicked out of their universities and institutions and sent away from Alma-Ata. Many of the survivors of the bloodshed later remembered that they wanted to run away from the city to forget the horrors they had witnessed on the square. It is still unclear how many of the survivors, *zheltoqsanovscy*—Decembrists, as they were later called—ended up in psychiatric institutions.

While the protestors were sentenced to long years in prison, Kazakhstan's gendarmes received medals and prizes 'for courage'. What type of courage did the riot police display against the unarmed and mostly peaceful protestors? What weapons of mass destruction did the ordinary people, among them many women and teenagers, have? The snowballs[61] they threw at Nazarbayev and Kamalidenov, who demanded that the protestors go home?

Kolbin spent three more years as the first secretary of the CPK. He pretended that he was a real leader, but Moscow's influence reached across every governing institution—from the KGB and Ministry of Internal Affairs to the socio-linguistic surveying of Kazakh society (see the next chapter). But while Kolbin remained in his position, any investigation into the violent and repressive crackdown of the December 1986 protest was disallowed. Anyone who disagreed was immediately denounced as a 'nationalist' and stripped of their job and whatever privileges they may have had.

Mourning families were not allowed to open the coffins to see the bodies of their dead children. The funeral of Asanova, the sixteen-year-old Kazakh girl who allegedly jumped from the fifth floor of the KGB building between interrogations, was held in secret, and her parents were denied the chance of seeing her face for a final time. But word of mouth spread quickly—one of the former police officers who knew what had actually happened to Asanova (she had been raped and tortured) resigned from his post and was traumatised for years, saying it was the worst memory of his life.[62]

For years, people who experienced the atrocities of Moscow's settler colonialism had to mourn in silence, unable to speak about their trauma. In Soviet history, the Alma-Ata December 1986 'events' became a transitory date before the more publicised protests or 'events' in Tbilisi, Baku and then Vilnius and Riga from 1989 to 1990. The repression of the protests in these countries, and the repetition of the Blizzard 'special operation' in the case of Tbilisi, with sapper shovels breaking the bones of the protestors as in Alma-Ata in 1986, became the founding myths of these respective nations' paths to independence. In Riga, where at least six protestors died in

January 1991, monuments commemorate the names of the victims, and there is a special museum dedicated to the protests. In post-1991 Kazakhstan, when Nazarbayev assumed full power, activists from the Zheltoqsan movement literally fought for the victims to be commemorated, and only in 2006 was a monument to their suffering unveiled. The real number of victims and their names are still unknown. There is a colloquial saying in Kazakhstan—'until Nazarbayev dies, we won't find out about Zheltoqsan'.

'We are only the party's soldiers'

> What I've seen in the police station did not make any sense. It resembled films where fascist actions were shown. Soon after the [December 1986] events, minister [of internal affairs of Kazakh SSR] in private conversations several times suggested that I didn't 'show myself up' [chto ya sebya ne 'pokazal'].Within a year, I, the chair of political control [politupravleniya], a colonel, member of the audit commission of the Central Committee [of the CPK], sought admission at the Central Committee and could not get an appointment with any of the party officials. The reason was still the same—I 'didn't show myself up' properly [ne tak sebya pokazal]. Six months later [they] started hinting that I should find a different job for myself because they didn't trust me with the political work anymore. At first Vietnam was on offer [Predlozhili snachala Vietnam], then Afghanistan and then it was announced that: 'You are an internationalist [ty je internatsionalist], so go and serve your duty.' I spent eleven months in Afghanistan and returned from there because our [Soviet] troops were withdrawing [from Afghanistan]. After that I still could not find a job for three months.
>
> Murat Kalmataev's testimony to the December 1986 investigative commission. In 1986, Kalmatayev was a chair of political control at the Ministry of Internal Affairs of Kazakh SSR.[63]

The life stories of the people who were on the different sides of the barricades on the three cold days of December 1986 developed in very different ways. Kolbin left Kazakhstan in 1989, leaving the country's leadership to Nazarbayev. Kolbin died of a heart attack in a Moscow metro in January 1998. Solomentsev died in Moscow in 2008. His career in Kazakhstan was dogged by scandals, including a sexual harassment allegation that was covered up and the rumours killed off even though the high party officials were aware of his behaviour. Viktor Miroshnik, the head of the Kazakh KGB, continued his career in Moscow and died in March 2016. None of them was legally prosecuted for the repression and violence they had unleashed against the peaceful protestors.

Those now competing for political power—Kamalidenov and Nazarbayev, as well as other local elites, including young Komsomol leader and future contender for the position of Nazarbayev's successor, Imangali Tasmagambetov—had to live in Zheltoqsan's shadow. Those who had direct access to secret documents on the protests and the crackdown did all they could to erase them from the archives and secret KGB 'kompromat' holdings. Kamalidenov, who lost the political competition with Nazarbayev, later acknowledged that the protests were the first signs of 'democracy' in the Soviet Union but claimed that the old elites did not understand this at the time. Nazarbayev quickly understood the importance of December 1986 for the public. In the post-independence period, he created myths that he was 'at the head of the column of the protestors' and had helped them in their demands. Many commentators have cast doubt on his version of events, but since the KGB documents have been destroyed, it is difficult if not impossible to prove what role he had played. In the remaining documents, especially his testimony to the investigative commission, he merely claimed that 'we were only the party's soldiers'.[64]

Protests in solidarity with the students of Alma-Ata erupted in all the major cities of Kazakhstan that December, and people demanded open and independent investigations throughout the perestroika period. The chairman of the investigative commission, Shakhanov, was becoming increasingly popular among ethnic Kazakhs, who saw him as the voice of the people, leading Nazarbayev to change his narrative and claim that he was the one leading the protestors:

> I say that this approach [of appointing Kolbin as the first secretary without consulting party officials in Kazakhstan] to the future

destiny of Kazakhstan really shocked the members of the Bureau of the Central Committee of the Communist Party of the republic. Everyone entered a state of hypnosis, and no one even thought of an idea, of the need to at least discuss the candidacy [of Kolbin] 'at least for the protocol' at the bureau's meeting. Honestly, there was nothing to discuss—none of us knew him [Kolbin]. The plenum of the Central Committee of the Communist Party [of Kazakhstan] went ahead in a very enchanted atmosphere. The whole procedure took eighteen minutes. Everyone raised their hands and Kolbin became the first secretary. The syndrome of insane obedience to the centre ruled yet again; the syndrome of the barrack psychology [*sindrom kazarmennoi psikhologii*]—'we are only the party's soldiers'. No one [including Nazarbayev himself] thought about the consequences, and these arrived fairly quickly.[65]

The square where the protests happened in 1986 continues to serve as a space of contestation. It is home to the ruling regime's first attempts at nation-building—the 91-metre stela of the Golden Man and the 'History of Kazakhstan' series of monuments. This central monument is a favoured space for opposition rallies, most of which remain prohibited by the country's law on 'unsanctioned rallies'.[66] The square is also home to the local city administration and at one point hosted an underground cinema and a shopping mall. In a snapshot, this is what Kazakhstan represents to both the regime and its people (*narod*)—rapid neoliberalisation, banausic nationalist projects, male-dominated visual state representations and continuous contestations of the meaning-making mechanisms.[67] Is it possible to create a consistent and truthful politics of memory on a square that became the site of so many deaths? Although more protestors lost their lives on the same square (see Chapter 5) in early January 2022, the mundane politics of the everyday means that those visiting the square today will remain oblivious to the various tragedies that have unfolded there. New cafés and even clothing stores opened during my fieldwork in the summer of 2022 and 2023, and it feels like the regime prefers to silence our history instead of contesting and openly questioning it.

THE DECEMBER 1986 PROTESTS IN ALMA-ATA

The December 1986 events are at the heart of these contestations. The real number of victims is still unknown, and their names are yet to be fully recovered. The tragic spirit of the violent repression of December 1986 still walks through Almaty. Growing up, we often heard stories adults shared among themselves about what really happened in December 1986, and on every anniversary of the protests, different groups of people come to the square to commemorate the victims. Some of the survivors of special operation Blizzard continue to organise, and many receive welfare payments from the state, but their trauma has never been fully and openly acknowledged in the post-independence period.

At a symbolic level, the 1986 protests laid the basis for the national myth of independent Kazakhstan—16 December became the country's Independence Day, but for many it remains a day of mourning. Shakhanov even proposed commemorating 17 December as a Day of National Mourning. The trauma does not seem to have healed, as during my interviews with a completely new opposition, the independence generation who were born in or after 1986, the members of the Oyan, Qazaqstan (Wake Up, Kazakhstan) political movement, also believe that 16 and 17 December should be days of mourning.

Every decade in Kazakhstani history brings a new tragedy to the winter months—first December in 1986 with Zheltoqsan and December 2011 with the mass killings in the city of Zhanaozen, and then Bloody January in 2022. In the commemorative events I attended in Almaty after 2022, some activists were lamenting that the winter months were months of sorrow in Kazakhstan. 'Let's pray there won't be Bloody Aqpan [February in Kazakh] anytime soon, but with this leadership, who knows?', an anonymous activist said during a commemorative evening on the anniversary of the Bloody January protests in Almaty.

The December 1986 protests became the founding myth for Kazakhstani nation-building against the odds, given the censorship and repression of the Moscow-backed elites and the allegations that the protests had divided the country along ethnic lines (see the following two chapters). The narrative of the protests may be retold differently—especially in the official pro-regime school textbooks—but it continues to unite different, post-ethnic political movements like Oyan, Qazaqstan. The protests were a manifestation of popular discontent with Moscow's settler colonialism and its policy of dividing ethnicities from one another, particularly in the cities, where ethnic Russians dominated. But these policies at the same time placed ethnic Russians in Kazakhstan in the precarious position of being 'settlers', potentially making them vulnerable relative to their other, non-Russian compatriots who saw them as a more privileged ethnicity, even if many of them did not want this status. Major protests like those in December 1986 posed crucial questions about the Soviet model of ethnic politics and challenged ethnic identities in hybrid contexts (for example, Kazakhstani Russians), unintentionally paving the way for the discourse of the ethnic Kazakhs' trauma over the violence on Brezhnev Square on 17 December 1986.

I am not a proponent of the idea that the indigenisation of an ethnic group's colonial trauma can lead to a potentially fruitful outcome in nation-building or other socio-political projects. Yet the outburst of protest in Soviet Kazakhstan discussed in this chapter brought to the fore questions of settler colonialism, and the violent suppression of that protest gave rise to the 'remedial' nationalising incentives[68] that highlighted the need to remedy the ethnic Kazakh side of the story as the main victim. And this was the dominant narrative for most of the post-independence period among Kazakh national-patriots. But what was the role of the ethnic Kazakh elites in the repression and then denunciation of the protestors? And how were these same elites able to continue ruling the country, often using the same colonial blueprints as the Kremlin? Was it only ethnic Kazakhs who were the victims of the December 1986 protests, or the whole of Kazakhstani society? After all, any hopes for democratisation or any transparent political decision-making came crashing down on the evening of 17 December 1986, and any further attempts at democratisation were suppressed for a long time.

3

WHO ARE THE FOURTH *ZHUZ*?

ON RUSSIANS AND KAZAKHSTANI MULTICULTURALISM

I come to Russia, and they say, 'oh Kazakhs came!' even though we are Russians.[1]

In the aftermath of the December 1986 protests, a group of Moscow-led sociologists formed an internal committee chaired by Dmitry Tolstukhin and landed in Alma-Ata with a secret mission to research the relationship between ethnic Kazakhs and ethnic Russians.[2] Moscow state officials believed that the nationalistic mood among ethnic Kazakh youth posed a significant threat to the republic's interethnic relations. No questions were raised about the reality of Russo-Kazakh relations, and there were no investigations into whether Kazakh nationalism had really been the catalyst for the protest. The decision was made in the early hours after the 17 December violence on Alma-Ata's Brezhnev Square—all protestors, regardless of whether they were alive or dead, were proclaimed Kazakh nationalists. The Moscow-based Tolstukhin Committee, however, did not have a mandate to deal with the problems that had caused the protest, nor did it have time for prolonged, in-depth and multi-layered research.

The committee's final report, produced solely for the party leadership, claimed that there were 'complex' understandings of the December 1986 events in Kazakhstan, that 'a third of the population did not adequately assess the December [1986] events in Alma-Ata, considering these [protests] as only hooliganistic actions and not [actions] with nationalistic sentiments'.[3] Those who shared this view of the events were 'respondents of the Kazakh and partially German nationalities and to a lesser extent, the respondents of the Russian and other nationalities'.[4] The sociological survey and its findings separated the respondents into ethnic Kazakhs and ethnic Russians. According to the report, the Kazakh respondents tended to have 'negative' and 'wrongful' assessments of the protests and failed to fully condemn the protestors, which the report attributed to their nationalistic, pro-Kazakh tendencies. The report went on to specify that

> there is a specific contradiction in the mass consciousness [*v massovom soznanii*] when it comes to the assessment of the December events, there are significantly negative tendencies in the opinions of the population. One of these [contradictions] is in the [opinion of the respondents] that the protestors supported the previous leadership [Kunayev] and the previous order of things in the republic and that they connect it to the interests of the Kazakh people. Those who support the other tendency think that the protests reflect the interests of the Kazakh people but [that the protests] were not supporting the previous leadership and the order of things in the republic. Both of these tendencies, despite their differences, reflect a wrongful understanding of national interests and the deformation of the political consciousness among certain groups of the population. ... [T]he majority of the Russian population [in Kazakhstan] considered that the [December 1986] events contained a nationalistic character. The Kazakh population did not consider that the protestors supported the old regime but that [the protestors] rallied for the interests of the Kazakh population. December events are widely discussed, and many respondents do not consider the republican media coverage [about the protests] as enough and look for the answers in the foreign sources.[5]

Tolstukhin's committee reported back to Moscow that the 'low degree of the culture of interethnic communication' and the 'inadequate evaluation of the role of the Russian language as the means of interethnic communication', which was particularly evident among the 'Kazakh population', were the main reasons for the problems in the republic's interethnic relations.[6] The report's authors claimed the situation could be improved by the Kazakh population speaking better Russian and using it more widely in their everyday life; little thought seems to have been given to the possibility of the non-Kazakh population learning at least basic Kazakh to contribute to interethnic harmony in Kazakhstan.

Russian was considered the lingua franca of the Soviet Union, and this unspoken rule was rarely questioned in Moscow or any of its affiliated political institutions. As we saw in the previous chapter, some of the members of the Politburo who were sent to Kazakhstan to deal with the crisis in December 1986 scolded local elites for the 'issue' of the growing ratio of ethnic Kazakhs studying at Alma-Ata's elite higher education institutions. Moscow thus had a negative view of the spread of Kazakh-speaking communities in the main urban centre of the Kazakh republic.

Hiding behind the banner of peoples' friendship, the Politburo was openly engaging in a settler colonialist strategy of Russification and sought to exacerbate urban–rural divisions in Soviet Kazakhstan. Ethnic Kazakhs were subject to quotas in the allocation of housing—the *propiska* housing regulations—and the provision of education, as well as employment in public institutions. Most of these orders were kept secret and directed to the republican institutions from the top of the system. Solomentsev's hysterical speech in Alma-Ata during the 1986 protests openly revealed the Politburo's position—ethnic Kazakhs should not make up a majority of the urban population of their own republic.

Tolstukhin's committee was perplexed by the difference between what it described as the 'values' of those it identified as 'Russian' (mentioned in the report simply as *russkie*), who stated that the Second World War, known in the Soviet Union as the Great Patriotic War, the Soviet space programme and the cultivation of the Virgin

Lands (*tselina*)[7] were the main values of their people, and those of the Kazakh respondents, who did not share the same opinion.

The Kazakh respondents' views differed completely —they took pride in simply 'being Kazakh' and spoke about the 'Kazakh people's will to freedom [*svobodolubie*]' and their 'fight against the colonisers'.[8] Kazakh respondents were also anxious about the possibility of the Kazakh ethnicity withering away, that 'Kazakh people [will] forget their language' and that most of this was happening 'because of Russians', who, 'while living in Kazakhstan, do not respect Kazakhs and consider them second-class citizens [*lyudi vtorogo sorta*]'.[9] What happened to these divided communities after the Soviet Union collapsed is the question guiding this chapter.

Tolstukhin's committee did not come to Kazakhstan to formulate solutions to what they saw primarily as 'interethnic divisions' by encouraging unity among the different socio-lingual communities but to further divide them by imposing the Russian language and values on what they called ethnic Kazakh communities and respondents. The Russian language and Moscow's vision of what '*druzhba narodov*' (peoples' friendship) meant to the Soviet population had to be read through the indisputable domination of the Politburo and its Russified mentality. Though couched in the language of internationalism, these were settler colonial policies, with the Kremlin, the metropole, ruling over all colonised people and imposing internationalism by making everyone Russian first.

The report concluded there were sufficient reasons to predict that 'nationalistic actions of a different nature would continue to happen in the republic for a long time' and that this could lead to 'extremist actions by certain people and groups of the population'.[10] Even though this statement had not yet played out, Tolstukhin and his team at the time (1987) cautioned Moscow that the party elites should 'expect covert, masked resistance to perestroika and especially to [any further] political reshuffling among the [party] cadres', as the tension 'among the groups who consider themselves wrongfully discriminated' against was still present. These groups of discriminated people 'often portray themselves as those who speak for the interests of the Kazakh people, when in reality, they ignore their interests'.[11] The Tolstukhin report was not the only internal document that condemned Kazakh nationalism for the December 1986 protests while calling for more action from the party leadership in Moscow to resolve the divisions between ethnic Kazakhs and ethnic Russians.

Kolbin, who refused to leave his position as the leader of the Kazakh republic amid the protests, seemed to take the report as a personal blow and called for an audit of the republic's internal affairs. He received reports from special committees that re-read and censored the five-volume *History of the Kazakh SSR* (1979) book series because it placed too great an emphasis on Kazakhstan's pre-Soviet history.[12] The report went on to detail how the focus in Kazakh history books on the steppe rulers and the glorious days of the Golden Horde in the period before Russian colonisation had fostered nationalistic sentiments among the Soviet Kazakhs and how this was detrimental to Soviet values and the values of perestroika. Kolbin also received a number of letters condemning the protestors in the December 1986 'events' (*sobytiya*, a Soviet euphemism used to downplay any protests and their political meaning). Some of these letters condemned the celebration of the Kazakh writer Ilyas Esenberlin, who died of a heart attack in 1983 after a long battle with KGB censors over his historical novels, which were highly popular among ethnic Kazakhs. These letters deemed Esenberlin a 'nationalist element'; however, withdrawing his books from private homes and libraries would have caused further uproar at a time when the nation was still unsettled after the fateful days of December 1986.

Kolbin was no newcomer to the politics of ethnic division in the Soviet Union, nor was he the first leader in Soviet Kazakhstan who had to implement settler colonial policies in the republic. But unlike his predecessors, he faced a more acute problem given that his appointment had exacerbated growing interethnic divides, together with it being made at a time of other serious problems in the country, as people were also protesting against the Polygon located in the heart of the republic. Radiation levels in the vicinity were causing a rise in cancer patients and children born with various forms of disabilities and genetic illnesses. The country was facing an economic crisis and shortages. That the December 1986 protests, Zheltoqsan, were still officially attributed to nationalistic elements and the protestors had not been rehabilitated caused further social problems and hardened resistance to Kolbin's rule. Despite holding the highest position in the country for three years, Kolbin did next to nothing to bring people closer and allow traumas to heal; he was not a popular leader, and people were counting the days to his departure. When he left Kazakhstan in 1989, the Kazakh- and Russian-speaking communities were more divided than ever.

This chapter seeks to demonstrate how the category of 'Russian' (*russkii*) or Kazakhstani Russian (*kazakhstanskii russkii*) has transformed over time, and how the regime, first Soviet and then postsoviet or Nazarbayevite, viewed Russian identity as cohesive, unambiguous and always in connection—whether in competition or in the anticipation of potential conflict—with Kazakh ethnic identity. But while Russianness, as a group identity, builds on important linguistic and cultural—including religious—signifiers, different individuals within this group often have divergent personal histories and connections to their localities. Pavlodar-based Russians may not be the same as Zhetysu-based Russians. Moreover, the top-down approach to the all-Russian identity in Kazakhstan often led to a crisis of identification, as some of this chapter's data and interviews reveal. Russianness was often used as a weapon of division, but this also led to significant issues in group formations, at times separating Kazakhstani Russians from their sincere desire to belong in Kazakhstan.

Regime divisions and the discourse of parallel communities

Nazarbayev, who succeeded Kolbin in 1989, used the Russian–Kazakh divide and deepened it even further. Nazarbayev continued to view Kazakh society as divided into ethnic Kazakhs and ethnic Russians, together with a smaller proportion of other ethnic minorities. Policies based on these divisions increased the possibility of future conflicts, for example by fostering separate values among ethnic Russian and ethnic Kazakh communities. Proposals were made to establish fixed boundaries separating one group from another, even in areas where there was a great deal of interaction between Russians and Kazakhs and they could understand each other's languages.

Some of these policies in turn influenced people's perceptions of their own group identity, as parts of this chapter will demonstrate. These tendencies continue to co-exist even today along with the discourse that Kazakhstani Russians form the 'fourth *Zhuz*'. Traditionally, Kazakh society has been broken down into three *Zhuz*, or hordes, with which most Kazakhs still identify. Each *Zhuz* is made up of numerous tribes or communities with their own unique customs, forming a complex, multi-faceted identity: one can be Kazakh but from the Middle Horde and of the Argyn tribe. According to this discourse about the fourth *Zhuz*, ethnic Russians can belong to this additional *Zhuz*, and some go even further to specify that different regions and different cities can often have significant cultural identity components, meaning that Pavlodar Russians, for example, may identify differently from Atyrau Russians, despite both groups being ethnically Russian. The fourth *Zhuz* paradigm aims to accommodate Kazakhstani Russians to a more localised identity group and highlight their difference from Russians from Russia, Latvia or even Uzbekistan and Kyrgyzstan. I dwell further on this idea in the discussion of 'our Russians' later in the chapter.

In 1989, when all Soviet republics implemented the new language laws, centring them on the languages of the titular ethnic groups, for example Estonians in Estonia and Kazakhs in Kazakhstan, it created further public debate. Soviet Kazakhstan was drifting towards a dual lingual approach of favouring the Russian language over the Kazakh language. It was only in the late 1990s that policies were adopted that established Kazakh as the state language, slowly elevating it to the language used in state documentation (*deloproizvodstvo*), though Russian still remained widely spoken and was officially known as the language of interethnic communication.[13]

Nazarbayev, who was fluent in both languages, continued to address his nation in Russian and Kazakh well into the post-independence years, a practice that has been continued by President Tokayev.[14] As we have seen, Nazarbayev believed that Kazakhstan was divided between Kazakh-speaking minorities and Russophone majorities, even if many among the Russophone population identified as ethnic Kazakhs, and even though many ethnic Russians have a more complex understanding of local Kazakhstani identities.

An era of parallel socio-linguistic communities began. Some political observers went as far as declaring the Kazakh- and Russian-speaking groups as communities living in two parallel realities that were incapable of understanding each other;[15] however, this is largely a stereotype that has yet to be confirmed by serious research.

The regime's narrow and simplistic understanding of Kazakhstan's complex societal and ethnic relations was shared by the Kazakh national-patriots, who often attributed the Russophones' lack of Kazakh-language proficiency to their limited understanding of 'Kazakh problems'. In my interviews with Kazakh national-patriots and even with Mukhtar Shakhanov himself, I was asked whether I went to a Kazakh-speaking school,[16] and many of my respondents referred to Russians and Kazakhs as living in 'parallel communities'. To them, the question of Kazakh-language proficiency remained the top priority and the biggest problem in contemporary Kazakhstan.

This problem also came up in an interview with an opposition leader, who told me that 'if we all start speaking Kazakh here and even wearing Kazakh national costumes in our everyday life, it will not solve our political and economic problems',[17] hinting that the language issue was secondary to the more pressing questions of democratisation and better governance. In the new wave of Kazakh activism, the younger generation places the issue of Kazakh-language proficiency into a different paradigm and asks for greater consideration of the non-Russian-speaking communities, who are often discriminated against in public spaces due to a lack of simple translations to Kazakh, for example in menus in restaurants and cafés. 'Living in a space where lack of Russian-language proficiency creates more and more problems on an everyday basis is something very few people take into consideration', complained one of the Kazakhophone activists.[18]

Linguistic divisions continue to haunt Kazakh society. Russia's invasion of Ukraine in February 2022 further complicated the problems created by the linguistic division. Many non-Kazakh speakers quickly began learning Kazakh, and improvised Kazakh-language clubs appeared in cities across the country. In an interview, Alexey Skalozubov, the founder of the popular Qazaq-language discussion club Batyl Bol, said that the war had led to 'a wave of hatred against Russia: against citizens of Russia in general and against [ethnic] Russians in particular', and that his decision to specify on video that he is a 'Kazakhstani Russian' who claims Kazakhstan 'as my homeland' and the Qazaq language as one of his languages allowed him and others like him to 'calm people down'.[19]

At the same time, the Russian media in Russia proper have sought to manipulate this issue by reporting on Kazakh-language 'patrols' and linguistic discrimination against ethnic Russians in the country, viewing the treatment of ethnic Russians as a potential premise for Russian intervention. Opinion polls indicate that the number of Kazakhstanis who believe in a possible Russian invasion of Kazakhstan doubled between November 2022 and May 2023. Around 15 per cent of the Demiscope and Paperlab survey respondents believed that an invasion was a possibility, with 23.3 per cent agreeing that an invasion was possible 'under certain circumstances' and 70 per cent stating that they had been personally affected by the war.[20]

The long postsoviet goodbye posed problems for ethnic Russians in Kazakhstan in terms of their identification with a nation that is no longer Soviet or Russian. According to state statistics, those who identify as ethnic Russians number 3.5 million, plus around 300,000 officially registered Russian citizens who entered Kazakhstan after Russia launched its full-scale invasion of Ukraine (the numbers of those who entered and left Kazakhstan are much higher).[21] If the identification of those who have recently left Russia—who prefer to call themselves 'relocates' (*reallokanty* in Russian)—is more or less stable, the identity of those who have lived in Kazakhstan for a long time is still largely fragmentary (including, for some, even on the question of whether they belong to the Russian or the Kazakhstani state), ambiguous and in search of more stable signifiers. Who are Kazakhstani Russians? This chapter is dedicated to their narratives and searches for belonging. I will return to the problems of the Kazakh language in the following chapter to offer a more complex understanding of how it creates challenges for and discrimination against Kazakh speakers and non-Kazakh speakers among ethnic Kazakhs and the types of divisions this creates.

In any political analysis, Kazakh groupness can be distinguished based on distinctive identities and divisions stemming from whether they are 'northerners' or 'southerners'; there are also ubiquitous discussions over the 'western' accent and whether it can be classed as its own version of the Kazakh language. Yet the regime almost never questions the identities of 'Russians', with their groupness rarely discussed as a potential 'identity in crisis'. Russians, in other words, are a static category in the regime's eyes, rigid and all-encompassing. Data collected about Kazakhstani Russians often reinforce this view of conflict-potentiality and rigid groupness. State surveys in Kazakhstan seldom question who Russians in Kazakhstan are, what their main identity signifiers are and whether they differ from Russians in Russia. The approach to rigid groupness that Nazarbayev's regime imposed on ethnic Russians in Kazakhstan was the same as the rigid Soviet approach to minority ethnic groups like the Kazakhs.

In the Soviet period, surveys considered ethnic Kazakhs as a problematic group with the potential to cause interethnic conflict; however, since the 1990s, the tables have been turned, and surveys now target 'Russians' as a potential source of conflict and secessionism. The Nazarbayev regime inherited these problematic positions from the Soviet system, in which ethnicities were deliberately divided and people strictly identified by their dominant ethnic group—excluding their mother's ethnicity from the official fifth paragraph in ethnically mixed families. But what is more important is that the persistence of the Russo-Kazakh division and the competition to become the majority population is impeding the further development of supra-ethnic projects and meanings that people of all ethnicities actually practise on the ground.

Faces of the 'specific' nationality[22]

The debate over whether the Soviets were the makers or breakers of the Kazakh nation is still ongoing, and it is unlikely that it will be resolved in the near future. The idea that the Soviets created nations 'that didn't exist there before' returned in Putin's claims that states like Ukraine were 'invented' by the Soviet Union[23] and that Kazakhstan only came into being as a state in 1991.[24] The politicisation and manipulation of the complex historical phenomenon of colonised peoples turning into Soviet republics often dismisses historical trajectories and local conceptions of nationhood and alternative forms of political subjectivity.

The Soviet categorisation of ethnicities led to a system where the state had control over prescribed ethnic difference based on 'centralized rule, serving as a complement to force and coercion' over what the Soviet state identified as different 'ethnic groups'.[25] For the Soviet Union's purposes, this served as what Francine Hirsh calls 'double assimilation'—'the assimilation of a diverse population into nationality categories and, simultaneously, the assimilation of those nationally categorized groups into the Soviet state and society'.[26] In reality, this often meant everyday ethnic discrimination and the proliferation of ethnic hierarchies and slurs. Terms like 'the faces of a specific nationality', for example those of a Caucasian nationality—*litsa kavkazskoi natsional'nosti* or *sredneaziati*—are often used to refer to all Central Asians, regardless of their ethnicity, as part of the everyday Soviet and postsoviet grammar of discrimination and objectification. People with a facial appearance associated with other nationalities are often juxtaposed against the Russians, who, in some cases, especially in urban contexts in Central Asia, are called the 'Europeans'. In the context of the Soviet national republics, Russians occupied similar or in some contexts even higher positions than the so-called titular ethnicity group—Uzbeks in Uzbekistan, for example, were considered the titular group of the Uzbek SSR.

In its Sovietised form, ethnicity became a fixed and all-pervasive privilege or a source of discrimination, a rigidly applied form of codified identity. No single person could choose to enter an ethnic group they identified with, and no single person could freely exit an ethnic group they considered discriminatory or inferior. And as with any colonial term, the Sovietised form of ethnicity had its own hierarchy and logics of inferiority and superiority. Not everyone was equal in the supposed 'friendship of peoples'. The collapse of the Soviet Union did not end the discriminatory ethnic divisions and the use of terms such as 'non-Russians' (*nerusskie*) that are often still used in imperial centres like Moscow.[27]

The Kazakh regime inherited the Soviet Union's rigid definition of ethnicity—also termed nationality or *natsional'nost'* in Russian—

and continued to view Russians as a cohesive, ethno-cultural, sociolinguistic and, at times, even socio-political group. In the early 1990s, when Kazakhstan was taking its first steps as an independent state, the political elite had to reckon with the question of Russian colonialism and the legacy of the Soviet Union and its colonial policies, periods when the people of Kazakhstan had little to no say in the governance of their country.[28] In his speeches and policies on multi-ethnic Kazakhstan, Nazarbayev continuously stressed the codification of ethnicity and division of people according to their ethnic background. His use of the slogan 'multi-ethnic Kazakhstan', a country with more than 100 different ethnic groups, sounded like an attempted re-brand of the policy of peoples' friendship, which, among other things, the Soviet regime had tried to propagate under the national-theatrical banner of ethnic minorities dancing in their national costumes on 1 May each year.[29]

The main problem with Nazarbayev's nation-building project was that the regime's elites were not eager to involve citizens in the wider discussion of their national identities. Since the regime intended to control all aspects of nation-building in order to circumvent the work of different ethno-nationalist groups on Kazakh or any other identity (including Russian), the same approach to controlling the nation-building process was also used elsewhere. In other words, the state constructed a closed-off entity in which all ideas about and policies towards the nation and nation-building emanated from Nazarbayev himself, turning it into a highly personalistic and authoritarian regime[30] that excluded citizens from the political decision-making process and strictly policed social movements and grassroots activism. The early postsoviet years, with civil wars and ethnonationalist conflicts all over the Commonwealth of Independent States, allowed Nazarbayev to promote the need to maintain 'stability at all costs', and citizens who were fearful of civil wars and ethnic conflict came to view the country's stability and that of their own lives as a collectively shared value in itself.

The regime continues to view ethnic Russians in almost the exact same way the Soviets viewed ethnic Kazakhs in the aftermath of the 1986 protests, namely as the potential source of an interethnic conflict. Official surveys ask ethnic Russians if they are part of specific

WHO ARE THE FOURTH ZHUZ?

Russian organisations and communities like the Republican Slavic Movement (known by the abbreviation LAD),[31] which was established in 1992 and deals with cultural–political relations between ethnic Russians in Kazakhstan and Russia; the cultural-educational and religious society Svetoch; the Institute of Cossackness (*kazachestvo*); ANK, which represents local ethnic Russian communities from each of Kazakhstan's cities; and other organisations. But at the same time, these surveys do not ask about deeper ideas of self-identification and instead serve as spaces to determine the potential dangers emanating from Kazakhstan's ethnic Russian communities.

Local ethnic Russian communities exist alongside other formalised and institutionalised ethnic communities, such as the Tatar and Ukrainian communities in Kazakhstan. But since there are significantly more ethnic Russians than other ethnic groups, including Kazakhs until the 1990s, the Russian institutions often assume a role beyond mere cultural centres and play an important part in local dynamics, particularly where ethnic Russian communities constitute a significant proportion of the population, such as the cities and Kazakhstan's northern and eastern regions. The real number of people who actively participate in these cultural centres is hard to pin down, as most people only visit them to attend major events such as concerts, though some also use them to seek help with grants and education or for help when applying for higher education in Russia.

The respondents in one national study of ethnic Russians, conducted in 2014 and based on opinion polls and focus groups, were aware of the existence of Russian centres and other organisations but did not engage with them very often. 'There was one organisation at the beginning of the 1990s, I think it was called LAD. But I don't know if it exists now or not', said one of the respondents in the city of Uralsk (Oral in Kazakh).[32]

Many of the study's respondents stated that the ethnic cultural centres did not play a particularly important part in their everyday lives. One of the respondents in Oskemen, a city in Eastern Kazakhstan, even went so far as to say that 'if the number of Russians was minimal [in Kazakhstan], then this kind of community would have formed, maybe people would have organised themselves. But as there are quite a lot of us [Russians in Kazakhstan], we can communicate among ourselves; the [Russian] celebrations are well promoted.'[33] A respondent from Almaty remarked that he had no need to attend what he called 'Russians' anonymous groups'[34] because 'we all grew up and developed here [in Kazakhstan], and we have no need [for special ethnic centres]. A Ukrainian choir came out, sang, danced [at the concert]. I don't have any natural requirement to enter any of these [ethnic and cultural] organisations.'[35]

Many of the ethnic Russian respondents did not see any need to engage in cultural and ethnic centres in their cities or regions because they viewed them as something for the 'ethnic minorities'— the ethnic Korean community or the ethnic Greeks. The study's Russian respondents did not see themselves as an ethnic minority. Their identities had often developed over a long period: they and their relatives had been born in Kazakhstan and had grown up in the country, and their histories were frequently intertwined with Soviet history. In the words of some of the respondents in the 2014 survey of ethnic Russians:

> The thing is that I am not an immigrant. I didn't come to this country [Kazakhstan]. My parents did not come to this country [*moi roditeli ne priehali v etu stranu*]. This country [Kazakhstan] does not pay me welfare payments. This country [Kazakhstan] does not give me anything except for the minimal package for me to live here. My ancestors equally built this post-war Kazakhstan, in the same way [*da, tochno takzhe*]. In other words, I think that I have 100 per cent right to speak in Russian here. I don't say that *they* [Kazakhs] should speak only in Russian, but that it all [language policy] should be done in such a way that there is a compromise [between two socio-lingual communities]. (Respondent in a village in Almaty region)[36]

> I have everyone here: my grandmother, my grandfather, my mom and my dad. Three generations, all Kazakhstani [*vse kazakhstancy*], the whole of Almaty [*vsya Almaty*]. (Respondent in Almaty city)[37]

> Before, when there were fewer Kazakhs *here*, we communicated more. But now when Kazakhs came, we rarely find a common language [*my menshe nahodim obshego yazyka*]. They [Kazakhs] came here and feel like the owners [*khozyaevami*]. But we live here longer

and also want to feel like the owners [of the land]. So far, we don't have interethnic conflicts though. (Respondent in Pavlodar city)[38]

The identity of ethnic Russians in Kazakhstan has undergone a transformation in the postsoviet period. Survey and other data show that people's identities vary depending on where they live—for example, the Russians of Kazakhstan view themselves as separate from the Russians of Russia, and Russians in Pavlodar or Northern Kazakhstan view themselves differently from Russians from Almaty. It is not unusual for citizens to identify with the categories prescribed by the state—for example, as Russian rather than Ukrainian or Korean (both of which are also predominantly Russophone communities). It is still unclear what meaning these respondents attach to their 'ethnic identity'—that of Russianness or Kazakhstani Russianness (which can also be considered a civic identity)—though this could be studied further ethnographically or through in-depth interviews (discussed in the next section). Surveys, with the addition of focus groups and discussions, allow us to tap into some of the group-think and stereotypes about the current state of interethnic affairs in Kazakhstan.[39] In focus groups, discussions often centre on the differences between the southern—predominantly Kazakh—and northern—predominantly Russified and Russian—parts of the country, as can be seen in the following responses to focus group questions:

> I was born in Northern Kazakhstan and the way of thinking while I lived here changed. Right now, it is different, there [up north] it is also Kazakh but there are still divisions. People from the south [of Kazakhstan], *yuzhnye*, became a problem now. (Respondent in Almaty city)[40]

> We [Kazakhs and Russians] live in friendship. But it [the ethnic divide] is still felt, for example, in the *marshrutka* [minibus], Kazakhs give seats to mostly Kazakhs, they give seats to Russians but not as often as to Kazakhs [*russkim men'she ustupayut*]. (Respondent in Pavlodar city)[41]

> I am telling you, they [Kazakhs] think about it and when they get drunk, it starts: 'Russians, go away' ['*a kogda nap'yutsa, nachinayetsya: 'Uhodite russkie*']. (Respondent in Semey city)[42]

> If we take the perspective of the 1990s, yes, I said it. [My] classmates who grew up with me, my ex-friends [start]—it is all because of this constant dictatorship of all sorts of nationalist chauvinistic publications, books and the history rewriting. Before [they] were completely adequate people, but now they all move to the nationalistic side. It is very sad, unfortunately. If we take the older generation [of Kazakhs], then they remained as they were. But our generation—those aged forty to fifty—it is changing. And the youngsters, they are complete nationalists. (Respondent in Oral city)[43]

Many of these stereotypes and discriminatory encounters were shared out of anxiety. As one of the respondents stated, in the city of Karaganda, 'we feel that the [interethnic] situation can change, and everyone is afraid that it would change not in our favour, not in the best scenario'.[44] Many of the respondents connected their worries and anxieties to the uncertainty surrounding the transfer of power from Nazarbayev to a potential successor (at the time of the focus groups, it was still unclear whom his successor would be). And most of the surveyed ethnic Russian respondents viewed Nazarbayev as the main guarantor of interethnic stability in the country and thus as the most important actor in Kazakhstan when it came to interethnic policies at the time of the study in 2014. They praised his ability to maintain a balance between the various ethnic groups; as one respondent remarked, no ethnic group, whether Kazakh, Russian or German, should be allowed to develop nationalistic sentiments. Respondents agreed that no single ethnic group should take priority or ownership over the state. Some respondents believed that Kazakhstani meant 'citizenship':

> The government makes interethnic policies, and this is why we are all the same and citizens all in our equal rights, whether you are Ukrainian, Russian, Kazakh or German. We are all people; we are all citizens. We are just of different nationalities, but we

all have equal rights. No one should discriminate someone else's rights. (Respondent in Kokshetau city)[45]

Other respondents connected Kazakhstani to the shared culture or mentality of all people living in Kazakhstan and their cultural, social, historical and political experiences:

> Of course, [what matters] is to get into this mentality [*vlit'sya v etot mentalitet*], to understand these relations, especially at work, especially in the collectives, all of these relations connected to people. Understanding this [Kazakhstani] mentality is very important, especially if you are a chief [*rukovoditel'*]. (Respondent in Oral city)[46]

> We [Russians] must be as peace-loving as Kazakhs. We do not exacerbate the situation [*my ne obostryaem situatsiyu*]. Because when we come to Russia, they [people in Russia] are so aggressive. And we [Russians in Kazakhstan] are a lot more friendly [*dobrozhelatel'nye*]. Maybe [we, Russians in Kazakhstan, are like that] because we are a multinational state. It is our strongest point. (Respondent in Pavlodar city)[47]

There were many positive responses to the possibility of claiming Kazakhstani identity. Some respondents even claimed they would accept their nationality being taken away, with only their Kazakhstani identity remaining. Many referred to the 'international' experience in dealing with this 'issue'. For example, in the focus group conducted as part of the 2014 survey, respondents shared that they would willingly adopt a Kazakhstani identity:

> Focus group interviewer: And this idea of the united nation, Kazakhstani [nation].
>
> Respondent 7: I would accept it normally.
>
> R2: This is tendency of all developed countries—don't divide [people] into ethnic groups [*ne razdelyat' na etnosy*]. If you live in Germany, you are German, [if you live] in Turkey, then you are Turkish.
>
> R1: I think this is actually a really good [tendency].

R2: Of course.

R5: Here [in Kazakhstan], it is the other way around. No one is saying that I'd be written down as Kazakh but what nationality I accept no one would ask me.

R3: And this is better.

R8: [I think] this is a positive [development]. Kazakhstani, let it be Kazakhstani.

R5: I am saying this too. I come to Russia, and they say, 'oh, Kazakhs came!' even though we are Russians [*v druguyu stranu priezhaesh, hotya b v Rossiyu, govoryat: o, kazakhi priehali. Hotya my russkie*].[48]

The 2014 focus group data with ethnic Russian citizens highlighted a seeming paradox. On the one hand, the respondents spoke of how deeply they valued the system Nazarbayev had built and how they saw him as the guarantor of a 'peaceful' and prosperous future. Yet, on the other hand, respondents also emphasised that it was the ordinary people, the Kazakhstani citizens themselves, who allow peace and interethnic stability to flourish in Kazakhstan.

The study's respondents had a very one-sided view of the situation in Ukraine. Very few of them spoke about the Euromaidan as a struggle for democracy, focusing instead on the negative outcomes of the political situation more generally. This can partly be attributed to the respondents' consumption of Russian propaganda, which was and still is widely accessible in Kazakhstan via Russian state television channels:

> I think that it is the absolutely balanced out and deliberate policy [of Nazarbayev] that allows to keep the situation [stable] in Kazakhstan, well, in comparison with Ukraine, for example, or Russia where all of these nationalist attitudes [are in full swing] and where all of these nationalist attitudes mushroom day by day. (Respondent in Karaganda city)[49]

> We all have it [nationalism]. May I say something: for example, the fact that we have our president, twenty years, independence, and I think that no other republic after the collapse of the Soviet

Union has what we have, for example, the Assembly of the People of Kazakhstan. Many people from different [postsoviet] republics come to us [Kazakhstan] every year, and to be honest, it is not like they envy us, but they approve this [interethnic policy in Kazakhstan]. Because the head of the state really pays a lot of attention to this issue [of interethnic relations in Kazakhstan]. (Respondent in Oskemen city)[50]

Yes, there were these cases and if they said, 'you are no one in here [*ty tut nikto*], you are Russian [*ty russkii*] and I am Kazakh', if it happened, there were measurements taken. In our case it is all immediately stopped, and if someone is caught with this [type of language], they can be immediately thrown out of the university. (Respondent in Oskemen city)[51]

If we compare to different countries, we do not have it [nationalistic divisions]. When it all started in Ukraine, then Kazakhs themselves said, 'oh, thank God we don't have this war' [like in Ukraine now]. (Respondent from a village in the Pavlodar region)[52]

This is the reality [*eto deistvitel'nost'*] because [in Kazakhstan] things never reached that level of serious clashes. There were no riots, no military actions, no setting things on fire, no pushing people of a specific nationality to move out, none of it happened. Here, it is true, peace and harmony exist in our country. (Respondent in Oral city)[53]

There is this feeling—deep down inside, in your soul you are very scared of something like that [war in Ukraine] happening here [in Kazakhstan]. And for now, there is a sense that our [country] is calm, stable and everything is great. (Respondent from a village in the Aqmola region)[54]

It is not like you are expecting it [war or conflict in Kazakhstan] but there is this fear deep down inside [*etot strakh kakoi-to est' vnutri*]. (Respondent in Semey city)[55]

The Russian Kazakhstani respondents made comparisons between the situation in Ukraine in 2014[56] and the Baltic states—where they believed ethnic Russians were discriminated against—and concluded that if any ethnic conflict erupted in Kazakhstan, it would (1) be between Russians and Kazakhs and (2) driven from the top-down—by the elites and the people in power. These beliefs were built on respondents' evaluations of Nazarbayev's monopolisation of the nation-building process and his approach to maintaining peace between the country's two biggest ethnic groups. Many of the stereotypes that were openly discussed during the focus groups as a way of starting conversations and fostering shared beliefs stemmed from the legacy of the Soviet approach to ethnopolitics, in which ethnicities were divided into rigidly defined groups.

When the conversations turned to everyday life and interactions in multilingual and multi-ethnic communities, ethnicity played a less rigid and more fluid role and took on a contextual form. Most respondents agreed that it was important to learn the Kazakh language, for example, though people of the older generation remarked that it would be hard for them to do so. One respondent stated that 'learning Kazakh' was 'crucial' for all those who wanted to build their future in Kazakhstan. Other respondents stated that there was nothing unusual about their children learning Kazakh in school, and that anyone interested in staying in Kazakhstan had to acquire some knowledge of the language, even if only later in life. On the question of celebrating different religious or cultural events like Ramadan or Orthodox Christmas, respondents spoke enthusiastically about how this cultural diversity was central to the multiculturalism that Nazarbayev often boasted about as his and his regime's own achievement.

They are our Russians

'I live and work in Moscow and I largely attribute my success in my job to my Kazakhness', said a young Russian woman in one of our conversations.[57] Why so?

> You see, I'm very social and great in communication. Russians in Russia are not like that. They are cold and suspicious; it is hard for them to build communications that are crucial in my line of work with clients. But I'm different because I was born and

raised in Kazakhstan, I am Kazakh in all the senses. Everyone knows how Kazakhs are great communicators. It is impossible to grow up in Kazakhstan and not have a skill to get along with practically anyone. When I moved to Moscow, me being Kazakh was a game changer at work. I instantly became the employee of the month, and my boss praised my communication skills. I told him, it's because I'm from Kazakhstan, it is a different kind of culture here; we're all, *Kazakhstanis*, naturally open-minded and friendly.

Her use of the phrase 'my, Kazakhstancy'—or 'we, Kazakhstanis'—highlighted the deep meaning she associated with the term. She mentioned how the experience of leaving Kazakhstan and living abroad—she considered Moscow and Russia 'abroad' and often mentioned it as 'zagranitsa' (the Russian word for abroad)—meant she associated 'home' with Kazakhstan, while Moscow and Russia were places of 'immigration'. 'I am from here, I am Kazakhstani [*ya kazakhstanka*], and in Moscow, I'm a migrant [*a v Moskve ya migrantka*)]', said my interlocutor, mentioning the very ethnicised word *migrantka*, used for 'non-Russian migrant workers', for example those from Central Asia.

My interlocutor chose her words in this conversation very carefully, as she wanted to show that she is *svoia*, 'ours', and not 'Russian-Russian', which in her mind meant a Russian citizen who had never lived in Kazakhstan. The sense of *svoia* or *svoi* (plural for ours)—our, Kazakhstani Russians—signals a deeper sense of belonging to Kazakhstan and often a specific locality where the person grew up, for example Northern Kazakhstan. At the same time, it also reinforces divisions between those Russians from Russia and 'our Russians' from Kazakhstan.

These divisions became even clearer when it came to opinions on Russia's full-scale invasion of Ukraine in February 2022, which often separated communities into those who supported the war and those with a neutral or pro-Ukrainian stance. These divisions in Kazakhstanis' understandings of the war are revealed in survey data from Central Asian Barometer and local Demiscope and PaperLab studies in Kazakhstan. In Central Asia Barometer data collected in both the spring and autumn of 2022, a significant number of people answered 'do not know' to the question 'to what extent do you think Russia's special operation in Ukraine[58] is justified or unjustified?'—23 per cent in spring and 27 per cent in the autumn. A similar number had an anti-war stance—28 per cent of respondents in the spring and autumn agreed with the statement that the war was 'completely unjustified', the highest disapproval rates in Central Asia.[59]

The responses to the war are deeply rooted in what people watch and whether they are receptive to Russian propaganda. But their responses also depend on their personal lives. In my work, I have seen fervent supporters of Putin in Kazakhstan suddenly become disenchanted with the war once they began seeing the effects of mass mobilisation—such as the sudden spike in rent prices as large numbers of Russians sought to resettle in Kazakhstan—mass deaths, the strange mutiny of Wagner Group leader Yevgeny Prigozhin in June 2023 and his even stranger death two months later, as well as the inflation stemming from the war and its impact on Kazakhstan's economy. At a personal level, as well as dividing ethnic Russians in both Kazakhstan and Russia, the war has also shaken their established frames of what they considered to be their Russianness and their connection to Russia if not as a second homeland then as a space for opportunities, business, familial ties and frequent travel before the war. The war and people's worries about it spilling over into Kazakhstan exacerbate the existing anxieties and fragment their already ambiguous understanding of Russianness outside Russia. Let me explain this using data from an interview with a middle-aged woman I anonymise here under the name 'Kay'.

Kay was one of my long-term respondents.[60] Our interviews were conducted at her workplace, where she worked with six other women, all of them non-Kazakh but only one of whom was Russian. The rest were Greek, Chechen, of mixed Caucasian origin, one mixed Russian and one Ukrainian. Kay paid little attention to ethnicity before the war, aside from when people spoke about 'Chechen traditions' or a special 'Armenian dish', which she understood as referring to specific groups of people. Everyone still spoke local Russian—a form of the Russian language with words and concepts predominantly from Kazakh mixed with some other languages, which would often not be understood outside Kazakhstan, or at least that is what Kay told me. It was also natural to her that a different form of Russian was spoken in different places, with its own slang words and colloquialisms.

I never asked about Kay's origins, but she often spoke of her travels to Russia and even told me she kept some of her savings in Russian roubles, some in US dollars and some in Kazakh tenge.[61] She also incentivised her children by giving them money for every good grade in school, and the children kept their small savings in Russian roubles.[62] 'Money is a good motivation', Kay used to say while explaining her decisions. I once asked her where she would spend Russian roubles given that she lived many miles from the Russo-Kazakh border and travelling to Tomsk or Novosibirsk from her part of Kazakhstan would take several days. 'Everyone travels. In a car, it is about a three-day drive if you have a co-pilot. We are all nomads *here* [in Kazakhstan], aren't we?' Kay replied, laughing.[63] Indeed, she was a frequent traveller and spent most of her vacations and some weekends roaming around nearby cities, going to China and Russia due to the business her partner had there.

For Kay and her family, the war changed everything. She told me she had never considered Russia her homeland (*rodina*) or a place she'd call home: 'If we wanted, we could have moved there years ago but we didn't', she said. She then told me that her partner had a Russian passport, even though he was born and grew up in Eastern Kazakhstan. 'Even he [Kay's partner] doesn't want to go back [to Russia]', she explained in the summer of 2023. The war and mass mobilisation were part of the reason for her partner's decision, but there was something more to her feelings about this issue.

Kay looked down at the ethnic Russians returning from Russia to Kazakhstan. 'They ran away from *here* in the 1990s and now they're coming back claiming for it to be their home when it is not. Russia is their homeland, not Kazakhstan', Kay said in one of our longest conversations in the summer of 2023. Then she told me the story of her family line and how her father had been born in Northern Kazakhstan and how her mother and her family came from central Ukraine to Northern Kazakhstan to work on the Tselina—the Virgin

Lands campaign—and how the two met, married and moved to the warmer parts of Kazakhstan where Kay and her siblings were born.

She became very emotional when discussing Ukraine: 'I remember going to Ukraine when I was little, you know. Back then it also took us days to travel by trains and cars to get to the village where my Ukrainian family lived', Kay remembered. She could not say which side of the conflict was more responsible for provoking the conflict. Like many of her compatriots, she found this question difficult to answer. At the same time, she felt like Russia had become an alien place for her and that she did not want to go back there. She also told me she had now stopped using Russian roubles because the currency had become 'incredibly unreliable' and was often 'worth nothing'. The war strengthened her identity as a Kazakhstani: 'I don't even know what being a Russian means anymore. I don't even look Russian, and most people call me Ukrainian [*ukrainka*]. I am a mix of things and importantly, I am from here, from Kazakhstan. I am *kazakhstanka*.'

Kay shared many interesting ideas with me when discussing her own identity and often asked me if I felt like her—a mix of different group identities that meant I was Kazakhstani. She knew that part of my family identified as Tatar but that our roots and genealogies were far too complex for us to be defined on the basis of a single ethnicity. To Kay, visual representation played a role—thick hair, dark hair, the smallest facial indications of Asiatic roots and eye colour, but rarely language or religion. Kay worked with a lot of people from various ethnic backgrounds, and through these interactions she tried to pinpoint some cultural connections—how people spoke, how they celebrated, what they ate. Kay found some of these things perplexing because she felt that growing up in Kazakhstan also made her Kazakh simply due to the experience of doing the same things most ethnic Kazakhs do—she knew, for example, about the cultural norms of the *toi* (big celebration), or when one had to keep quiet for the ceremonial Islamic prayer before the start of a meal, and how and when to slaughter a sheep for the Muslim ritual (and, more importantly, how to buy a good one at the market beforehand). At the same time, she was also learning how to make Korean salads and bake Tatar pies.

WHO ARE THE FOURTH ZHUZ?

The war brought turbulence to Kay's own understanding of her Russianness and, together with the mass protests of January 2022, which Kay called 'our war' (*nasha voina*),[64] contributed to her feeling more at home in Kazakhstan than in Russia or Ukraine. As one of Kay's Kazakh friends said, she is 'our' Russian, 'our' Ukrainian (*ona nasha russkaya, nasha ukrainka*). Kay concluded that this external connotation of *nasha*, 'ours', especially as often pronounced by Kazakhs—'she is ours'—made her feel closest to her sense of identity. *Ours* as *nasha* in Russian is slightly different from *svoia* (also ours). Both can be translated as one's own, rooted in *here*—in Kazakhstan, rather than the ambiguous 'there' (Russia, Ukraine or anywhere else in the world)—and it gave her a greater sense of belonging.

After February 2022, her understanding of Russianness quickly changed. She had previously associated it with religion and observing Orthodox celebrations—as much as she enjoyed observing Chinese New Year, as well as Ramadan or any other local celebration—and as belonging to a specific group. For her, 'we, Russians of Kazakhstan' changed to 'Kazakhstani people', and the term Russian dropped out of the equation. 'We are not really Russian, are we?', she told me in the summer of 2023 after announcing that her grown-up daughter was finally settling down with a 'Kazakh guy'. She said that 'she [Kay's daughter] is also now becoming Kazakh, through love. You know, she never liked any Russian or Slavic guys, only real Kazakhs', using the colloquial word *nagyz Qazaq*—the real Kazakh.

The question 'We are not really Russians, are we?' came back to me a day or two later when I met two young Russian men who refused to accept the label of 'relocate' (*reallocant* in Russo-Kazakh). Kay's Russianness went through a long process of becoming Kazakhstani, but it was the war, which she struggled to find the words to describe—'was it Russia's war or was it NATO's war?', she asked me—that made her more clearly realise the boundaries of her Russianness: what separated her self-identity as part ethnic Russian from Russia proper. Even though Kay attempted to smooth out this process in her own self-narration, there was a moment of intense and abrupt conflict in her narrative. She stopped going to Russia and had no plans to visit it again. This decision was personal, and Kay did not want to go into too many details. She differentiated between 'our war' (*nasha voina*) and 'their conflict' (*ikh konflikt*), between 'our [local] Russians' (*nashi, mestnye russkie*) and 'Russians in Russia' (*rossiiskie russkie* or *rossiyane*), between 'home' here and non-home *there*. Kay did not mention having any anxieties about someone potentially asking her to leave Kazakhstan. When I asked her about this, she said: 'I felt like I needed to cut the Russian propaganda out of my mother's tv but if I need to cut it across other people's minds, I would.'[65]

Relocates, exiles or migrants?

'When Russia started the invasion of Ukraine in February 2022 and then when [Russia] announced the mass mobilisation in September 2022, we [in Kazakhstan] had a "rain of men" [*muzhitskii dozhd*'], there were [Russian] men literally everywhere', an Almaty dweller tried to explain to one of my foreign colleagues in July 2023 when he asked her about 'current affairs' in the country.[66] Indeed, in September 2022, the Russo-Kazakh border, the second longest land border between two states—7,644 kilometres or 4,750 miles—experienced a massive influx of Russian citizens after Putin called for a mass mobilisation on 21 September. Almost 3 million Russian citizens had entered Kazakhstan by the end of 2022, about 300,000 of whom stayed in Kazakhstan.

The term '*reallocant*' (relocate) quickly stuck to the Russian citizens in Central Asia. While Central Asians in Russia are still called 'migrants' and 'gastarbeiters'[67] and are often racially profiled, Russian citizens I spoke to claimed they were met with open embraces in Kazakhstani cities.[68] In Oral, the city many knew by its old Russian name Uralsk, local cinemas opened a space for reallocating Russians to sleep in, and many local businesses offered free food and water. Telegram chats flooded with useful information on how to organise life as an immigrant and questions about whether children of the recently migrated Russian citizens would need to learn Kazakh or Uzbek in the local schools. This latter question seemed to bother many newcomers when I read relocation chats on Telegram or during my preliminary fieldwork in Almaty in July–August 2023.

WHO ARE THE FOURTH ZHUZ?

When I approached two young men who my acquaintances told me had recently come from Russia, both instantly said: 'Oh no, no, we are from *here*, we are not Russians [*my ne rossiyane*].'[69] 'I'm from Oskemen', one of them said proudly instead of the Russian Ust-Kamenogorsk for the same city. 'And I'm from Semey', said the second one, also mentioning the city's Kazakh name, which many Russian citizens still refer to by its colonial name Semipalatinsk. I did not want to insist but stated that someone had told me that the two men were 'from Russia' (*mne skazali, chto Vy is Rossii*): 'My family moved there when I was fourteen and we lived there for a bit, mainly for my education but I am *svoi, oskemenskii* [Oskemen local]', said one of them, who later declared he was turning twenty-one that month and had thus spent only seven years in Russia. 'I also moved around different cities in Russia but never felt that I belonged there, I am Kazakhstani [*ya kazakhstanets*]', said the other one. His friend visibly objected when I mentioned that someone had suggested to me they were from Russia—'We are from here, from here [*my otsyuda, otsyuda my*]' and waved his hands in protest. There was a very strong feeling of not wanting to be Russian, and one of them even said, 'we are not *rossiyane* [Russian citizens], we are from Kazakhstan'. 'We are all here', and one of them pointed to our small circle with his finger moving around all of us. 'We are all from here', he repeated.[70]

This encounter reminded me of a sketch on the Russian comedy panel show *KVN*, which was popular in the mid-2000s. In the sketch, a team of comedians from Kazakhstan portray what they call a 'usual day in Russia', where an ethnic Kazakh couple pretend to be 'Russian to their bones' in order to rent an apartment that a Slavic landlord will only rent to Slavs. The whole point of the joke was in the Russian expression 'sdayetsya tol'ko slavyanam'—rented only to Slavs—or 'licam slavyanskoi natsional'nosti', literally, the faces of Slav nationality. The Kazakh team was made up of a blonde Kazakhstani Russian comedian—who played the racist landlord—a beautiful Kazakh female actress—who played the spouse of the man who was trying to rent an apartment, all dressed up in traditional Russian costume—and a Kazakh comedian, whose role was to speak Russian with a bad and very obvious Kazakh accent, often mixing up words in both languages to make things 'funnier' for the non-

Kazakh-speaking audience, to whom Kazakh often sounded like a made-up language.

So, in the sketch, the Kazakh couple do their best to pretend they are 'Slavs' to get the contract for the apartment. They speak in what they present as old (medieval) Russian, sing Russian folk songs and play into the most stereotypical understanding of what it means to be a Russian/Slav. All their acts are accompanied by the landlord asking, 'Are you sure you're really Russian?', and them replying (with an accent) 'of course we are'. There were many layers to this particular sketch, for example the team would often play on distinguishing their Russian colleague as someone who sometimes spoke Kazakh and how unusual it was for a Russian to live in an Asiatic place like Kazakhstan (the show, which was borderline racist, played on the general population's lack of knowledge about neighbouring states like Kazakhstan and Ukraine).[71]

The reason I remembered this rather problematic sketch was because, once Russians escaping from mobilisation started coming to the Central Asian states, some local comedians and TikTok users reversed the joke, instead applying it to Russians from Russia. Videos were uploaded about 'apartments rented only to non-Slavs'— 'sdayetsya tol'ko NE-slavyanam'—and a trend began of asking the new Russians 'to whom Crimea belonged' (*Krym chei?*) in an effort to ridicule the Russian propaganda slogan 'Krymnash'—'Crimea Is Ours!' Many online questioned why Central Asians in Russia were called 'migrants' (*migranty*) while the Russians coming to Central Asia were called 'relocates'. In my brief initial encounter with my two interlocutors, I had no intention of interrogating or criticising them, but their reaction demonstrated that perhaps that is what they were expecting.

When I got to know them better, one of them told me there was nothing interesting in his responses to my questions. Yes, he had moved back to Kazakhstan to avoid mobilisation, as well as more generally not supporting the regime in Russia or wanting to live in or be associated with a country that had started a war. 'It is amoral and shameful [to live in Russia or support Putin]', he explained, believing this 'was an obvious thing'.[72] On top of that, he found Kazakhstan far more 'hospitable': Kazakhstani people were 'friendlier' than people in Russia, and he could finally overcome the feeling 'of not belonging' that he experienced in Russia even after he gained his citizenship. 'Here I belong and there I was always an outsider', another respondent (a female from Russia) told me several days later.[73]

The notion of 'coming home' to Kazakhstan was interesting. For my initial interlocutor, there were aspects of life in Kazakhstan that were familiar, but there were also things he was re-discovering and new things he was getting used to. But Kazakhstan was still home, a home that had changed over the six to seven or even ten years he had spent outside Kazakhstan, but it still felt like home. I shared that feeling with him.

Being in Kazakhstan evoked different memories of smells, forgotten maps and broken mosaics on the walls, but it also involved discovering that an old café from my undergraduate years had now turned into a posh restaurant and lost its old glory. It is about *reclaiming home* no matter how much it changes over time, often turning old places significant to my memories (a huge casino outside my old window has been completely demolished and turned into a major mosque in the span of few years) into completely new things in the present. And maybe therefore the term re-allocating-person or a returnee (*oralman*, an old and disused term in Kazakh for ethnic Kazakhs returning *home* from Mongolia, Uzbekistan, China) applies well to people like the young man whom I met on the first day of my July fieldwork, who shared some personal history with Kazakhstan.

The problem is that most people reallocating from Russia want to claim the term 'relocate' instead of 'migrant'. The vast majority of the people I met in Almaty tried to find some connection to Kazakhstan—a distant relative was part of the Virgin Lands campaign, an estranged parent was from 'around Almaty', third cousins who still live in Shymkent, a great-grandmother was a half-Tatar from Semipalatinsk. All those who were lucky enough to find some connection to Kazakhstan held on to it like a lifebuoy on which they could build their new identity, an identity not associated with Putin's Russia and the war. And all those who did not have that lifebuoy, those whose genealogical searches did not bring up any evidence of

Kazakhstani-ness in them, were looking forward to acquiring that identity in the present day.

In the cultural circles that Almaty is known for, the newly arrived *rossiyane* attended Qazaq indie band concerts, read Kazakh history books and tuned in to all the latest bilingual Kazakhstani podcasts. In their attempts to become the new Kazakhstanis, they were often more informed about contemporary Kazakhstani or Almaty affairs than I was. Some even attended Kazakh-language classes. In this very specific milieu of the creative class of Russian relocates to whom I had access via my friendship networks, and prior research on contemporary art in Kazakhstan, I could clearly observe an insatiable desire to acquire the Kazakh language as soon as possible.[74]

To many Russian relocates, Kazakhstani cities were both familiar and utterly strange. They could recognise some old Soviet-style buildings and newer supermarket chains; they could understand local Russian, which had its own specific cultural context together with a lot of Kazakh words for slang. For some, coming to Almaty in particular also coincided with learning what 'decolonial turn' meant and how it affected the locals' reading of history and more recent events. But above all, no one in Kazakhstan was shy about calling what is happening in Ukraine a 'war', and even many local Russians were often openly critical of Putin's actions. This level of freedom in an authoritarian state was 'strange'. My compatriots' questions about why these recent migrants were not protesting the war while living abroad was another strange and painful encounter.

When I came to Almaty for fieldwork in the summer of 2023, discussions were dominated either by the post-January political processes and court hearings or about the attempts to organise another pro-Ukrainian rally (the first one happened in early March 2022). At many of the public talks, exhibitions, film festivals, seminars and popular parties, locals identified themselves clearly by occasionally threading Kazakh words into their conversations or speaking fully in the Qazaq language as a form of protest against the use of the Russian language and the Kremlin's propaganda. The Kazakh language even started becoming popular in Almaty, a city that has claimed its coloniality for so long (see the next chapter), where speaking perfectly articulated Russian was a sign of cultural capital. Many of the people I spoke to told me that their decision to go back to studying Kazakh was triggered by the start of Russia's full-scale invasion of Ukraine.

There was also much talk about what to do with the Russian language and whether it is even possible to 'decolonise Russian', to which a Kazakh friend replied, 'our Russians are the fourth *Zhuz* here', repeating a popular local phrase meaning that Kazakhs are formed of three *Zhuzes* (tribal conglomerates) and Russians form the fourth one. In a different conversation, my friend, Anuar Dyussenbin, a Kazakh decolonial poet, told me that our Russian language should be renamed and reclaimed by calling it 'kishi Qazaq'—the *small* or junior Kazakh language, because 'our Russian' was different from the core Russian, or the Russian spoken in Moscow.[75]

These linguistic distinctions in conversations among the new cultural elites of Kazakhstan, people who were never Soviet nor postsoviet, people whose childhoods and teenage years were lived under independence, also hint at the changing landscape of Russianness and Kazakhstani Russianness.

If the Kazakhstani Russian language became 'kishi Qazaq', or *orusskii tili* (a slight grammatical change to the Qazaq spelling of the Russian language), then how would it translate to the identities and experiences of local Russians and even more so to the 'new Russians' (relocates), some of whom consider Kazakhstan their new home? 'Our Russians', I am told, do not need to search for an external homeland, our Russians claim home in Kazakhstan by expanding and enriching the notion of Kazakhstani and hopefully bypassing the Russian–Kazakh divisions established by the Soviet elites.

But anxiety remains—will Northern Kazakhstan's Russian communities become the new Crimea for Putin? This question remains pertinent in Kazakhstan not so much because of the Russian communities themselves but more because of Moscow's imperial ambitions and imperialist narratives, which claimed the territory of Northern Kazakhstan as early as 1990–1, first with Aleksandr Solzhenitsyn's *Kak nam Obustroit Rossiyu?* (How shall we rebuild Russia?) and then in the writings of Eduard Limonov and other Russian imperialists. The danger is in these narratives and ambitions rather than in entire communities labelled as 'Russian speakers' or 'Russians' without further investigation into their own self-identification.

The main theme of this chapter requires a field of enquiry of its own: What is the 'Russian question' outside Russia and perhaps also within Russia itself? In this snapshot of a social portrait of the category of 'Russian', I have tried to highlight how swiftly it changed under different political regimes, and at different periods of time, after the annexation of Crimea in 2014 and more than a year after the full-scale invasion of Ukraine. The category of 'Russian' works as a stable identifier on paper, but in reality, and just as with any other group identity, it is a complex mix of varieties of identities, often conglomerated from the regional and religious but also micro-contextual and personal (the idea of *becoming* Kazakh through love, for example). My point is not to imprison that contextual and often challenging idea of 'who is Russian?', especially who is Russian in Kazakhstan. Perhaps the complexity of personal subjectivities, knowledges and perceptions of self-identification describes these processes and praxis better. I have instead sought to find a way to disrupt the rigid frameworks of 'ethnicity' that often convolute the lived experiences of multiple identities and belongings and to show how different communities, including those who identify themselves as different Russians, experience the same burden of fixed identity boundaries prescribed by the Soviet system that was adapted by the Nazarbayev regime after independence. After all, Russians and Russianness, in Kazakhstan, at home or abroad, in Russia, is an identity that is always in-flux, in-conflict and in-search of redefining itself.

4

MANKURTS VERSUS *MAMBETS* (THE 'M'-WORD)

ON DIVISIONS AND HYBRID IDENTITIES

Several Russia-based journalists described the January 2022 mass protests in Kazakhstan as a 'riot of the *mambets*'[1] (*bunt mambetov*).[2] This famous 'M'-word has a long history that can be traced to Kazakhstan's colonisation and remains a slur against Kazakhs as a group, as it can sometimes be used against people deemed 'uncivilised'. The term was widely used in Almaty and other major Kazakh cities in the 1990s to distinguish the urban and supposedly more educated residents from people from the 'peripheries'—villagers and those who lived away from the lights of the big cities.

The term originated with Russian and Soviet colonisation and the division of people into sub-classes, where those called *mambets* needed to be 'civilised', often via assimilation to an urban lifestyle and Russification. In the post-independence period, some claimed that *mambet* no longer applied solely to those of a particular ethnicity and could be applied to anyone who did not meet certain social norms, in a similar way to the Russian word *bydlo* (which is a no less horrific and divisive word for marginalised groups). However, this does not address the problematic nature of the M-word and the history and stereotypes it continues to signify. Similar slurs are used to identify co-ethnics of less 'developed' or 'civilised' backgrounds in other parts of Central Asia—the equivalent in Kyrgyzstan is *myrk*, and in parts of Turkmenistan it is *shatyr*. All these words are used as slurs and are offensive.

In this chapter, I discuss two M-words that continue to symbolise the legacy of Soviet coloniality in Kazakh society. The first, *mambet*, is used to distinguish between those who are cultured and those who are lacking in civilisation; the second, *mankurt*, refers to those who have forgotten their roots while seeking to adopt aspects of a foreign culture. *Mambet* is one of the names of the Prophet Muhammed and, thus, was a name given to many Kazakhs, often in different variations—Mambetali, Mambetkhan and so on. But at some point in Soviet and postsoviet history, it became a slur against mostly Kazakh-speaking Kazakhs.

The second M-word, *mankurt*, stems from the Central Asian legend described in Kyrgyz writer Chingiz Aitmatov's novel *And the Day Lasts More than a Century* (1980), where a captured warrior turns into a mindless slave after his mental capacities and memories are erased. In the end, he kills his mother who comes to save him because he has forgotten who she is and whom he was. Partly because the novel was such a hit in Soviet times and partly because the term translated so well to the daily encounters and anxieties of those people who believed they were losing their native language, traditions and sense of belonging, *mankurt* became a popular term in post-independence Kazakhstan and Kyrgyzstan.

Both words and their heavy historical, colonial and divisive baggage are two sides of the same coin—Russian colonialism and the divisive hierarchies it created that continue to haunt Kazakhstan long after the imperial collapse. Both words signify a hierarchy of developed or developing groups of people and those who are still catching up and require civilising. Things are more or less stable with the *mankurt* idea.

In Aitmatov's novel, the captured protagonist's hair is shaved off, and he is forced to wear a sheep's stomach on his head. The stomach quickly dries under the sun, but he is not allowed to take it off or scratch his head, from which it soon becomes inseparable. When his hair starts growing, it is unable to penetrate the cap made of sheep stomach, and while he survives this gruesome procedure, he become mindless and utterly obedient to his captors.

If a *mankurt* is a slave to his colonial master, then a *mambet* is the defiant Other, someone who refuses to be fully colonised and, as such, remains on the margins of the dominant narrative—uncivilised, half-barbarian, dirty, disobedient and dangerous. Stripped down to their initial meaning, both terms are terrifying and painful. Yet their usage persists in the everyday context of mundane life in Kazakhstan. 'Look at these *mambets* throwing trash on the street!', someone might say in disgust at certain behaviour. 'Look at these *mankurts* who forgot their own mother tongue!', someone might say, equally critically. Normalising these terms brings with it even more violence. But critically re-evaluating them will hopefully allow for collective healing and reconsideration, allowing the term 'mambet' to return to its initial and positive meaning—the Kazakh name for Muhammad. And hopefully one day the term 'mankurt' will simply refer to a concept from an old legend used in Aitmatov's and other writers' work.

The two terms are also legacies of the unfinished project of the Soviet man (*sovetskii chelovek*) who was supposed to share Soviet values and not local traditions, build communism and not 'narrow-minded nationalism', and who was supposed to be fully Russified and thus forget their local language or mother tongue (*ana tili* in Qazaq). But what would happen to those who refused or failed to become full-fledged 'Soviet people'? In this vicious circle, are we only able to be *mankurts* and *mambets*?

Kazakhstan is particularly revealing of the effects of this failed experiment perhaps because Russification was so potent here that it produced generations of people who were Kazakh but who do not speak the Qazaq language—*mankurts*, *shala* or asphalt Kazakhs, who gave up their roots for the mirage of Soviet cosmopolitanism but ultimately failed to become full-fledged Russians. But the failure of the project to create a 'Soviet people' can also be seen all over the former Soviet space, and in some places, the failed project of sovietness (and making people Soviet) transformed into a project to make people Russian, as for example in a 2022 video from Russia where schoolchildren in present-day Tatarstan are forced to sing the

'I Am Russian' pseudo-patriotic song by the Russian singer Shaman. In the video, children are asked 'aren't you Russians?', to which they reply 'obviously, not'. The tragedy of the un-making of Soviet people continues to haunt no-longer-postsoviet societies, often in the form of dehumanising and denigrating labels like the two M-words discussed in this chapter as well as those who remain in the Soviet project long after it has collapsed (see this chapter's discussion of Madina Baideldinovna).

The fortress

In our article on the protests of January 2022, Marlene Laruelle and I spoke about 'a division operationalized during the protests ... between urbanites and *mambety*, a very derogatory term used to brand the rural population as "rednecks"'.[3] There are several works that touch upon this slur in connection to another phenomenon, mainly rural–urban migration[4] or online comments referring to a lack of culture and civilisation.[5] Kazakh decolonial scholar Aizada Arystanbek has attempted to define *mambet* according to its use in public forums and in response to a domestic violence case where '*mambet* culture' was referred to by one of the commentators, claiming that it disregarded people's and women's rights. And this is what is so problematic with the use of this slur—it assumes too much on the part of the Other without ever giving the Other the right to speak for themselves. The *mambet* slur is always used by someone who not only identifies outside this group but also someone who assumes a position above the M-group, placing themselves higher on the hierarchy of development and culturedness (*kul'turnost'* in Russian). As Arystanbek writes in an explanatory footnote, '*mambet* typically means a person who comes from a rural area; only speaks Kazakh (or speaks Russian very badly); lacks proper education; and has bad manners. It is typically used by the urban Russian-speaking public to disparage others.'[6] Nobody would openly accept or adopt this label given that it signifies the persistence of the coloniality that permeates every aspect of everyday life and divides society into the cultured, privileged, educated and often urban population and the less fortunate, usually poor, less educated people who lack culture or are 'uncivilised'.

In many ways, *mambet* is connected to the urban–rural divide that still separates people into the more urbanised and cultured and the more provincial. In her study of urban migration, Kazakh anthropologist Alima Bissenova argues that

> the perception of migration as rural and as detrimental to the city is particularly prevalent in Almaty, a city that from its founding was conceived of as a proper imperial city against the background of native backwardness and as a bulwark of European civilisation on the edge of the empire.[7]

Astana, in contrast, which became the new capital, was at the same time a centre of internal migration, meaning that 'the "rural" and the "native" were incorporated into the identity of the city from its very inception and throughout its development have been seen as an integral part of the city'.[8]

In the juxtaposition between urban and rural dwellers, the rural Other is demonised and presented as an alien and negative element in the city. Unfortunately, this level of discrimination is associated with the Soviet terms 'development', 'civilising' and 'culture', where the rural Other either lacks all of these or is considerably lower on the hierarchy of development and culture. Kazakh political analyst Kanat Kabdrakhmanov divides Kazakhs into two groups—'those who [are] predominantly committed to traditionalist Kazakh values and those who are committed to universalist values'.[9] The members of the first group are orthodox in their attempts to claim traditionalist Kazakhness and thus, are *mambets*, while the more universalist and cosmopolitan value group are 'urban Kazakhs', according to Kabdrakhmanov, and the two groups exist in antagonism. Their difference is highlighted by the differences in their values, Kabdrakhmanov claims. For him, *mambets* are ethnocentric and nationalistic and strive for 'Kazakhstan for Kazakhs!':

> In *mambetism*, the national pride is strangely entangled with slave's swagger [*rabskoe chvanstvo*], the archaism of the obviously obsolete [*ustarelogo*] and our instinctive aspiration to be a contemporary

people who have their own cultural face. 'Mambets' embody the stigma of the obsolete. Behind their backs 'the urban' [Kazakhs] look at each other. But the biased sight [of the urban Kazakhs] cannot miss that 'mambets' are indispensable and full-fledged participants of the national spiritual and cultural dialogue [*natsional'nogo dukhovno-kul'turnogo dialoga*]. Without 'mambets' and without dialogue with them, 'urban Kazakhs' will certainly get lost, and many are already lost in the emptiness of the civilisational forms.

What is surprising in this division into urban and rural Kazakhs is the normalisation of the colonial division into 'civilised' and those 'lacking civilisation' or who are 'uncivilised'. The division seems almost natural to some who until recently attempted to defend the *mambet* term by qualifying it, claiming that it can also be used to refer to someone outside the ethnic group or to someone who lacks manners or comes from a village, as for example in the problematic term '*mambets*' riot' in reference to the January 2022 protests, suggesting that there were large groups of impoverished ethnic Kazakhs among the protestors and that many of them were among the looters (see the next chapter). Again, the juxtaposition between the rural and impoverished barbarians and the lavish neoliberal cityscape conquers the imagination of the ordinary city dwellers in this highly problematic discourse. Was it really *mambets* who were destroying the city or the organised crime groups who wanted to create violent chaos amid the instability in order to hijack the pro-democratic forces and their agenda?

In these discussions, many of my respondents stated that a lack of culture or good manners is 'not a sign of a specific ethnicity' but a marker 'of a lack of upbringing or lack of experience of living in the city', as one Almaty interlocutor told me in April 2022, right after the January protests.[10] People who support this idea of an uncivilised Other 'beyond ethnicity' also believe there are other terms that do have ethnic connotations, for example the old term for *oralman* (now *qandas*)—ethnic Kazakhs repatriated from abroad. If *mambet* does not have a specific ethnic identification, then *oralman* is a different type of ethnic Kazakh. In the 1990s, President Nazarbayev started a repatriation programme to welcome back ethnic Kazakhs whose ancestors left Kazakhstan before or during the Soviet colonisation of the region at the beginning of the twentieth century or especially during the Asharshylyq, the Great Famine of 1931–3. Unsurprisingly, Kazakh repatriates from Mongolia, China and Afghanistan did not speak Russian and were divided by the subgroup name 'oralman'. The repatriates from Turkmenistan, Russia, Uzbekistan and other former Soviet republics spoke Russian and could quickly assimilate and adapt to the post-independence realities, thus leaving the status of *oralman* and its discriminatory policies behind. Non-Russified *oralmans* who could only communicate in Qazaq were often cut off from the Russified public sphere and fell into a category below the M-word, meaning that the O-word is inherently discriminatory—which is why these people are now known as 'qandas'. Widespread discriminatory practices excluding Kazakhophone Kazakhs from the urban, Russophone and 'civilised' sphere created further stereotypes reflecting their position in the colonial hierarchy of culturedness. Some of the respondents in the 2014 survey of ethnic Russians' attitudes to ethnic politics in Kazakhstan, discussed in the previous chapter, viewed the state's programme for ethnic Kazakh repatriation in a negative light:

> According to the opinions of the focus group participants, the majority of those [ethnic Kazakhs] who returned had a low level of culture [*s nizkim urovnem kul'tury*] and education, and their only advantage was their knowledge of the Kazakh language. Nevertheless, the status of 'invited by the president [Nazarbayev]' allows them to feel their privileged status and is reflected in their behaviour, acting as though they are missionaries who can teach [locals] how to live right. According to the opinions shared in the focus groups discussions, this position [of repatriates] causes rejection not only among the Russian-speaking population but also among local Kazakhs.[11]

The unproblematic reading of the coloniality embedded in these divisions into 'civilised/uncivilised' or 'rural/urban' encourages the stigmatisation of certain sections of the population, non-Russian speakers in particular. Among the returnees, there is very little talk of them holding a 'privileged position', as described in the report on interethnic policies in Kazakhstan. In her interview with the Kazakh writer, poet and translator Tilek Yrysbek, Kazakhstani social anthropologist and expert in the study of Kazakh kinship, Zarina Mukanova, notes that Yrysbek 'was bullied in school for being an *oralman*' in the late 1990s.[12] Moreover, the lack of Russian-language skills positioned repatriates and many other non-Russified ethnic Kazakhs quite literally on the fringes of the job market and the more prestigious positions in the society. Mukanova and colleagues noted this discrimination in further interviews, stating that

> [e]ditor-in-chief of the *Exclusive* magazine, Rasul Zhumaly, in 2011 said that the lack of Russian [language] skills led to *oralmans* being treated as second-class citizens both by fellow citizens and the state ... Many settlements of *oralmans* reportedly were not provided with running water, sanitation and crucial infrastructure. Tilek Yrysbek pointed out that just like the Russians had treated Kazakhs as second-class citizens in the Soviet institutions, now the *oralmans* were treated as second-class citizens by the local Kazakhs. In his words, the *oralmans* have become the new *mambets*. Only this time the stigma was placed by the very people who had been victims of the same type of stereotypification a few decades earlier.[13]

'Mambet' continues to be a term of stigmatisation and hierarchisation—it places those who use it in a position of superiority where they can talk down to and dominate the Other, the impoverished, un-cultured and un-educated, and call them out for their lack of privilege. Masa, an independent Kazakhstani media outlet, dedicates a whole page of their online glossary to the term in order to specify how 'due to colonial Soviet policies and Russification in the [non-Russian] republics there was a widespread opinion that the use of national languages [non-Russian] was a sign of low education, lack of development and of un-culturedness [*beskulturie*]'.[14] The end of Soviet rule and mass Russification should have ended the need to divide and shame the non-Russian speakers in this crude and discriminatory fashion, but in Kazakhstan the term 'mambet' took on a different and not just linguistic (lack of Russian) category.

With mass migration to the cities in the 1990s, some urban dwellers viewed the rural population as 'as second-class citizens'. The Kazakh state took over the Soviet system of internally registering all citizens according to where they live, called *propiska*. Although officially only used for bureaucratic purposes, in practice *propiska* creates a dividing line between those with 'golden *propiska*'— Almaty dwellers and owners of elite housing—and those with no *propiska* and no privileges. Residents coming to the city from different parts of the country or from rural areas and those who cannot afford to own housing in this major Kazakhstani city, an economic hub, often cannot get *propiska* and are only able to stay there temporarily. Without *propiska*, people cannot get free medical provision or register their children in urban schools. Some landlords might consider giving their lodgers *propiska*, but these cases are rare. The challenges involved in getting *propiska* are linked to the shortage of housing. On the one hand, the regime kept promising its loyal citizens all the fruits of economic development and the Kazakh oil booms, while on the other it made a segment of the population feel 'homeless' in their own homeland, in the words of British social anthropologist Catherine Alexander's interlocutors in Shanyraq district.[15] The Sovietised practice of excluding rural residents from centres of urban 'civilisation' repeated itself again. As anthropologist Saulesh Yessenova writes:

> [T]he Soviet passport system that excluded *kolkhoz* members until 1974, effectively regulated urban migration thereafter. Students from rural areas were given temporary residence permits (*vremennaya propiska*) that provided them with legal status in the city and access to university dormitories and healthcare facilities. A regular residence permit (*propiska*), normally stamped in one's passport, could be obtained only on the basis of a job offer from a limited number of organizations, which were in need of cadres unavailable in the city. Urban-based public services, including healthcare, retail trade, social work, and cultural institutions, that launched massive recruitment between 1959 and 1970,

were some of those organizations that invited recent urban migrants and graduates. The representation of ethnic Kazakh workers in public services doubled during this period, reaching 45–50 percent in 1970.[16]

This new post-1970 urban Kazakh population found ways to discriminate against other Kazakh urban newcomers who had migrated because of the economic collapse of the 1990s. Many of the recent urban migrants whom Yessenova interviewed and communicated with during her 1998–9 ethnographic study of Almaty's massive bazaar, Barakholka,[17] were pressed to leave their native villages due to the collapse in agriculture and state support for the rural economy. As new urban migrants in the city, these impoverished and disoriented people found themselves in a liminal space, Yessenova argues, as not yet urban residents but also no longer rural subjects: '[A]s they arrive in the city, urban migrants [were] pressured by their new environment to reassert and correct their statements of identity as a strategy for repositioning themselves within the larger society, as well as in relation to urban culture', which marginalised them for lacking the facets of this same urban culture and the urban life it entailed.[18]

The problems and discrimination that the *mambet* slur reveals in terms of accommodating non-urbanite communities in the cities also existed during the Soviet period, when the cities were considered centres of cultural life that rural folk would only be privy to occasionally and then only for a short time,[19] say on a *kolkhoz* workers' visit to an opera house or a tour to a sanatorium if it was located in a big city.[20] If the city is a colonial fortress from which the *mambet* is prohibited, then the *mankurt* is the defender of that fortress.

The slave

What does *mankurt* really mean? Like *mambet*, *mankurt* is a colonial and postcolonial term that exists to create internal difference and a hierarchy of status. However, unlike *mambet*, *mankurts* possess all the colonial features that a *mambet* lacks—they speak perfect Russian, often at the expense of their native language, are educated and live in urban areas and are, thus, 'civilised' (in colonial terms). But despite all this, the *mankurt* is lost between two worlds—the world of their master, in which they will never become *Russian enough*, and the world of their supposed indigeneity from which they were violently uprooted. *Mankurt* is the condition of not belonging to either world and staying in between, in the limbo of the Russified Kazakh or 'asphalt Kazakh'—someone so rooted in the cityscape they can no longer find a way back to their roots of steppe and *aul*. In other words, a *mankurt* is also stuck in a liminal space unsure or unwilling to move forward and away from their colonisation.

Some *mankurts* are nostalgic for the Soviet past and the times of their youth and glory, while others see little point in learning Kazakh, which they find useless in spaces that are predominantly Russophone or that have now globalised, where English spellings are used. They are not willing to start a dialogue and walk in the shoes of the mono-Kazakh speakers, those for whom living in a city full of alien words and bad Kazakh translations, in a city that lacks such simple things as menus or bank services in Kazakh, which is often the only language they feel comfortable communicating in, is an everyday torture. Kazakhophones often feel *invisible* to their co-nationals who believe that 'there is no market for Kazakh services, news, menus, and entertainment'.[21]

What does this phrase 'no market' mean when there are so many Kazakhophone audiences that would prefer to read their favourite Instagram or Telegram channels in Kazakh rather than constantly having to translate it from Russian? 'Qazaqsha Jaz' (Write in Kazakh) and 'Qazaq Grammar' Instagram accounts grew out of linguistic activism for Kazakhophones who find themselves invisible or undervalued in the Russified and globalised economy of Kazakhstan's urban centres. Their work essentially consists in reminding others not to forget about the people who do not speak Russian or English fluently, people who mainly communicate in Kazakh in their everyday life, people who migrated to Kazakhstan from the Kazakh-speaking communities of China, Mongolia and other places whom our state assigned the category of *oralman*. Thus, *mankurtism*, the state of being a *mankurt* or a culture of sustaining linguistic hierarchies according to the old colonial order, requires that we constantly and critically engage with this issue. To those who feel discriminated against in the urban centres because they are predominantly Kazakh speaking, *mankurts* are the core of the problem. It is *mankurts*' inability to understand or empathise with them that recreates these colonial divisions. But those called *mankurts* believe they are being singled out for things and conditions they did not choose—in interviews, many of them asked me why they are blamed for others being unable to study in their native language. The conflict remains unresolved.

I know many people who are ethnic Kazakhs but do not speak Kazakh. Many of them blame the Ministry of Education, the schooling system and the lack of good teaching technologies to make Kazakh-language acquisition effective. 'I learned it for eleven years in school but can barely get by', a friend told me, a native resident (*korennoi zhitel*') of Almaty for three generations, which he disclosed with pride on his face. 'The only people who spoke Kazakh in my family were my grandparents, but even they soon started speaking in Russian. It is not their or my fault', he said, and described his upset at being unable to follow a basic conversation in Kazakh with a group of young researchers and some visitors from East Turkestan (known to him as Xingjian).[22] 'Not speaking Kazakh does not make me less Kazakh', he concluded in perfect Russian.[23] I think ours was the last generation of activists, scholars and cultural producers who worried about the lack of Kazakh-language knowledge making us less or *shala*, or *mankurt* Kazakhs.

In my interviews with Gen-Z Kazakhstanis, most people spoke a combination of three languages, often interchangeably and with no difficulty transferring from Kazakh to English to Russian and back. The lines of Otherness or the boundaries between different tongues were suddenly erased. In a brief encounter in the winter of 2023 in an underground bar in Almaty, during an event commemorating the first anniversary of the Bloody January protests, a young queer Qazaq activist narrowed his eyes at me and immediately spoke to me in Qazaq: 'Diana, Diana, what a strange name for a Kazakh', he said. 'Well, my mom is not Qazaq', I replied in the same language. I had learned this phrase the hard way in primary school, though everyone teased me not so much for my name but for my fair skin and green eyes and my lackadaisical approach to learning Abai poems by heart (a bare minimum to claim your Kazakhness in my postsoviet Kazakhophone primary school). 'But you're still Qazaq' *(bari bir Siz qazaqsyz goi)*, he replied, half laughing. 'Arine',[24] I nodded.

After Russia launched its full-scale invasion of Ukraine, the number of people who started learning Kazakh online and in special talking clubs and the number of people who suddenly started speaking Kazakh increased even in very Russophone spaces like Almaty. According to the most recent census (2021), only 20 per cent of the Kazakhstani population has no knowledge of Kazakh and is unable to speak the language. 'After the war, speaking Kazakh became *natural*', one of my long-term interlocutors told me. Growing up in a household where Russian was predominant, it was hard for them to acquire Kazakh, but they claim 'it was the right thing to do'.[25]

The Kazakh language made several comebacks in the Russophone sphere of influence, predominantly in cities like Almaty, where being a 'native-native' *(korennoi-korennoi almatinets)* permanent resident automatically came with the city's colonial past and adoration for everything Russian. The first was when Kazakhophone music suddenly became popular, which was initially due largely to Moldanazar, an indie-rock band with a lead singer from Kyzylorda who prefers to speak Kazakh; then the introduction of Q-pop with the band Ninety One[26] and their Kazakh lyrics and the bilingual Russo-Kazakh rap band Irina Kairatovna.[27] This was followed by a wave of Kazakh decolonisation, when the local art scene became an intellectual hub for rethinking the legacies of Russian and Soviet colonialism. The second wave coincided with the crisis of Nazarbayev's rule in regime–society relations in the late 2010s and after the Zhanaozen 2011 massacre. Visual art and then the contemporary Kazakhstani writing scene started rethinking their coloniality and incorporating the Kazakh language into narratives that sought to decolonise the mind.[28] However, the biggest incentive for many Russophone speakers to start using Kazakh in their everyday encounters, even if on a very basic level, with accent and errors, was Russia's full-scale invasion of Ukraine. The experience of the 2010s had a greater influence on the popularity of the Kazakh language than thirty years of the regime's promises and programmes to 'empower' the Kazakh language. Kazakh sociolinguistic expert Juldyz Smagulova claims that from 1995 to 2006, there were at least twenty major laws, state programmes and presidential decrees designed to strengthen Kazakh-language policy.[29] But the problems with Kazakh-language acquisition continued to linger in Kazakhstan well into the post-independence period.

One other problem connected to *mankurtisation* is the Soviet legacy, where some people, including ethnic Kazakhs (see the next section), still identify with certain Soviet values. The question remains of whether the failed project of making a new, Soviet people has left people with distorted and hybrid identities in the wake of the imperial collapse. I discuss one of these potential stories in the following section.

The Soviet Union faded away, but sovietness remained

In late August 2018, Kulshat Medeuova, a renowned Kazakh philosopher, took me and a group of fellow researchers on an improvised tour of 'Fading Astana' to show us some sites of historical interest that were rapidly disappearing with the construction of new real estate projects. For a long time, Astana was a very Soviet city, with buildings housing cultural and municipal institutions where Soviet workers came to be indoctrinated in their belief that they were the *real* Soviet people. There were monuments to Soviet workers (*truzhenniki*) and cinemas and cultural houses (*dom kultury*) where workers attended concerts, listened to party speeches and came to socialise and spend their free time.

Formerly Tselinograd, Astana was at the heart of the Soviet Virgin Lands campaign in the scarcely populated northern regions of Kazakhstan. From the late 1950s, this vast territory, which the Soviet leadership considered 'empty', was colonised by agricultural development and became a meeting place for the multi-ethnic groups of Soviet workers who flocked here from all parts of the country, but predominantly from Russia. They required an infrastructure of institutions and monumental art that would remind them they were still Soviet people even if Moscow or anything connected with sovietness was far away. Lenin's portraits and monuments were placed across the city's space, competing only with the monuments to the workers on the Virgin Lands (*tselinniki*). Lenin and his portraits were the most important signifiers of Soviet rule and its propaganda in the farthest points of the empire.

Medeuova stepped into a messy construction site dressed in her fashionable boots and a light raincoat.[30] 'Here's where the famous Lenin mural was', she said loudly, pointing to the blank wall of a 5-storey apartment block. We were unable to see even the mere outline of the former mural. The wall was blank and grey, stripped down to its concrete base. 'But where is Lenin?', someone from the group asked. Medeuova joked that he was 'dead and gone' and then kicked some stones at the bottom of the wall with her boots. 'Oh, here it is!', and she picked up colourful pieces of the former mosaic. We quickly squatted and started collecting colourful pieces of the mosaic from the ground, some fully covered in wet and dark northern soil. These were 4 centimetre-long pieces made from shale-like rocks but all permanently coloured into yellow, light blue and even violet. I ended up with about ten bright yellow pieces in my hand. It was hard to picture what the original mosaic looked like from the handful of small pieces we had gathered. I then asked Medeuova if anyone on the construction site had attempted to preserve the artefact and donate it to a local cultural institution, like the state museum, for example. 'No, they threw everything away. These are perhaps the last bits of history that you have in your hands', she said and looked at the colourful pieces in my hands.

Lenin was no longer valued in post-independence Kazakhstan, I thought, while stuffing my pockets with a historic souvenir. There were no pictures of this mosaic on my quick Google search, and I remained puzzled about where they had placed the bright yellow and purple pieces in the mosaic. I grew up with a colourless understanding of Soviet and postsoviet times, where Lenin was depicted in plain brown and pale beige colours painted on a faded red background. There was no yellow on the portraits I remembered.

Stripping old mosaics and portraits of long-gone leaders is one thing, but it is quite another to deal with the Soviet legacy, which remains an open wound in many people's lives. In 2018, 2019 and even in 2023, when Russia's full-fledged war in Ukraine was in full spin, Kazakhstan remained a society with complex views about its Soviet past and Soviet legacy. The voices of the decolonial activists who called for an open discussion of Soviet colonisation and the colonial residue it had left on the country coincided with the voices of those who associated a lot of good things with the Soviet period.[31] Beyond the usual discourse—'but Soviets brought us [Kazakhs, Tajiks, Uzbeks, etc.] opera houses'—I want to focus on the micro- and contextual understandings of the Soviet period and people's experiences of their pain at having lost the promised Soviet future. Let me explain through an ethnographic vignette.

Madina Baideldinovna[32] identified as a proud Kazakh woman. She cherished her Kazakh genealogy and carefully kept her family's *shezhire*, the family tree and genealogy printed in a special book, in her home library. There were also collections of classic Russian literature, some essays and the collected writings of Lenin and Stalin, *Az I Ya* by Kazakh writer Olzhas Suleimenov and some new volumes of reprinted Kazakh literature someone had given to her after 1991. Madina did not see the paradox in taking pride at being a true Kazakh—which, for her, meant speaking Kazakh without an accent and being a Kazakh patriot—and taking pride in having once been a fervent Communist functionary. She spent many years of her career in the Komsomol and other Communist institutions, and had it not been for the collapse of the Soviet Union, she would have had a long and successful career as a party functionary, perhaps even coming close to the highest echelons of power. She always speaks of 'Nursultan Abishevich' (Nazarbayev) as though he were a close relative, despite having only met him once, during one of his visits to meet local bureaucrats. Although he probably never remembered her name, she kept his pictures in her house as a reminder that she had once met him and had even shook his hand.

To celebrate her seventieth birthday, Madina booked a popular restaurant, a renovated Soviet building that had been turned into a hotel. She invited 200 guests, old friends and colleagues. As part of the celebrations, she compiled and printed 200 copies of a book dedicated to her life. It was not a memoir, because it contains little text aside from some reflections about her parents and her early childhood in a village in South Kazakhstan. Most of the book was instead filled with photos of her as a young lady who had just joined the Komsomol, and as her life progressed, each photo in the book represented a different stage in her life as a Communist and the life of her countries—the Soviet Union and post-independence Kazakhstan.

The black-and-white photos of Madina's family at the start of the book made it clear that this was probably a pre- or post-war period in the Soviet Union. The end of the book had around twenty pages filled with numerous photos of Madina visiting different tourist attractions in Kazakhstan or in the near abroad. In every photo, she made sure there was a flag and a portrait of Nazarbayev on the wall to signify that the photo had been taken in independent Kazakhstan. Madina's aging face also served as a signifier of the progression of time from the Soviet to the postsoviet and post-independence periods. The only period that was frozen in time was the 1970s and 1980s, two long decades that occupied most the book. These were not only the times of Madina's youth, when she was aged twenty to forty, but also when she was at the height of her career. The period was indicated by the carefully collected photos of her award certificates (*gramota*) for passing courses on Soviet propaganda or for completing training with the Komsomol. She had also meticulously collected all her party membership booklets, *partbilet* in Soviet terminology, and every single medal she received in the Komsomol.

Lenin's face glanced at the reader from every page of that part of the book. He was on Madina's medals and photos and was even printed on the official postage stamps. The book had no images of the Soviet money where Lenin's face was also immortalised for years, though there were many potential reasons for why this was the case. In the 1990s, she lost a large sum of money in Soviet roubles that she kept in savings inside the sofa in her home. The money, which had been enough to buy two Soviet cars, 'burnt' (lost value) overnight, stealing her sense of security and stability. But the Soviet collapse stole something a lot more significant than the money she had saved for years—it also stole her aspirations and ambitions of becoming a party boss, perhaps the first Kazakh woman to occupy a high Soviet post. At the age of forty, she had to reinvent herself to adapt to the conditions of the new state and pursue a new career, having spent her whole life climbing the Communist Party ladder that suddenly collapsed along with the Soviet Union. Madina was able to navigate life in post-independence Kazakhstan by working as a minor bureaucrat in her city in Southern Kazakhstan, but the pain of a lost future haunted her for the next thirty years. When she turned seventy, she felt like she could openly boast about the brilliant Soviet career that had failed to materialise. It was not her fault—she was a great Communist, and all of her certificates and medals spoke volumes to that. She was sincerely happy that Kazakhstan had gained its independence, but she was still unable to heal from the pain of losing a Soviet future that never happened. Presenting her life story as a Communist-turned-patriot in the 200 copies of the colourful and well-printed book she gave out to everyone who attended her birthday party was an attempt to overcome this past. At least this way, people would know or remember that she was once a Communist with great career prospects. In the book, she was still a thirty-year-old party soldier full of potential and aspirations; the Soviet Union was still alive, and so were her unrealised dreams. In this book, her phantom pains found some sort of closure.

The story of Madina Baideldinovna, who found nothing paradoxical in cherishing her Communist past—the book even included letters addressed to her from numerous Komsomol committees—while also being a patriot of independent Kazakhstan, reminded me of the numerous stories of other people who had similar phantom pains stemming from the Soviet legacy in Kazakhstan. In my fieldwork, many people reported that they had kept their red Soviet passports as souvenirs from a time when they believed they were happy. These were more than just some accidental old photos of Soviet pioneers in red ties that many of my brother's generation kept at home as long-forgotten pieces of their childhood in a state that had ceased to exist.

Soviet passports, medals, pins from Soviet summer camps (Artek, for example), army certificates (*voyenniy bilet*), tins of old Soviet tea and even old Soviet money (roubles) formed a museum of personal memories. One of my respondents told me they kept their Soviet passport until the late 1990s, hoping that maybe the Soviet Union would be reincarnated in some form—'maybe without the

Baltic states [*Pribaltika* in Russian]', they told me—and that the old passports would be needed again. The same respondent had an internal Kazakhstani ID but did not get a new, Kazakhstani passport until 1998.[33] The meaning attached to these pieces of sovietness played a significant role in how people responded to the new realities in which they found themselves after 1991.

A collection of Leninist writings in their home library, a Soviet medal exposed in a central sideboard (*servant*) in the living room or an old Soviet passport kept in the drawer by the bedside served as physical remnants of sovietness that to many people meant more than just the state that had ceased to exist or a motherland (*rodina*) that was now divided into numerous independent states. It represented more than just a space or time where someone used to live, used to be happy, experience major life events—graduating from school, serving in the army, going to university, getting married or building a career.

Sovietness represents the pain of a lost future. Different people feel it in their own way, and it is not the case that it is ethnic Russians who experience it the most or that being Russian is a prerequisite for such pains to exist and influence one's life. It is also not entirely beneficial to place these complex feelings and emotions under the all-embracing category of 'nostalgia'. While many people feel nostalgic about the Soviet past, this does not mean that everyone experiencing the phantom pains of sovietness can explain their feelings by reference to nostalgia. Sovietness is a lot more complex than that.

When the Soviet Union collapsed, borders were redrawn and erected, sometimes causing internal conflicts, secessionism and wars. But the feeling of sovietness remained, and though Madina would not put it in these words, her experience of phantom pains stemmed from losing a future she had been promised but had never experienced. Her way of dealing with this was to explain it in the book about her life-story, where she could take a leading voice in explaining that she was powerless to stop the collapse but was unable to let go of it. Instead, she harboured a sense of a long collapse in her personal life and then exposed it when she turned seventy—the age when most Soviet people are 'allowed' to reflect on their life's journey. Her own narrative about sovietness is still and rigid. It is stuck in old photos and letters dated '1979' or '1981' and hastily written by hand. She does not want to return to that past; nor is it possible to do so. Her story often reminded me that we sometimes measure the independence years through the lifespan of the youngest generation, people born in the 1990s, but rarely via the lifespan of those who, like her, experienced the collapse of the Soviet Union when they were in their mid-thirties or early forties and entered their later lives over the thirty years of independence.

All that is left of the Soviet Union is a pastiche of cafeterias playing on the supposed idea of what Soviet life represented or the old Soviet buildings that can be still found intact in parts of Minsk, Russia or Russian-occupied Crimea. Madina is not eager to visit those places. Even Moscow seems too alien and far away to her from the context of her present life in Kazakhstan. All she wants is to heal from the loss of the bright future she once had ahead of her. Even in the 1980s, she realised this future was unlikely to be one of true communism, but it was a future where pensions would be guaranteed by the state and where, as she says, 'there were hopes for tomorrow and the next day' or hopes that tomorrow would be as good and peaceful as today.

This short vignette demonstrates the complexity of postsovietness and its influence on people who might live in the same neighbourhood but share completely different perceptions of what it means. Some might be nostalgic for a 'lost future', while others lament or are even angry about their 'lost past'—the time Kazakhstan could have spent developing its own independent statehood and dealing with the legacy of discrimination inherited from the Soviet period.

The future: decolonising mambets *and* mankurts

It is sometimes claimed that a true Kazakh nation will not exist until all Kazakhs speak the Kazakh language. However, colonisation and Russification, as well as the failed project of making all people, including Kazakhs, Soviet people, has left Kazakhs as a polylingual group. Kazakhs can be Kazakhophone, Russophone, Francophone or Anglophone; more recently, many have also begun learning Korean,[34] Turkish,[35] Arabic[36] and Italian and Chinese. Many of my interviews and conversations in Kazakhstan over the 2010s were conducted in different languages. Only rarely would someone ask why we spoke a polyphony of different languages based on Kazakh with the inclusion of English when speaking to a Kazakh person from East Turkestan, where the Kazakh language is free of Russian words but often features Chinese inclusions that most Kazakhs are unable to understand.

Kazakhness is multi-faceted, and it still bears the legacy of colonial division and difference. It is hard to say which side suffers the most—the one that speaks or does not speak the Russian that we have made our own Kazakh Russian (*qazaq-orys*)—but it is clear that both sides suffer nonetheless. Further divisions, especially influenced by the artificial colonial divides into *mambets* and *mankurts*, and the newer forms of *shala*, asphalt, urban Kazakhs and *nagyz* (real) or Kazakh-speaking Kazakhs, only exacerbate the situation further. In the words of the multilingual Kazakh German writer and philosopher Gerold Belger, these divisions create further cleavages in places where there should be unity:

> *Mambet* is the Kazakh from the soil. This Kazakh is very dear to me. But the fact that Kazakh from the soil [*ot zemli*] does not always like *shala* Kazakhs [Russified Kazakhs] is very bad. What is it *shala* Kazakhs' fault? Or *shala*-German? Or *shala*-orys?[37]
>
> ... So, all of these divisions are arbitrary and will not lead to anything good. I know many of my colleagues among the *nagyz* Kazakhs [real Kazakhs as they call themselves] who believe that a *shala* Kazakh is not to be trusted. Because, so to speak, he is an imperfect Kazakh [*nepolnotsennii kazakh*], he will for sure lie to you, he leads the country somewhere where it shouldn't lead. But I think it is a very debatable understanding [about *shala* Kazakhs] and I cannot agree with this statement. Because these same *shala* Kazakhs (among them many of my friends) are the people who received a great education. They cannot blame Russian language or Russian culture ..., they won't look for an enemy in it. ... I know that Kazakhs who incorporated themselves into the Russian culture, graduated from Russian school, who were brought up in the Russian spirit, who think and write in Russian—are not at all the worst Kazakhs. And national-patriots, or the so-called

'mambets', are also not the worst [Kazakhs]. I am myself *mambet*, I am a Kazakh from an *aul* [village] and I am proud of it.[38]

While Belger was ahead of his time in describing himself as a *mambet*, many in Kazakhstan still shy away from adopting this label, considering it something marginal, bad and dirty. This self-colonisation and self-discrimination through the act of using the M-words could lead to further divisions. On the eve of Russia's invasion of Ukraine in February 2022, there were widespread calls to prohibit the use of the first M-word, *manbet*, and the war has only strengthened these calls. The concept of *mankurt* and *mankurtisation* as a process of making one into a captive colonial subject, however, has only recently gained traction in local, Kazakhstani and Central Asian discussions on decolonisation. Attempts have been made to decolonise 'mankurt'—rather than it being seen as a slur, local activists have proposed using it as a tool in a productive decolonial dialogue. For example, the Bishkek-based memory association Esimde's second annual conference, 'Mankurt Dreams', was designed to initiate a public discussion about coloniality and the normalisation of the colonial relations that remain part of our everyday life.[39]

In the autumn of 2023, young Kazakh artist Aiganym Mukhametzhan made headlines with her work 'Mankurtizer' ('Mangurttendirgish', in Qazaq), which openly invited Kazakhstanis and other Central Asians to discuss their colonial past. Her installation depicted the mechanism of torture by which people were made into 'slaves without memory and self-awareness':[40]

> The installation 'Mankurtiser' is a [depiction of the] mechanism of torture that turned people into *mankurts*—slaves without memory and self-awareness. In the artist's new interpretation, this construction is surrounded by ribbon fences and stripped of its original function, becoming a symbol of decolonisation and the end of an era of oppression. These fences emphasise that the old methods are no longer applicable. The work invites us to rethink the past and regain our lost memory. In contemporary Kazakh society, where the terms 'mankurt' and 'mambet' reflect cultural differences, the installation offers unification and

acceptance of ourselves, each other, and our common history as a way to true liberation and overcoming collective trauma.[41]

Mukhametzhan's powerful visual language echoes her generation's desire to fight for a better, no-longer-postsoviet and no-longer-authoritarian future. In her paintings, Mukhametzhan, a native of Shu, a town in Southern Kazakhstan, has even created her own aesthetic of the decolonial Kazakh *aul* with the aim of empowering places less central than the urban hubs and making them more attractive. In her work, Mukhametzhan, as well as many other artists of her cohort, of the new Kazakhstan, creates a space full of new meanings, where *mambet* ceases to be a slur or associated with something dirty, instead becoming desirable, central and beautiful. In Yessenova's words, Mukhametzhan and people like her are helping create a new Kazakhstan, 'a "nation" representing a symbolic space bounded by cultural markets made of and for its members, created within a unified field of communication and social exchange', one free of colonial divisions and labels.[42]

This discussion of *mambets* and *mankurts* highlights the continued influence of Soviet coloniality on Kazakhstani society. These divisive, racialised, discriminatory slurs infiltrate visions of common identity and erect harmful hierarchies among co-nationals and compatriots. The major crises that Kazakhstan has experienced in the past decade have also accelerated discussions about the colonial foundations of these divisive M-words. The grassroots project of building a Kazakhstani identity can potentially resolve these colonial traumas and heal the fault lines in communities that were forcefully divided to allow the metropole direct control over identity politics. The aftermath of the January 2022 protests, discussed in the next chapter, gives hope that these divisions can eventually be overcome.

5

'WE ARE THE ORDINARY PEOPLE'

THE JANUARY 2022 PROTESTS IN KAZAKHSTAN

The winter months are bitterly cold in Kazakhstan. The itchy, frosty feeling on your face and the needle-like ache in your feet when the cold air seems to almost reach your bones are perhaps the worst. But the early days of January 2022 did not feel like any other winter. Cities across the country roared with crowds of protestors undeterred by the winter temperatures. The protests started in Western Kazakhstan, the oil- and gas-rich region that has been developing a real culture of political contention over the course of the past decade. And overnight more cities across Kazakhstan joined forces in the most unprecedented mass protests in the country's recent history.

On 1 and 2 January 2022, oil workers in the cities of Zhanaozen and Aktau in Western Kazakhstan started gathering on the main squares of their cities and held peaceful rallies. The protestors, who were ordinary citizens, took to the streets to speak out on a variety of political and economic issues, even if the immediate catalyst of the protests was the sudden spike in liquefied petroleum gas (LPG) prices.[1] There was a certain irony that the protestors lived in oil- and gas-rich regions but could not afford the highly popular LPG after the Ministry of Energy dramatically increased the price at the start of 2022. Remarks by Olzhas Baidildinov, an advisor to the energy minister, only added fuel to the fire. At a press conference about LPG prices in Astana on 3 January 2022, Baidildinov stated that 'those unhappy with the LPG price hikes' should take public transport instead.[2] For many on the streets and in the public squares, it was clear that the elite were completely divorced from ordinary citizens' everyday lives.

As crowds gathered on the central squares, it was also clear that the price of LPG was only the first item on a list of demands being voiced to the Ak Orda—the presidential palace in Astana— and the president himself. It was an open secret that while Western Kazakhstan was the richest region and thus contributed more than any other part of the country to the state budget, the share of the region's residents who were living below the poverty line was growing rapidly.

Social and economic inequality was rampant in the region, and workers and their rights were not protected by state law—which was written mostly to benefit foreign companies—and the state had banned formal labour unions. As Paolo Sorbello, who has studied labour disputes in Western Kazakhstan, explains:

> [I]nequalities in pay and conditions, limitations of freedoms, and neoliberal corporate practices were gradually introduced by TNCs [transnational corporations] in the oil sector and had a direct effect on the relationship between labour and capital and indirectly aided the government's authoritarian project, because precarisation of work is ultimately also an instrument of control.[3]

The protestors in Western Kazakhstan organised into informal networks and came to the central squares to demand real change instead of more empty promises. The protests were peaceful and self-organised. No official leaders or political parties were involved in the first days of the Aktau and Zhanaozen protests in that frosty January of 2022. Women and men gathered on the square, feeling compelled to speak out at the regime's failures. Every speaker who emerged from the crowd and took to the stage asked attendees at the predominantly Kazakh-language rallies to stay calm and not resort to violence. Every provocation was stopped by groups of protestors themselves.

As well as LPG prices being returned to their previous level, the people who gathered on the squares in Aktau and Zhanaozen wanted the regime to come and listen to what they had to say. Shouting slogans like 'Sack the Government' and 'People Should Be Electing Their Own Governors!', their economic demands quickly became politicised.[4] Protestors in Zhanaozen, where the Bloody January 2022 mass protests began, knew only too well that economic change would only be permanent if it was also accompanied by a political transformation at the very top of the system.

The protestors' demands were clear and loud. The country needed a new government with genuinely fresh faces, not the long-time elites reshuffled from one post to another every six months or so. From a hastily erected stage, the protestors in Western Kazakhstan called for the people to be able to freely elect their representatives and for the president to reinstate the 'truly democratic' 1993 Constitution. They voiced these demands to the governor of Mangystau region, Nurlan Nogayev, who emerged from his office to speak to the crowds after the first days of protest. President Tokayev also responded swiftly, dispatching a committee to address the protestors' demands.

The committee flew to Aktau to address the issues causing discontent, and the government was immediately sacked. But Pandora's box had already been opened. On the evening of 4 January, crowds of protestors began gathering in Almaty. Hundreds of unarmed people walked in columns through the city's streets, singing the national anthem and waving the Kazakh flag. Eyewitnesses and journalists on site reported that people from nearby apartment buildings were shouting out in support and singing along.[5] The following day, unprecedented mass protests took place in over sixty cities and towns across Kazakhstan. Although peaceful, the protests were violently suppressed in three cities in the southern region: Taraz, Taldyqorgan and Almaty. The Bloody January protests claimed the lives of at least 238 people.[6]

In this chapter, I discuss how Kazakhstan's emerging protest culture has changed the frames of national identity and national imagination. I argue that the Bloody January protests did not make

145

Kazakhstan more ethnonationalist, even though ethnic Kazakhs were the dominant group by dint of being the 'ethnic majority' in the country. Leaving aside the regional and other divisions between the protestors themselves, there were other factors that mean these protests cannot be described as ethnonationalist—there were no calls to amend the language law, for instance, or claims against the country's numerous ethnic minorities.[7]

Instead, the wave of protests served to foster civic identity and increase citizens' engagement in politics. The various organised and spontaneous protests calling for democratisation inspired many Kazakhstanis to believe that they could become active participants in everyday politics and demand changes from the dictatorial regime. Opposition groups have thus been successful in their efforts to 'awaken' Kazakhstani society and make it more active in voicing public demands to the regime's elites.[8] These demands united people of different ethnicities and paved the way for a new civic culture of grassroots political engagement.

Protests—once unthinkable in the dictatorship built by Nazarbayev—became ubiquitous after 2011, clearly demonstrating the disconnect between the politics of the regime and society's needs. For more than a decade, Kazakhstani society experienced protests that in one way or another expressed the demands of broad social groups. In those regions and cities where protests were more consistent and frequent, a special form of protest culture emerged: people joining rallies knew how to behave to avoid conflicts with the police, for example. In Western Kazakhstan, groups of workers formed informal groups to take collective action. In Almaty, the hub of opposition forces and new political movements like Oyan, Qazaqstan, activists even distributed leaflets containing information to help those detained by the police. Protestors organised crowdfunding to pay fines and retain lawyers, as well as attending public court hearings.[9] Kazakhstani society was ready to contend with the regime—people were tired of its endless unfulfilled promises, and mass protest was the only way they would be seen and heard by the president.

The Almaty chaos

My friends and acquaintances were among those on the streets and in the public squares of Almaty, Kazakhstan's largest city. They told me they did not feel the frost on their faces or the aching of their bones in the freezing temperatures of early January. Instead, they were preoccupied with feelings of deep solidarity, mixed with fear and anger.

In Almaty, peaceful protestors gathered into several groups and walked through the city singing the national anthem and expressing solidarity with the protestors in Western Kazakhstan. But the Almaty protestors—like their counterparts across the country—knew that the protests were not just about LPG gas but rather about inequality and authoritarian rule.

Groups of protestors gathered in front of the Auezov theatre, close to the city's main stadium. Another group, organised by the Oyan, Qazaqstan political movement, formed near the Park of the First President on Navoi Street, farther away from the centre, where young people held banners, one of which read 'Kazakhstan without Nazarbayevs'. Soon after, Oyan, Qazaqstan activists, among them young women, were stopped and beaten up by the police. On the other side of the city, a large group of protestors gathered around Almaty Arena. The arena was already well known to many of the protestors, as it had been the site of the spontaneous June 2019 rally against the election of Tokayev as the new president. According to Kazakhstani opposition leader Zhanbolat Mamay, people knew where to meet by 4 January, having already seen numerous discussions on social media. He came to the area around Almaty Arena in the early afternoon in the hope he could stop the police from clashing with the peaceful protestors. He had also hoped that Almaty's mayor, Bakhytzhan Sagintayev, would speak to the protestors, just as the governors of the Atyrau, Mangystau and Kyzylorda regions had done.[10] In the event, however, the Almaty mayor hid for most of the January days and was subsequently sacked by President Tokayev on 31 January 2022.[11] The columns from different parts of the city started gathering on the main square in front of the city administration building, *akimat*, marching from their respective points of initial organisation on each side of the city.

In Almaty, the police started clashing with the crowds on the main square on the evening of 4 January 2022.[12] Around this time, the state also blocked internet access to prevent 'the spread of disinformation', as they would later claim—or, more likely, to stop crowds of protestors in different parts of the city from communicating with one another. The late evening of 4 January marked the start of Kazakhstan's descent into complete chaos and violence.

'Suddenly, it felt like a war had started', one of the protestors told me in a short phone call in mid-January. 'For days we stayed at home with no internet, no food and no information' said another acquaintance who had two small children at home. Meanwhile, people on the streets reported cannon-like sounds, and some eyewitnesses described seeing bullets flying around. No one knew who was shooting.[13] 'We thought these were rubber bullets used by the riot police alongside the tear gas', another eyewitness reported. Tear gas was everywhere on the main square; Mamay reported that 'it was hard to breathe', so people started running from the square to the nearby streets. All the while, news about the protests continued to spread even without the internet, and by 5 January many more protestors thronged the streets and the city's main square, which had previously been named after the Soviet leader Leonid Brezhnev.

There were all sorts of people on the streets, eyewitnesses told me.[14] Some went to protest against rampant inequality and unemployment, while others looted local shops.[15] Still others, as an anonymous activist told me, went simply because 'they wanted to be heard'. There were also those who were just curious, having never seen anything like this in their lives: 'It felt like a revolution had started and it would be a shame to miss it', said one activist who rushed to the main square in Almaty on 5 January to witness the events with his 'own eyes'.[16] Then there were those who spread violence and disorder: cars lacking numberplates shot sporadically at people; violent mobs and their 'curators',[17] who allegedly wore red puffer jackets, arrived on the streets and gave orders to the organised crowds. Finally, there were crowds of peaceful protestors who were trying to voice their political demands and stop the violence.

All these groups managed to co-exist within the framework of the street protests at the time of the worst violence, the shootings and killings. The *akimat*, a Soviet landmark, quickly caught fire, and news agencies worldwide started reporting on the 'mass violence in Kazakhstan'. It was not clear who had set the building on fire or how coordinated the looting was. Those who were on the square when the violence intensified reported a sense of total collapse. 'Once the *akimat* was on fire, the crowds of people started screaming that we needed to storm the presidential residence', an eyewitness told me. The residence was located right behind the *akimat*, behind the main square in Almaty.[18] The residence was not accessible to the public, being heavily guarded by security personnel even when unoccupied.

For the angry crowds of protestors, destroying anything that personified Nazarbayev's long dictatorship was an end in itself. The storming of the residence was 'quite chaotic and violent'—as large crowds of men rushed at the closed gate, shots rang out. 'Then we saw bloodied people falling on the ground, but it did not stop the crowds of people rushing to the residence', recalls one of those who stormed the closed gate.[19]

When the gate fell and ordinary people could get into the building, many of them were 'stunned by the level of the luxury inside ... there were images of Nazarbayev everywhere [inside the residence]; even the library had a lot of his [Nazarbayev's] books', remarked another eyewitness. He added that storming the residence was 'a historic scene not to be missed'. For him, it was the moment of Nazarbayev's downfall. 'The people showed their rage against the dictator who thought he was super-popular among the masses; most people who stormed the residence spoke Kazakh', he concluded.[20]

At the time of the storming of the residence, the protestors—squatting in underground spaces on the main square or watching burning administrative buildings and cars—did not know that the state was already calling them 'terrorists' who posed a threat to the social order. Given the complete internet blackout across the country, state television was almost the only source of information. Only a small number of people, and mainly in the big cities, had access to the internet through VPNs; they communicated with the outside world primarily via Telegram, the social media platform of choice in Kazakhstan. Many people in Almaty later reported they were unable to use their mobile phones to call their relatives, and some even had trouble communicating via landline phones.

The complete information blackout served as an important tool to sway public opinion, enabling the government to frame the mass protests as a threat to the entire country. State television reported relentlessly on the '20,000 terrorists' allegedly involved in these events: in the first version of the narrative—and according to President Tokayev himself—these people were foreigners, but later media reports began to claim that many of the so-called terrorists were Kazakhstanis.[21] In one instance, an alleged 'foreign terrorist' was interviewed on national television, but it was later revealed that he was Vikram Ruzakhunov, a famous jazz musician from the neighbouring Kyrgyz Republic who had been arrested and beaten up by the police in Almaty during the protests. He appeared with bruises in an interview broadcast on state television and claimed he had received 200 USD to participate in the January protests. When the video went viral, his friends and family demanded his immediate release.[22] After his release, Ruzakhunov shared that he had been beaten up by the police and told to say he was a 'foreign extremist'. Other Kyrgyz citizens with numerous injuries were later found in police detention centres and reported police brutality and torture even though they had not participated in the protests.

People feared the violence might spread and enter their homes, that their property would be damaged, that the country would fall into a long and violent period of uncertainty. State propaganda played on these concerns about instability, rarely describing the protests as peaceful or mentioning the groups that were demanding democratisation and regime change via open and freely contested elections. And even though there was no proof that 'foreign terrorists' were involved, the January 2022 protests remain a point of contention for many Kazakhstanis. Those citizens who experienced or witnessed the most severe violence in Almaty, for example, tend to view the protests in a negative light, as having threatened the social order in the city and the country as a whole.[23] Nevertheless, few Kazakhstanis supported the arrival of CSTO troops[24] in Kazakhstan to establish order.

At the end of 6 January 2022, Almaty remained in chaos. Peaceful protestors gathered around the Monument to Independence and tried to clear the space of rubbish and burning particles of nearby buildings and burned cars. They had just received the news about the 'terrorists' attacking Kazakhstan and wanted to make handmade posters to specify that the peaceful protestors were not terrorists. It was hard for them to communicate with the president directly. The situation in the city was highly unstable.

Several official buildings, including the offices of the 'party of power', Nur-Otan, were set on fire; major banks and their ATMs were vandalised and looted. The streets were covered in rubbish; burnt-out car carcasses stood silently in the middle of the roads. Almaty dwellers used their phones to video the masses of people marching down different central streets. The police were nowhere in sight. Hard-to-verify rumours spread around the city. Was it really a coup? Would violent mobs come and attack civilians? How many were dead, and who was doing the shooting?

In the midst of the news and the war-like sounds on the streets, it emerged that some protestors—or 'violent elements'—had taken over the city's airport. Locals reported that 'bandits' were driving cars without numberplates and shooting people at random. 'Almaty looked like a scene from a sci-fi movie about Armageddon', a resident who went out into the streets to document the scene later told me in a private conversation. 'It just felt surreal.'[25] Yet the official rhetoric about the 'events' in Almaty still made little to no mention of the peaceful protestors.

The Tokayev regime clearly rejected the protestors' demands for further democratisation, preferring instead to portray these events as a dangerous threat to state sovereignty with the potential to lead to civil war. The regime could have co-opted the traumatic memory of the protests as part of its own project of building a national identity and the process of de-Nazarbayevification that began as early as 6 January, when Tokayev sacked and imprisoned the once-omnipotent head of the security police, Karim Massimov. Instead, the Tokayev regime, in order to gain complete power and step out of the shadow of Nazarbayev, felt the need to turn a new page.

In Taldyqorgan, the police found and arrested a group of young men who had toppled a monument to Nazarbayev before dragging it around the central square in an act of public humiliation. Allegations quickly spread across the city that these young men had been mistreated in detention. Activists started collecting money to help one of the protestors pay for medical care for injuries he allegedly sustained during detention. Activists also alleged mistreatment of protestors in other cities. And as Kazakhstan slowly began to recover from the bloodshed of the first weeks of January and news agencies started reporting on civilian deaths during the clashes, President Tokayev and his administration declared that the state investigation into the 'January events' (*yanvar'skie sobytiya*) would be completely closed to the public. In Almaty and other southern cities, the regime portrayed the organised violence as an attempted 'coup'.

While eyewitnesses reported that 'curators' had been directing the attacks by violent mobs, a lack of information about who these people were raises more questions about what happened in Almaty and other southern cities in January 2022. The lack of a transparent investigation thus exacerbates the problem.

'Biz Qarapayim Halyqpyz' — *'We Are Ordinary People'*

'Through the sounds of the shootings, we could hear how the protestors sang the national anthem. I heard my own voice going, "and my [dear] Homeland, my Qazaqstan!" singing the familiar words of the anthem.[26] We were peaceful protestors, not bandits, not terrorists, as state TV and the president [Tokayev] told the whole world. There were others who set things on fire; we were cleaning up [the mess] and voicing our political demands', one of the protestors who stood on the square in Almaty during the long days of early January 2022 told me.[27]

The peaceful protestors who gathered on the main square in Almaty next to the Monument to Independence started making banners. One read 'We Are Ordinary People; We Are Not Terrorists' and 'Don't Shoot!' in an attempt to shield themselves from the coming days of total violence. It was the late afternoon of 6 January—a day that many of my interlocutors and fellow citizens will remember forever. The sounds of gunfire drew ever closer, and as darkness fell, the people standing on the square started to see their comrades fall too, their blood running down the pavement.

'A woman right next to me was shot in the head and fell down dead', remembered one activist. Another told me of a young man who died of his wounds, unable to escape to the nearby apartment buildings. People were screaming and running around trying to find help and get the wounded to hospital as the air filled with the sound of flying bullets. 'It smelled like death, and any one of us could have ended up dead', another activist related.[28]

Few of them want to remember the details of those days in the dark, cold January of 2022, especially in Almaty, which witnessed the violence yet returned to 'business as usual' in just a week. Qantar became one more addition to the litany of Kazakhs' traumatic collective memories, along with Asharshylyq, the mass famine of the 1930s; Aqtaban Shubyryndy, the eighteenth-century bloodshed that ended in defeat to the Dzhunghar (Kalmyk) tribes; and two fresh wounds, Zheltoqsan—the deadly mass protests of December 1986 in Soviet Alma-Ata—and the 2011 Zhanaozen protests that claimed the lives of dozens of people following brutal police suppression.

In the chaos that followed Qantar, citizens of Kazakhstan—a country that has proudly and fully digitalised—were cut off from reliable sources of information as the country fell into a total internet blackout. In Almaty, as in other cities, most people had become accustomed to paying for goods digitally using their phones and had long forgotten where they kept cash. 'We started searching for change all around the house because without internet we could not even pay for bread!', some local interlocutors told me. Other people recalled they had landline phones but could not reach their loved ones—even the telephone connection failed. 'The only source of information was the TV, and like Big Brother, it only showed the state version of what was happening on the streets. This was how we found out that the CSTO troops were coming down. The panic started once again!', remembered another Almaty local. Meanwhile, the protestors and political activists on the main square responded with the only weapons they had—banners emblazoned with the words 'CSTO, Withdraw the Troops' appeared on the Monument of Independence.[29]

An opinion poll organised by the Kazakhstani polling agency Demoscope almost a year after the protests demonstrated that public opinion remained divided over the involvement of CSTO troops. Of those polled, 43.6 per cent disapproved of the deployment, while 36.8 per cent supported it.[30]

When the gunfire stopped, CSTO troops started clearing the streets. A year later, the citizens of Kazakhstan still have unanswered questions about what the official narrative describes as the 'chaos'. Who were the organisers? Are the people who were tried in closed court hearings in 2022—former security chief and Nazarbayev strongman Massimov and young, charismatic opposition leader Zhanbolat Mamay—really the ones to blame? And, if so, how many more people in power escaped the allegations and investigations? The January 2022 protests remain one of the biggest challenges for Kazakhstan as a nation and a stumbling-block for the Tokayev regime's efforts to consolidate power.

The story of the peaceful protests is still marginalised in the official discourse. However, their importance to Kazakhstan's post-independence history cannot be underestimated. During the bloodiest days of the January protests, they represented Kazakhstan's growing—and thriving—civil society. In the midst of the protests and before the violence broke out, the protesters were largely united in solidarity and then in their growing understanding that they could claim power and stand up to the authoritarian regime and its politics. When an ordinary citizen emerged out of the haze of tear gas and fog holding a large Kazakhstani flag, he symbolised the hope shared by many of those standing on squares across the country.[31]

The January 2022 protests resulted in the formation of a specific post-January identity and a new sense of what it means to be Kazakhstani. This identity is rooted in civicness, in an understanding that being Kazakhstani is about being part of a community of citizens who are able to protest and demand political change from the regime. In other words, the January protests altered the balance of regime–society relations: society became more powerful and ceased to see the regime as omnipotent. The aftermath of the protests, including the torture of protestors, further engaged citizens and contributed to a growing civic culture. Kazakhstani citizens are now united, beyond ethnicity, on the basis of their civic identity and their political belonging to Kazakhstan.

The aftermath

In July 2022, I was in an Almaty bar meeting some activists of the #Qantar2022 volunteer initiative. Sat on the bar was a transparent container full of donations (see Figure 5.1) to the victims of Qandy Qantar. Shortly after the violence erupted, when independent observers started collecting stories about the protestors being tortured in police custody, the hashtag #Qantar2022 emerged on Instagram. Some posts featured the families of those who had been shot dead during the protests, while others sought donations and to aggregate resources for the ongoing court hearings of peaceful protestors who had been falsely accused of engaging in acts of violence. Stories were shared in both Kazakh and Russian and sometimes gave the bank account information of the families who needed financial help.

Hundreds of people did indeed need help after the protests, and the Qantar movement's tireless work is a testament to that. The movement's page on Instagram, one of the most popular social media platforms in Kazakhstan, continues to fundraise money for the families of those protestors who died or are still imprisoned. The activists behind the initiative prefer to stay anonymous and for their posts to 'speak' for them. From my rare and deeply personal conversations with someone connected to the movement, it seemed as though, for them, the violence had not ended in January but continued for months. 'We see so much sorrow every day, sorrow that goes unnoticed by many', they whispered.

They, and other activists like them, carry the horrors of Bloody January with them in their bodies—like bullets stuck in their bones, like wounds that fail to heal. Every time someone brought up Bloody January in a casual conversation, I could hear someone else crying or see them staring helplessly into space. The trauma permeated the city; it was stuck in the bullet holes left around the main square and in the burnt-out buildings still sticking out in Almaty in the summer of 2022. 'Even the air in this city is heavy, it carries the aura of that trauma', opined another interlocutor, a local activist who was in the city during the days of unrest and violence. 'Those who witnessed it all [the violence] are still in shock', they said.

I sat in Almaty's New Square—known in the Soviet era as Brezhnev Square—for hours when I first arrived in the city five months after the tragedy. Behind me was the burnt-out *akimat* that once radiated authority. I had crossed this square thousands of times in my lifetime, and it always left me feeling uneasy. But on this day in July 2022, I sat there silently, watching the cars rushing by. I wondered to myself how they could drive on the same asphalt that in

Figure 5.1. Jar with Qantar 2022 donations in an Almaty bar. Author's photo.

January had absorbed the blood of those who had been killed. How come this square had not been closed as a silent monument to the numerous tragedies that took place here between December 1986 and January 2022 and many more in between? How much more sorrow and human suffering does it have to witness?

There are several places in Kazakhstan that carry a similar heaviness and burden of history: the closed-down Stalin-era gulags in northern Kazakhstan; the endless steppes where starving people drew their final breaths during the mass famine of 1933; and the central squares that have witnessed mass protests. When I visited it in August 2022, the central square in the nearby city of Taldyqorgan, where protestors tore down the monument to Nazarbayev, remained in exactly the same condition as the protestors had left it. The monument had been located on a small plaza immediately next to the square, near a historical building—a wooden house that had been the home of a local writer in the early twentieth century. The monument's brown plinth had been broken; some of its stones had been ripped out and still lay on the floor. The plinth was empty, and its cheap gold lettering had been ripped off. It was here that the monument to Nazarbayev had once stood. The protestors took it down in early January 2022. They first attacked it with their bare hands and wooden sticks before bringing in a truck and some long ropes. They placed the ropes around the monument and connected them to the truck. With a couple of tugs from the heavy vehicle, the monument came down, cracking open and revealing that it was empty inside. The crowd cried out in support; some people clapped.

The remaining half of the monument, which still resembled Nazarbayev, was later pulled away with ropes and taken to the nearby central square. There, the protestors hung it by the neck from the second floor of the regional governor's office, the central building on the square. The crowd cheered and continued to celebrate. Later, videos taken on mobile phones showed the same monument, tied by a rope to an old sedan, circling the Christmas tree in the middle of the square. Loud music played, and a celebratory atmosphere prevailed as protestors revelled in vandalising the monument to Nazarbayev.

In the aftermath of the protests, the young driver of the truck that toppled the Nazarbayev monument in Taldyqorgan was beaten and tortured with irons, leaving him with severe burns. In February 2023, five policemen were sentenced to prison terms of varying lengths for torturing at least twenty-five protestors in Taldyqorgan. 'In Taldyqorgan the torture was particularly severe', an activist from abroad told me in a private conversation.

Around 10,000 people were detained in the aftermath of the protests, many of whom were tortured and forced to confess that they had been plotting violence. Some detainees were reportedly taken into the police station after their phones were checked: if the policeman found videos of the mass violence or riots—which were widely shared via social media in Kazakhstan once the internet was restored—that individual was apparently detained immediately. The joint report prepared by the International Partnership for Human Rights, the Kazakhstan International Bureau for Human Rights and the Rule of Law and the Kazakh NGO Coalition against Torture, in partnership with the World Organisation against Torture, documented numerous accounts of physical and sexual abuse, yet just twenty-four law enforcement officers have been tried and sentenced for torture.[32] According to the report:

> The vast majority of the people tortured were men aged 18–50, although there were also reports of torture against women and adolescents. Reported methods of torture included allegations of severe beatings, the use of electric shocks, being doused with boiling water, being burnt with a hot iron, pulling teeth out, and threats of sexual violence, among others.
>
> Torture was used to extract confessions but mainly also to extrajudicially punish most of those who were arbitrarily arrested during the first days or, in some cases, weeks of their unregistered detention.
>
> Individuals were reportedly tortured in pre-trial detention centres, police departments, as well as ill-treated on the street. In Atyrau in Western Kazakhstan and in Ust-Kamenogorsk [Oskemen], participants from the January protests, as well as mere bystanders, were taken to the Dynamo sport halls, owned by the cities' police departments. Witnesses say that in Atyrau [in Western Kazakhstan] up to 400 people passed through the sports centres starting 6 January 2022, most of whom were tortured

either at the sports hall or in separate rooms at the police station. On 13 January, the Atyrau Area Command Office denied that torture was being used in the Dynamo sports halls. The Human Rights Ombudsperson and members of the National Preventive Mechanism were allowed to visit Dynamo [sports hall] only on 24 January 2022, by which time the sports halls were no longer being used to hold detainees.[33]

The January protests were the latest in a chain of similar protests that have taken place in Kazakhstan since 1986. With every new protest, the number of civic-minded activists has grown and learned from past mistakes when it comes to navigating police violence, voicing concerns to the regime and collecting resources for the victims of violence. For its part, the regime has maintained its authoritarian character in dealing with the activists and protestors. State violence has become more institutionalised and more flexible as it has adapted to each new protest and social movement. Yet the regime's tactics have remained the same: using the police to intimidate anti-regime protestors. This has turned protests into a tug of war between the regime and the new political field of activism and opposition. The regime has continued to repeat this mistake, assuming that violence and intimidation will prevent more protestors from joining the rallies and the ranks of the opposition. Each protest wave has remained in the collective memory of Kazakhstanis as a painful legacy; their names reflect the state violence that protestors suffered, from Qandy Qantar to the Zhanaozen massacre.

Yet the aftermath of Qantar is not just a story of suffering; it is also a story of volunteers, of fundraising campaigns for its victims and of the fight for an open and transparent investigation. The tragic days of January 2022 have brought Kazakhstani citizens closer, helping to forge a new civic identity. The biggest crisis and trauma of the post-independence period has thus brought people closer together. In Almaty, when people could not buy food or bread because they were unable to pay for goods without their mobile apps and mobile internet, grassroots initiatives enabling people to help one another mushroomed across the city. People shared resources and came together in small neighbourhood communities to collectively deal with the problem. Every small act of kindness—a ride home when taxi services were shut down, a loaf of free bread given out by the local bakery—created a sense of community beyond state propaganda and celebrations of 'multi-ethnic diversity'.

When a foreign reporter asked me if the January protests would spill over into an ethnic conflict, I paused for a moment. The sociologist in me was thinking that in times of crisis anything can happen, but the citizen in me was horrified—someone prepared to use inter-ethnic tensions to achieve their own ends in a country already suffering from so much violence would have to be mindlessly evil. After all, in socio-economic crises caused by bad governance, most citizens suffer equally, but this suffering has little to nothing to do with ethnicity. As one Kazakh national-patriot once told me in an interview:

> [P]eople in the elite [*bilik*] do not have ethnicity, they are neither Kazakh nor Russian, not even Uyghur; people who allow corruption to worsen conditions of all citizens of the country cannot be called Kazakh, Russian or any other ethnicity. These people just do not care about their own country and its people.

As I walked through the places where protestors had squatted in downtown Almaty and in parts of Taldyqorgan, as I looked through the numerous videos of the protests that emerged during and after the fateful days in January, I could see there was a deep sentiment of shared solidarity. Peaceful protestors smiling into the camera frames and offering each other a helping hand; an old Kazakh lady showing people the way out of New Square as the air filled with tear gas on the night of 4 January. Did she care whom she was saving? Was the ethnicity of the policemen or the looters important to her or to anyone else?

Kazakhstan's history from 1986 to 2024 demonstrates that people tend to unite in times of heightened crisis. The January 2022 protests revealed Kazakhs' resilience and their civicness because people felt the power of society when speaking to the corrupt authoritarian system and because people also understood that they can often resolve problems after a crisis long before the state. This resilience was soon also evident in other more localised crises like the infrastructural collapse that left people freezing in Ekibastuz in December 2022 or in national crises like the public demands for the criminalisation of domestic violence after the killing of thirty-one-year-old Nukenova in early November 2023 and the prolonged trial of her husband, ex-minister Bishimbayev, who was found guilty of her murder in 2024. Collaboration in resolving shared problems, which the events of January 2022 accelerated through the waves of solidarity with the protestors and discontent with injustice, rampant corruption and bad governance, is the key element in the true Kazakhstani-ness, the civic belonging born out of social engagements on the ground and not in the pompous pamphlets frantically reprinted in Ak Orda.

6

THE LONG POST-JANUARY

FORMING CIVICNESS

In mid-July 2023, I was conducting a workshop entitled 'Beyond the Postsoviet' together with colleagues from local and foreign art institutions. Through an open call, we gathered a group of people interested in the theme, mostly young scholars and activists from Kazakhstan and Russia who resided in Almaty at the time. As part of the event, we went to New Square in Almaty, the old Brezhnev Square, where peaceful protestors and passers-by had been gunned down just a year and half earlier. Our aim was to explore the space as an open-air museum of the events and the new monument that had been unveiled by President Tokayev in January 2023, on the first anniversary of the protests.

It was a hot summer day. One of those days where there wasn't a cloud in the sky, and it felt as though the burning sun above our heads could almost melt the pavement under our feet. We walked from Mira (Peace) Street up to the monument to the December 1986 protestors and from there reached the square. Old Soviet buildings that had previously been used by the local telecom companies had recently been renovated to hide the burned-down spaces on the façade. Cars were hurrying from one side to another to avoid the notorious Almaty rush hour. The square was still open for the busy traffic, and we had to carefully navigate it as the pedestrian crossings were only available on both ends of the rather wide square. Certain memories rushed back to me. I remembered this square in the early 1990s and could still picture its blue pine trees, which were cut down to make it look less Soviet (because, for some reason, the poor trees represented sovietness). I remembered how my dad took me to eat lunch at an old *stolovaya* (canteen) that somehow survived in one of these same old Soviet buildings until the mid-2000s and showed me around the old party headquarters, which have now been transformed into the offices of radio stations and advertising companies. He wanted me to remember a piece of history once kept behind closed doors. Life was still and unremarkable inside these buildings during the slow passing of the mid-Nazarbayev era in the early and mid-2000s. At least that was how I remembered it, and maybe that was what my father wanted me to take a note of. The slow death of sovietness was soon to be replaced by the slow death of Nazarbayevism.

The presence of the cars on this square always puzzled me. The square was an open space that people were forced to share with the cars, yet it was also a space for mass gatherings, especially on commemorative dates. The traffic was only stopped for state celebrations or on the days when the protestors occupied the space and stopped the traffic themselves. This was not uncommon. Since 1986, this same square has hosted hundreds of protests, but the Bloody January protests are the most well known and caused the most deaths. The square has witnessed many rallies and many tragedies, yet the busy traffic rushing through it spoke of the mundane, of everyday business 'as usual'.

When we reached the Monument of Independence with the participants of the 2023 workshop, we could see bullet holes in parts of the monuments, especially in the figures of animals and people. Some were still open, while others had been hastily covered with a plaster material. One of the observant members of the group stood right next to the monument to check where the security forces had directed their bullets. 'They aimed at their [the protestors'] heads', she said. It was true, the bullet holes on the monument were level with the head of a person of an average height. We paused at this chilling realisation, and people stopped to observe a minute's silence. No one really wanted to speak even after the moment of silence. 'They were killing people here', someone finally said. The regime had turned the public square turned into a killing field, with the security forces using guns and snipers so precise they could be targeted directly at the protestors' heads. It was the mid-point of the square. Right around here, the protestors had gathered with their handmade banner 'We Are Not Terrorists, We Are the Ordinary People'. And right here, some of them had fallen on the ground, dead. No exit wounds. I knew people who had stood on the square during the protests. Even many months later, very few of them wanted to speak of that traumatic experience. As one of them once told me in a brief conversation in the summer of 2022, six months after the tragedy, *'words can't heal*, words can't do anything anymore', and subtly asked me not to bring it up any time soon. 'It triggers me that nothing has changed [since January 2022]', they said. For many of my interlocutors in Kazakhstan, we were still living in a long January, or as locals call it, 'we still live in Qantar'.[1]

We had yet to reach the monument that Tokayev had unveiled on the opposite end of the square when my phone started buzzing with messages. Right on this day, 11 July 2023, five activists were on trial for seizing Almaty's airport. The activists in the court, which was in a different district of Almaty, were texting me to come down to the court and take note of what was happening. Five people— history teacher Kalas Nurpeisov; taxi drivers Nurlan Dalibayev, Ermukhamet Shilibayev and Zhan-Aidar Karmenov; and journalist Aigerim Tleuzhan—were accused of taking control of Almaty International Airport in early January 2022. Alone, all by themselves, with no guns. A whole airport.

After inspecting the 'state-sanctioned' monument—a series of dark stelas with quotes from well-known male Kazakh writers and thinkers—I turned around to take a final look at Brezhnev/ New Square. With the burned down administrative building of the local *akimat*—once the headquarters of the Soviet CPK—behind me, the square felt like the Soviet creation it had been for decades. The writings on top of the main buildings on the other side of the square included words about the importance of obedience penned by the nineteenth-century Kazakh philosopher and thinker Abai. Just as in the Soviet period, the regime was again speaking to us through strange banners; the whole space was seeking to discipline anyone in its vicinity. 'Obey!', the banners screamed. Someone in the crowd started sobbing quietly. Seeing the bullet holes, the pavement that only a year and a half ago had been soaked in human blood and had witnessed the sorrow of hundreds of people who had been protesting here almost every year in December and January for forty years, proved unbearable for some of my companions. Five minutes later, my phone started buzzing again—the activists being tried in the 'airport case' had just been sentenced: the men on trial had been sentenced to eight years in prison; Aigerim Tleuzhan had been sentenced to four. It was time for all of us to cry.

Moments later, I decided I had to go to the court. People had been gathering there since the early morning. Some of them were the families and friends of the activists on trial, and it was reported that some of them had collapsed in court after the sentencing. Many people had been forced to stand outside, as there was not enough space for everyone inside the courthouse. Political activists of all kinds—the Oyan, Qazaqstan movement, feminist activists, art activists and independent journalists—were all there too. An unsanctioned rally demanding a fair trial and the release of the innocent protestors was underway inside and outside the court, my sources were reporting. 'You have to come now!', one message lit up on my phone. I left my group and told them to go home rather than risk being arrested for attending the rally at the court. Some of my friends still decided to come with me, and I advised everyone who was coming to the court to check their phone batteries, text their next of kin and make sure they had plenty of snacks, water and cash. I was accustomed to this checklist from the many stories of detention I had heard from political activists. Unsanctioned rallies were still illegal in Kazakhstan. Protestors would often end up in a police precinct and spend hours there after a rally, regardless of our constitutional right to free assembly. We could be arrested at any point after reaching the court. But the people around me, my friends and acquaintances, were determined to go.

The taxi ride took a very long time. I was counting the minutes, frantically checking my phone and unable to speak. I was impatient and anxious. My throat was dry, and my heart was racing. When we reached the courthouse, there were a lot of people sitting on the grass in the courtyard or on improvised benches. A long line of uniformed policemen stood ready to act on any order. They were silent, their faces emotionless, but their whole presence created an environment full of fear. Journalists ran around with their cameras and microphones. The crowd was agitated. Everyone had come to express their support and solidarity. There was an ambulance parked on the right side of the courtyard, as some people still needed medical help. Everyone was exhausted and frustrated. It was a hot July afternoon, but it felt like we were all still stuck in January.

When we saw the familiar faces of friends and activists, I still could not let go of the feeling that we were all police targets. In the small courtyard overlooking the mountains to the left and more buildings to the right, I felt surrounded, my every move surveyed; it felt like I was suffocating. There was no place to run from the police here. The court building had been strategically placed in an area where there was no possibility of escape. Yet everyone was calm and chatty. Activists shared bottles of water and handshakes; our brief conversations were mainly in Kazakh. 'How are you?', 'Good so far.' 'Were *they* already taken away?' 'Yes, people say they actually left from this gate and not where we all gathered.' 'Which prison?' 'We still don't know.' 'Relatives [of the people on trial] were not feeling well.' 'Yes, the medics took care of them.'

No more arrests were made on the day of the trial, though the police stood in line for almost an hour after I arrived, just in case any further protests took place. The face of one activist who sat on an improvised bench in front of me is stuck in my memory. He was smiling and joking. Every time someone new passed by or engaged in conversation, he added a bit more context to what had taken place. Just days later, my phone again began to ring with messages. Beszhan Toleubekuly, the smiling activist we spoke to outside the courtroom, had been arrested on the night of 14 July for organising an 'unsanctioned rally' after the trial.

In this chapter, I discuss the implications of what I call here the long post-January. This was a period when people needed space and time to reconcile with the tragedy and deal with the aftermath of the protest, including the court hearings and the imprisonment of activists and ordinary people accused of plotting some of the most audacious actions, from seizing the airport with their bare hands to attempting a coup. Every day, the news was filled with more details of the sentences and court hearings taking place in major cities across the country. Young men were being sent to prison for prolonged periods simply because they had passed by the squares or had come to the protests out of idle curiosity. Were these the real perpetrators? Had unarmed journalists and activists really been able to occupy a major international airport?

'We all speak the same language'

I did not come to the courthouse to take notes. Writing was not on my mind. I came to show my support. The morning of the sentencing, I still hoped the judge would release those on trial and start a proper investigation into the real perpetrators, including the organised crime groups. Five people, among them a schoolteacher and a journalist, could not stop planes from landing and disrupt a major infrastructural hub with their bare hands. But that was not the point. However absurd the trial was, the regime needed to punish someone to set a public example that would discourage other protestors, those who had gathered around the court told us.

Thus, like many others, I decided to come as an act of solidarity. I expected that just about anything could happen, and in the taxi on the way there, I was frantically checking if my friends and acquaintances were safe or if they had already been detained inside the police buses known locally as *avtozak*. For years, we have seen way too many people violently dragged into these buses: elderly ladies with their walking sticks, teenagers with colourful hair, people who became known political activists screaming the popular chant 'Shal, ket!'— Go away old man!—directly to Nazarbayev, and even a man who had been knocked off his bike while returning from a grocery shop in the June 2019 post-election protests in Almaty.[2]

When I saw dozens of uniformed policemen, a shiver went down my spine. Growing up in an authoritarian state, you quickly learn to stay out of trouble and out of the police's sight. You learn that when detained, you are no longer safe from allegations or random bags of suspicious substances being thrown into your purse. In short, you learn that the police are not there to safeguard you but to protect the dictatorship, and as an activist, you are a moving target for anyone in police uniform.[3] The police are an institution of fear, and their batons are a reminder that anyone can get hurt and that the police 'can get away with it'.[4] Fear of the police was a normalised response, an embodied feeling silently shared with others. At the same time, fear was something that many law enforcement officers I spoke to enjoyed seeing in the eyes of their detainees or people on the street. Fear reassured the police of their authority and power. In my interviews with protestors before Bloody January 2022, people openly spoke of their fear of physical punishment, especially torture or rape, which they had seen or heard about during the 2020 protests in Belarus. In conversations I had with people after the shock of the violence of Bloody January, fear became a sign of shame and guilt among the activists.

Virtually every person I spoke to, sometimes in conversations completely unrelated to my research and in contexts that had nothing to do with the horrors of the long January in Kazakhstan, knew someone who had been shot or of a family affected by tragedy. People told me about the experiences of their friends, when a family had lost their only son; I heard stories of denial and astonishment that lasted for days after someone learned they had lost a relative during the protests. And the whole country knew the horrific story of the Seitkulov family of three, whose car had been gunned down in Taldyqorgan, instantly killing their fifteen-year-old daughter Nuray and leading to her parents' horrific deaths from gun wounds and haemorrhaging on 8 January 2022.[5] As the investigation into the case would later find, their car had been sprayed with fifty-four bullets from a submachine gun; no one inside had any chance of survival.

Another story that rocked the whole of Kazakhstan was that of Aikorkem Meldekhan, a four-year-old girl who was shot dead while passing through the streets of Almaty in her family's car—her older sister was also injured—on 7 January 2022. A picture of little Aikorkem in Kazakh national dress became a tragic symbol of what had happened in Kazakhstan in January 2022 and a remainder of all the civilian deaths. Graffiti depicting her emerged around the city, sometimes with the question: 'Who Killed Me?' The car in which Aikorkem was killed had been struck by twenty-two bullets. The trial of the military serviceman accused of 'abuse of power with the usage of firearms that led to the death of a child' started at the end of July 2023 and concluded in mid-November 2023 with the Military Court of Almaty Garrison finding 'the defendant in this case, a military serviceman, Arman Zhuman, not guilty'.[6] The case was classified: the court doors were closed not only to the media but also to some of Aikorkem's relatives, who became active spokespeople in demanding justice for the four-year-old.

Every death became a lasting tragedy. Still in shock after the mass violence, activists and journalists had to investigate the allegations of people being dragged from their hospital beds or arrested in daylight on the street and accused of terrorist acts. The regime had to sustain its own line about how '20,000 terrorists' had attacked Kazakhstan. Some of Qantar's victims were accused of terrorism after they had been buried,[7] having been shot dead during the protests. Some journalists complain that people are tired of the numerous court hearings a year and a half after the protests, but more and more people are on trial, and most of them are the protestors, not those who had been in the firing squad.

When those involved in the 'airport attack' were driven away in an unmarked truck, people outside the courtroom stayed behind and continued to demand their release. New plans were being made in the shade; it is unbearably hot in July, so water bottles were being passed around non-stop. 'Zhana Qazaqstan'—Tokayev's brand new state programme, which literally means 'New Kazakhstan'—'is a lie', people say. Innocent people are still jailed in Zhana Qazaqstan, 'so it is an old Qazaqstan', someone says, and the small crowd cheers. I spot several people, most of them activists, and we take a photo. Two or three days later, news emerged that one of them had been detained outside his home for taking part in an 'unsanctioned rally' outside the courthouse on the day of the trial. Zhana Qazaqstan strikes again.

Country aflame

In the first days of January 2022, when people gathered in Zhanaozen and soon afterwards on the famous Yntymaq Square in Aktau, news of the protests spread swiftly across Kazakhstan. Telegram chats, a popular way for ordinary Kazakhstanis to seek information away from state-sponsored media, started calling on the citizens of Kazakhstan to show solidarity with Western Kazakhstan and with Zhanaozen. One of my interlocutors, whom I phoned after the protests had calmed down in Almaty, told me that 'we chickened out when it came to supporting the workers of Zhanaozen in December 2011, but we could not make the same mistake again in 2022'.[8] On the first days of mass protests, 3 and 4 January, there was a feeling of excitement and unity, a sense that every city in Kazakhstan was standing with Zhanaozen. Several activist platforms created interactive maps of Kazakhstan to show how rallies in 'solidarity with Zhanaozen' had spread throughout the country. Social media chats were full of encouragement and support, even if some commentators were visibly anxious, remembering how the Zhanaozen standoff had ended eleven years ago: in bloodshed, chaos, burning buildings.

The story of Qandy Qantar shares certain similarities with Zhanaozen—a protest with economic claims that became politicised, followed by its violent suppression—but it was also very different: Qandy Qantar involved protests throughout the country, not just one region. Once again, the regime failed to listen to the concerns of the population. Some limited attempts were made to establish a dialogue with protestors in Western Kazakhstan but none in Almaty and the southern regions. For his part, President Tokayev hastily labelled the protestors as 'terrorists' and spoke of paid foreign agents, including a beaten-up jazz musician from Kyrgyzstan who had nothing to do with foreign extremism. But most importantly, the regime failed to even try to understand society.

The Nazarbayev regime as it once was—an inviolable 'system'—began to crumble in 2011. Nazarbayev failed to address the societal problem in Zhanaozen, later claiming that he was not aware of the seven-month standoff where workers were held hostage by the system—some starved during the months of unemployment, and many others were killed when the protests were violently suppressed. As many Kazakhstani commentators have claimed, the Zhanaozen massacre was the first nail in Nazarbayev's political coffin.

The nation continues to mourn the victims of Zhanaozen 2011 and Qandy Qantar, and these personal tragedies cannot simply be brushed away by the new regime. State propaganda has engaged in an attack on 'looters' and 'bandits', and even if most court hearings are not televised, news about criminal elements among the protestors, such as crime syndicate leader Dikiy Arman ('Wild Arman') and others blamed for the violence, lands on fertile ground. The regime is attempting to sell the 'New Kazakhstan' as an effort to forge a more democratic future for ordinary Kazakhstanis. Tokayev has positioned himself as someone creating a 'listening state' that is open to citizens' concerns and grievances. He has even organised new parliamentary elections, removed Nazarbayev from his previous posts and called for political reform.

On the day of the parliamentary elections in late March 2023, voters in Almaty were reluctant to go to the polling stations, believing that voting in another staged election would do little to change the authoritarian system. Voter turnout in the Almaty region was as low as 29 per cent, but many independent observers still worked from early morning until late into the night, monitoring elections that were ultimately 'stolen' yet again. The workers in Zhanaozen have already informed the local authorities that they plan to organise peaceful rallies against the falsification of the elections.

Kazakhstan's protest culture has united some of the most divergent social groups: from Almaty's popular bloggers and new youth political movements to the workers of Zhanaozen, the farmers of Taldyqorgan and the feminists of Astana. 'Building a new Kazakhstan is in the hands of the citizens themselves, not some uncle [*dyadya*] in Ak Orda', declared an activist in Almaty as we sat in one of the city's most popular bars, in sight of a collection jar for the families of those who had suffered injuries or died during the January 2022 protests.[9] While we were there, people passed by and donated—the jar was almost full of paper bills, a rarity in this city, where people pay for almost everything digitally.

The opinion polls conducted one year after the Bloody January demonstrated that society was still divided over the main actors involved in the protests. To many respondents, it remains unclear whether the protests were part of a coup launched by rival political factions (37.9 per cent of respondents); a peaceful protest (28 per cent of respondents); or a violent terrorist attack (15 per cent). A quarter of the respondents found it difficult to say what had led to the protests.[10] Many were left with feelings of anxiety that violence could break out again and of empathy for the victims and their families.

State propaganda came up with its own narrative of the events, which it promoted in state-sponsored journalistic investigations and televised roundtables with Kazakh- and Russian-speaking experts, and by repeatedly emphasising the prosecutor general's conclusion about the organised nature of the violence. The state's journalistic investigations claimed that violent protestors had been intent on 'burning Almaty down', destroying local businesses, looting banks and causing mass disruption. While some of these acts did take place, most of the protestors were ordinary people and peaceful activists who were simply seeking to register their opposition to the Nazarbayev regime. Moreover, the state's focus on Almaty as the main site of the protests and violence ignored the mass, country-wide protests and sense of solidarity that had pushed people on to the streets. And though some investigations did take place into the allegations of police mistreatment, they were not open to the public and did not involve independent observers. In early January 2023, Berik Asylov, the Kazakh prosecutor general, concluded his investigation by stating that

> [i]t was an attempted coup. The investigation of the criminal case against the former heads of the National Security Committee … is top secret. The case contains information relating to foreign policy, counterintelligence, and surveillance. The materials are classified as they contain state secrets. Their disclosure may damage the interests of national security. The criminal case is now under consideration in court.[11]

Meanwhile, the ordinary Kazakhs forced to piece together disparate pieces of information from distrusted regime institutions—including the prosecutor general's office—were left in a state of trauma. Journalists who reported from the front line of the violent clashes often felt burnt out. Activists who tirelessly collected funds for the affected protestors, their families and for the many families who had been left without legal and financial support also found it difficult to cope with the sense of injustice. Communities shaken out of their previous stability were slowly rebuilding, often without any active support from the state. The Tokayev regime also had to find a way out of the crisis. State–society relations needed to be stabilised in the aftermath of the mass violence and Tokayev's own call 'to shoot without warning'.[12] This echoed one of my respondent's comments that in January 2022 Kazakhstan experienced its own 'war'—a war of the regime against its own people. Assel Tutumlu, one of Kazakhstan's leading political theorists, concluded that 'the old social contact created under Kazakhstan's first president, Nursultan Nazarbayev, is no longer satisfactory to the majority of Kazakhstan's people. The time has come to re-evaluate it, and the biggest question is if President Kassym-Jomart Tokayev is up to the challenge.'[13]

To remain in Qantar

While Tokayev was seeking to dampen the public's anger in the wake of the January protests, ordinary Kazakhs were searching for answers from a range of different outlets. The aftermath of Bloody January was thus characterised by widespread community-based work. People came together and organised for a social cause, for example collecting humanitarian aid for co-citizens or later, in February, for the civilians in Ukraine; different volunteer initiatives and spaces of community self-help started popping up online and throughout Kazakhstan. One of the activists concluded that if Kazakhstanis are able to organise themselves and fundraise for resources to help people, then there was little need for the corrupt regime: 'We can do everything by ourselves.'[14]

Local activists tirelessly investigated who had died or been subject to police brutality, eventually producing a list of the 'victims of Qantar'. Independent journalists and writers responded with more texts and reflections, giving space to the term 'to remain in January' or to 'remain in Qantar', which was not only about the dead but about all those who had suffered during these events or had lost loved ones. In one of his essays on the January protests, Daniyar Moldabekov, a famous Kazakh journalist and the author of a novel, *Qantar*, about the protests, wrote:

> On 6th of January [2022] like in all the following days, there was fog in the city. It smelled of gunpowder. On central streets [there were] burned down cars, broken shopwindows and very few people. The city [Almaty] was partially destroyed.
>
> But some destructions can be even scarier, like destructions in our souls. Now, when I finally get a chance to connect to the internet, I see the seeds of polarisation in our society: too often people who went out to the streets to protest against the status quo [authoritarianism] in our country are labelled as 'terrorists and marauders'. It is clear that there was looting. But for me it is also clear that [along with that] there was an attempt at a peaceful protest. I saw people with national flags singing the anthem who demanded [political] changes and not blood. If the morning of 6th of January smelled of gunpowder, then today [the air] smells of repressions. [We ought to] sustain our dignity in face of this danger.[15]

When the initial fears and anxieties faded away, Kazakhstanis were left with the lasting trauma of violence and the scenes of Russian troops first appearing in Kazakhstani cities and then, weeks later, in Ukraine. Russia's invasion of Ukraine shocked Kazakhstan at a time when it was still recovering from its own bloodshed. On 6 March 2022, Almaty dwellers organised a pro-Ukraine rally in Sary-Arka park on the outskirts of the city—the only place the local municipality would allow sanctioned rallies to take place. Despite the long distance, thousands of people took part; many were unable to find any space at the rally. People of all ethnicities brought Ukrainian flags and banners with writings in Kazakh, English and Russian, some with obscene language directed at Putin and many with anti-imperial slogans. Back in the 1990s, local authorities had moved the old Soviet monuments of Lenin and other party functionaries out of the city centre and to Sary-Arka park, and on the day of the pro-Ukrainian rally, yellow and blue balloons symbolising the Ukrainian flag were placed in the hands of an old monument of Lenin (see Figure 6.1).

As well as feeling great pain at the war in Ukraine, Kazakhstanis were also worried about potential Russian aggression against their own country, in the north of Kazakhstan. Since the January protests, many Kazakhstanis have felt that they are simply 'waiting for the war'. This feeling has played out differently for different people. During the initial days of Russia's full-scale invasion, some Almaty dwellers quizzed the mayor, Erbolat Dosayev, newly appointed by the president himself, about the conditions and availability of bomb shelters in case of a similar scenario unfolding in Kazakhstan. Others stocked up on supplies, having experienced the food shortages during the January protests that left many families with no provisions at a time when most of the supermarkets in the southern cities were closed. There were also those who openly supported Putin's decision

Figure 6.1. Lenin statue in Sary-Arka park, Almaty, pro-Ukraine march, 6 March 2022. Photo courtesy: RFE Europe and Petr Trosenko.

to invade Ukraine and blamed the 'collective West' for what they saw as lighting the fuse of a third world war. In Russophone circles in Russia, Kazakhstan and other countries that were once part of the Soviet Union, these people are sometimes branded as *vatniki*. Derived from the simple quilted jacket mass produced in the Soviet Union, the word now serves as a derogative term for those brainwashed by Russian propaganda. It also has the connotation of someone whose brain is made of cotton—*vata*, in Russian—a zombie who mindlessly consumes Russia's war propaganda. The term *vatnik* does not have a specific ethnic connotation. As my respondents told me, in Kazakhstan a *vatnik* can be anyone.

Vatnik is not a new term for the communities of the Russophone sphere. It first emerged in the Soviet Union, where it was used to identify someone who mindlessly towed the party line even in situations and contexts, such as the Soviet war in Afghanistan, where doing so was directly detrimental to their own life and livelihood. But the term really flourished after February 2022, when it was used to divide the pro-Putin supporters, the *vatniks*, from the supporters of Ukraine.

According to opinion polls by Central Asia Barometer, Kazakhs are still more likely to disapprove of Russia's war in Ukraine than people in other Central Asian states.[16] However, the availability of Russian television channels in Kazakhstan means that the divisions between *vatniks* and broader Kazakh society are likely to linger, with these divisions often being generational, as it is particularly people in their fifties, sixties and seventies who rely on television as their main source of news, while the members of the younger generation get their news from social media.[17] The contextual nature of these divisions and many people's reluctance to openly discuss their political support for Putin in the context of an interview or even a survey suggest that researchers need to combine different methods and triangulate their data.

In the aftermath of the Bloody January protests, many people felt unable to trust any source of information, whether regime-led, independent or Russian. Some of the pro-regime and Russian-led attempts to monopolise the discourse of Bloody January centre on the spike in the LPG prices as the main cause of the protests, reducing the events to a 'riot' by the poor—in some of the Russian sources, the protests have been described as 'a riot of *mambets*'.

According to the same discourse, the regime's decision not to increase LPG prices satisfied the protestors and solved their problems. However, in reality, in the aftermath of the January protests, there are still many structural problems, including the regime's failure to deal with widespread poverty, social inequality and the marginalisation of large groups of society, all of which remain a huge problem. The regime's and Russia's discourse also downplays the role that the violence played in forcing people off the public squares, including that of the violent, organised groups but also the regime and the army, whose participation in killing civilians remains a dark spot in the state's narrative of the protests, which it continues to describe as 'events' to avoid using the term 'protest'.

The concept of 'remaining in January' is thus a complex condition of living under a regime that killed, tortured and continues to imprison peaceful protestors while acquitting the real perpetrators. Remaining in January is also the feeling of not finding answers to questions that only an open and transparent investigation can produce, questions surrounding the illegitimate use of force and violence, of what scholars conceptualise as 'authoritarian resilience'.

How has the long post-January affected what it means to be a Kazakhstani? Like any trauma, it has had lasting consequences for people's identity and their relation to the state, their trust in state institutions and their sense of security. These factors and their influence on individual lives and contexts should not be dismissed. The process of enduring and living through the trauma and the search for a post-traumatic future has brought Kazakhstani citizens closer together through their demands for enhanced governance, a better legal system and greater protection of citizens' rights.

As I complete this manuscript in late 2024, another traumatic but also hopeful legal case is playing out in Kazakhstan—that of Saltanat Nukenova, which sent shock waves throughout Kazakhstani society. Yet even in such challenging times, people found ways to come together and collectively demand changes, including the adoption of a law criminalising domestic violence. The eventual adoption of the law on 11 April 2024 was preceded by an online campaign 'For

Saltanat' and for every victim of domestic violence in Kazakhstan. The campaign set in motion a tremendous process of civic engagement. Ordinary citizens sent senators more than 5,000 letters calling for the law be adopted. At the same time, dozens of people took part in rallies in different cities in Kazakhstan and abroad demanding justice for Saltanat, who became a symbol of the demand to criminalise domestic violence. Perhaps it was the post-January reality, the endless court hearings and the widespread sense of injustice that had pushed my compatriots to take matters into their own hands. When one petition failed, they started a new one; when one rally was sanctioned, they started an online campaign encouraging the Kazakhstani diaspora to take part in rallies across fourteen different cities in Europe and the United States.

The period since the January protests has been marked by unbearable feelings of injustice and insecurity, but it has also opened the way to a true sense of civicness, making the Kazakhstani identity stronger, more resilient and more meaningful. In the 'For Saltanat' campaign, that civicness acquired a full-fledged and fully embodied meaning for many of my compatriots—that as citizens we share a collective power to make changes in our own society and state. Our understanding of Kazakhstani-ness as a citizen-driven, empowering sense of belonging was thus strengthened in one of Kazakhstan's most challenging times.

AFTERWORD

DECOLONISING KAZAKHSTAN STARTS WITH DE-NAZARBAYEFICATION

The title of this afterword comes from Assem Zhapisheva, a famous Kazakh journalist and political activist of the Oyan, Qazaqstan social movement. We were filming a podcast together on decolonial thought in the postsoviet realm when Assem said that 'the real decolonisation of Kazakhstan starts with de-Nazarbayefication'.[1] After the podcast, we discussed this idea for a whole day. Nazarbayev was a true Soviet politician in everything he did, including a nation-building process that ultimately came to centre on Nazarbayev himself. But until we get rid of the Soviet legacy and its framework of ethnicity and overcome our inability to make the Kazakh language the state language, rather than something officials pay lip-service to in their speeches, we will continue to live in the world Nazarbayev and his regime were so keen to construct. Only when we are free of these things will be able to free ourselves from Nazarbayev's Kazakhstan (*Nazarbayevskii Kazakhstan*). As Tlostanova powerfully wrote in 2018:

> A merciless purging of the grand imperial myths, with their inhumane, unsightly colonial lining, and a decolonizing of collective and personal memory are the only remaining paths to any positive future that will not be stuck with imperial difference. It is hard to imagine this future today from the midst of the darkest imperial moment of its imminent death and its

stubborn clinging to life. Yet I do hope that even the phantom pains of the amputated empire will recede sooner than we imagine and a completely different geopolitics and corpo-politics of knowledge, being, and perception would (re)emerge. Multiple dependencies and intersections of oppression require a complex purification, in which the affective mechanisms are not less but more important than rational arguments.[2]

Letting go of the imperial myth of a hierarchy of ethnic groups, the brotherhood of nations and the friendship of peoples that technically promoted equality but was interwoven with racism, slurs, discrimination and inequality will be a challenging process, yet it can also be a hopeful one. Jettisoning old systems and beliefs, forgetting the Nazarbayevite slogans that soothed postsoviet anxieties and then became meaningless, useless pamphlets that polluted Kazakhstani cities will be another great challenge.[3] Yet the solidarity forged in Bloody January and its legacy of civicness and community-led initiatives offer a hopeful and radical re-imagination of a future, one where there is no post- or after-Nazarbayev.

One of the initial steps in uprooting and decolonising Kazakhstan's recent history will involve looking critically into what the regime achieved in dealing with what it viewed as the 'national question' and to give more agency to the ordinary citizens who contributed tirelessly to the peaceful 'multi-ethnic' state but whose efforts were negated by Nazarbayev's cult of personality.

In his speeches, Nazarbayev claimed to be the main guarantor of the country's stability and interethnic harmony. Many of the state-sanctioned secret opinion polls and focus groups, to which I have had access, propagated the idea that he had mass support among so-called ethnic minorities precisely because of his focus on maintaining interethnic stability.[4] The reports repeatedly mention his 'wise' approach to Kazakhstan's ethnic diversity and potential ethnic conflicts. And in every report I analysed, there was an underlying assumption that Kazakhstan was on the brink of an interethnic conflict, most probably between Russians and Kazakhs, and that Nazarbayev was the only person able to stop that conflict from happening.

AFTERWORD

But the myth that Nazarbayev was the guarantor of the country's interethnic stability came crashing down in February 2020, when Kazakhstan witnessed the worst mass ethnic violence in its history. Groups of ethnic Dungans and ethnic Kazakhs clashed in the transborder area most commentators call Kordai, with the violence then spilling over into several villages. The conflict, which began as a brawl, led to 'mobilised' and 'organised' violence against Dungan communities, leaving '11 people dead, 192 injured (including 19 police officers), and the mass exodus of some 24,000 Dungan fleeing into neighbouring Kyrgyzstan'.[5]

The stability many associated with Nazarbayev had given way to a 'pogrom', an extremely rare occurrence in Kazakhstan's history. Although Tokayev was the president at the time of the tragedy, Nazarbayev was the de facto leader of the country—he was the chairman of the country's Security Council and the self-proclaimed leader of the nation, *elbasy*, which gave him wide-ranging political powers. Everything that followed demonstrated how rotten the system was and how law enforcement and associated institutions wanted to depict the situation in a way that would be favourable to Nazarbayev's 'wise' policies in dealing with the interethnic situation. As Assel Tutumlu and Zulfiya Imyarova state:

> [T]here are testimonies of KNB [state security forces] instructing local people, both Dungan and Kazakh communities what to say during their meeting with the President of Kazakhstan, Mr. Tokayev (Interviews with Dungan community, 2021). As a result of these methods, actors who could have had a chance of intervening and protecting an ethnic minority, such as Tokayev and his Administration or central government officials and law enforcement representatives were largely blind to the informal pressure and fake confessions. Tokayev also offered two different messages when meeting with the Dungan community vis-à-vis the Kazakh community. First, the President met with the Dungans and said that they should draw the lessons from what happened and recommended them to resettle. A Dungan elder was forced to apologize for the tragedy in public by security forces. Then the President went to Karakemer where he had

dinner with Kazakhs and visited a Kazakh school with presents. Nationalist press used hate speech acts and blamed Dungans for disrespecting and even challenging Kazakh culture and traditions (Taizhan 2020), accusing Dungans for dodging the military draft and proposing to deport them back to China.[6]

The word 'pogrom' entered the Kazakhstani public lexicon and was no longer just a term used for historically or geographically distant events.[7] But could an authoritarian regime build an effective structure for dealing with potential interethnic conflicts when it borrowed so heavily from the failed Soviet tactics of the 1980s and 1990s? And could the old slogan of 'peoples' friendship' work when everyday life in the central cities of the former Soviet empire was incredibly discriminatory? Nazarbayev could not overcome his own sovietness. Old habits die hard, and he allowed the remnants of the old system to lumber on, even though it was always clear that it could fall to pieces at any point. The Kordai pogrom and many other localised conflicts broke apart this system's cracks.

Amid growing inequality, the state erected banners that screamed at us 'We live in a country of interethnic peace and stability!' These banners multiplied faster than the weekly pro-regime newspapers that were trying to convince us that everything was great and stable in Nazarbayev's Kazakhstan. Nazarbayev's portraits, his body always dressed in dark suits, became the symbol of this self-deceiving mantra of 'peace and stability'. Like many Soviet leaders before him, he appeared surrounded by children in different ethnic-national costumes or in the company of multi-ethnic Olympic champions, some of them Dungans, Russians, Koreans and Kazakhs, all of them proclaiming the same message of regime-sanctioned interethnic happiness.

Joseph Stalin famously defined the nation as a 'historically evolved stable community of language, territory, economic life, and psychological makeup manifested in a community of culture'.[8] This formula provided a simple way to standardise and construct communities. For politicians like Nazarbayev, who lacked formulas of their own, Stalinist terms for nationhood served as a blueprint to keep the disparate ethnic groups living in peace and supposedly progressing towards a specific point in the future where they would achieve a new form of nationhood. The problem for Nazarbayev was that people ultimately created this new form of nationhood without and often away from him and his regime.

Kazakhstani political observers often claim that ours is a society of parallel worlds. These parallel worlds are not just divided by class or who lives in proximity to the big cities or in the 'provinces'. Most commentators who use this concept mainly distinguish these worlds along sociolinguistic lines, which is also a very Sovietised and often simplistic way to understand Kazakh society. In a country where over 60 per cent of secondary education is in Kazakh,[9] there will inevitably be a shift to a more Kazakhophone or mixed linguistic reality where all three languages, Russian, Kazakh and English, will occupy somewhat equal positioning.

The generation of post-Nazarbayev youth who want to communicate in the new Kazakh—not the stigmatised language of the 'provinces' but the cool new language of upbeat Qazaq music, Qazaq rap and Qazaq new wave cinema—have no problem with linguistic switching. The more I interview younger people in Kazakhstan, the more my data are in Qazaq and English, as well as in Russian. And while there are limitations to the applicability of the 'parallel communities' paradigm to Kazakhstan, it is clearly the case that Nazarbayev cultivated and targeted different audiences over the thirty years of his rule, the first and most influential of which was the audience of his loyalists, especially the network of ageing bureaucrats and members of the Nazarbayev party, which once even featured part of his name—Nur-Otan. (The party's name was hastily changed to Amanat after the January 2022 protests.) But for the ageing bureaucrats, being loyal to Nazarbayev was perhaps the only thing they knew. So, if there are parallel communities or realities in Kazakhstan, then these are the realities of the regime elites who are deaf and blind to the country's ordinary citizens and their protests. Thus, in all my recent writing, I propose interpreting the authoritarian tendencies of Kazakhstan through the lens of regime–society relations.[10]

On 1 January 2022, in a less well-known episode of the Bloody January protests, a group of eco- and decolonial activists and artists gathered in front of the mayor's office in the old Communist Party building in Almaty to protest against the drainage of Astana's Taldykol lakes. The Taldykol lakes have existed on the territory of present-day Astana for centuries, long preceding Nazarbayev and his vision of a city that would one day, albeit very briefly, bear his name. But given the lack of local housing, an abrupt decision was made to drain the lakes and build new—and expensive—real estate projects in their place. The protestors started gathering in 2020 and soon formed a decolonial ecological movement called SOS Taldykol.

The movement's activities included public forums with ecologists, well-known architects and city planners, as well as scientists, experts and local residents, all of whom detailed why the drainage was detrimental to the local environment. Behind the scenes, the movement met online and connected people across many different locations in Kazakhstan and abroad (I connected from England) to discuss further actions as part of a broader intellectual, cultural and activist agenda. The pink flamingos that nest on the Taldykol lakes during the summer became one of the movement's symbols. Members of the movement managed to protest, organise trash-picking marathons, picnics and decolonial readings on the lakes every month for two years. On 1 January 2022, a group of SOS Taldykol activists brought their usual pink flamingo inflatable rings to the Almaty mayor's office and started dancing and singing the 'flamingo dance' to protest the drainage that was then in full swing. It was one of the many protests outside Astana that aimed to raise awareness of the issue across the country and connect the Almaty activists to their friends and fellow activists in Astana. All the 'flamingos' in Almaty were young women, most of them art activists and active voices in Kazakhstan's decolonial movement, which aims to critically rethink the imperial Soviet past and its legacies. As soon as they started singing, a man without a uniform approached them out of nowhere and asked them to leave.

Tlostanova, a leading voice on decoloniality in the Soviet context, asks us 'What is the afterlife of the coloniality?', that is, what remains of colonial and hierarchical relations when the empire disappears? And this is why the central square in Almaty is of such importance to me. Our coloniality is embedded in the unprecedented violence

AFTERWORD

the regime used against its citizens and sought to normalise; it is the afterlife of the dead sovietness that continues to live on in the rules and norms that Nazarbayev established and nurtured throughout his rule. It also lives on in his desire to portray himself as the father of the nation, the leader or, in Soviet terms, the *vojd'*, with authoritarian institutions and puppet bureaucrats so loyal to him that it took them a long time to adapt to the new realities in the cold post-January context when Nazarbayev's cult of personality had collapsed and the myth of his popularity had become apparent to everyone, including Nazarbayev himself.

Memes depicting Nazarbayev tearing up during his last Nur-Otan party summit in 2019 where he retired from the presidency became a popular way to highlight the collapse in his popular support. A satirical Instagram account '@shalmustbegone'—*shal* is a rude term for 'old man' and is part of the popular protest slogan 'Shal, Ket!' set against Nazarbayev and now Tokayev, which translates from Kazakh as 'down with the old man!'—has become an online sensation. The @shalmustbegone account shares reels in the form of a Brazilian soap opera ridiculing his 'family'—Nazarbayev's closest circle[11]— as well as memes about how tired people are of Nazarbayev's and Tokayev's policies.

The Nazarbayev regime was Soviet to its core, and it is no wonder that Nazarbayev concentrated all his might on creating a need to search for our common national identity, an identity that would keep society together and prevent neighbours of different ethnic backgrounds attacking one another. In short, Nazarbayev continued to think like the Soviets, and this informed his policy of 'divide and rule' towards Kazakhstan's vast multi-ethnic society. He had little to no interest in building a post-postsoviet identity that would unite us all. He believed we needed to 'grow our consciousness'—whatever that meant—if we were to become a united nation.

This constant searching also explains the anxieties shared by some of the mid-level policymakers who quizzed me about the possibility of writing up what they described as a 'solid' national identity 'project'. When I saw large numbers of policymakers flooding the Kazakh embassy in London in the 2010s, I started to wonder whether there was a private competition to design a new 'state programme' for yet another national identity project (similar to 'Kazakhstan-2030' or the later Mangilik El state programme). One such policymaker who had come to the UK for a professional 'internship' (*stazhirovka*) under a Bolashak state scholarship even asked me if I could draft a twenty-page document stating that there was no longer any need to look for a national identity. It sounded like something from the Russian writer Viktor Pelevin's novel *Generation 'P'* (1999), where a wealthy Russian businessman asks the novel's protagonist, a skilled copywriter, to draft a project setting out how great postsoviet Russia is. I politely declined the offer but engaged him in a more interesting discussion about why such a project was still needed. The policymaker shared his frustration about the Nazarbayevite 'search' for a national identity. The constant search for a sense of national belonging had made him yearn for some sort of ideological stability. Some years later, 'Rukhani Zhangyru' was announced, a state programme declaring that Kazakhstan had now entered a new golden age. I figured someone else must have been eager to write a twenty-page 'project' for it.

The deeper question haunting my co-nationals as I finalise this manuscript is what to do in the post-Nazarbayev era now that the regime has changed its main protagonists but continues to act in accordance with the same old script—repress–promise–never deliver–repress again. The fall of Nazarbayev's personalist regime only signifies that without major changes, there will be no further prospects for democratisation and good governance. Any hopes people may have had in the new generation of technocrats, who had been educated abroad and whose formative years were not those of the Soviet period, came crashing down in the wake of widespread allegations of corruption.[12]

At the end of 2023, two news stories rocked Kazakhstan yet again. The first was the allegation that Olzhas Khudaibergenov, a former economic advisor to the president, had harassed and abused his ex-wife, Moldir Kabylova. The second was the death of thirty-one-year-old Saltanat Nukenova, the wife of former economy minister Kuandyk Bishimbayev. Bishimbayev was arrested in connection with her death on 9 November 2023 and tried in a court in Astana in the spring of 2024. Earlier, in March 2018, he had been found guilty of receiving bribes and sentenced to ten years in prison and a lifetime prohibition on the right to hold leadership positions in the public sector. His name and the new allegation, the murder of his wife, shocked Kazakhstan. The Bishimbayev trial started in March 2024 and attracted an unprecedented number of online viewers when it was broadcast on YouTube and in Russian— the language Bishimbayev and his defence team preferred. In May 2024, Bishimbayev was found guilty of the murder and sentenced to twenty-four years in prison.[13] The court hearings and investigations into Nukenova's horrific and violent death shocked the public well beyond Kazakhstan, inviting new transnational dialogues about the pandemic of gendered violence and political elites who seemed to believe they could get away with murder.

But even in this traumatic picture, there is a glimmer of hope. Kazakhstani society united in the wake of Nukenova's death— reminded of countless other deaths, Kazakhs demanded, petitioned, protested for the implementation of a law against domestic violence, a law that was ultimately adopted by the Kazakh parliament in April 2024.

For years, Kazakhstani civil society mobilised outside the frames of the authoritarian regime. For years, activists, artists, writers and independent journalists came together to counter the dictatorship that was seeking to frame their lives and identities. The power of Kazakhstani society lies in its resilience and ability to organise, to nurture new ideas and new ways of resisting. The Kazakh-language speaking clubs that mushroomed across the country and became especially visible after 24 February 2022 and the defiant, decades-long campaigns to criminalise domestic violence that only grew stronger after Nukenova's horrific death are only some of the examples of Kazakhstani resilience that come to mind. The task of re-making Nazarbayev's regime and taking control of Kazakhstan's national identity is in the hands of these tireless civil society activists, who often pose the question of life after Nazarbayev not in terms of the postsoviet or post-Nazarbayev era but in terms of decolonising and de-Nazarbayefication.

Kazakh political artists have opened up a space to discuss these issues through their depictions of the regime's violence during the protests of January 2022. In a large room in the Dom 36 artistic space, Saule Suleimenova painted an entire wall in red to represent the main square in Almaty (see Figure 7.1), still symbolically 'soaked in blood', inviting her audience to meditate and converse about the trauma of the protests. Contemporary poet Samrat—known by the name of his band, Samrattama—responded with his fierce lyrics and music: 'What does your president sell? Heroin or the state?' (*Chto prodayet tvoi president? Geroin ili gosudarstvo? Geroin ili gosudarstvo*).[14] Suinbike Suleimenova ridicules state programmes and the 'sweet promises' of the dictatorship in her installation 'Colonise Me Now'—'good roads, come and colonise me now; fair and open elections, come and colonise me now'. Askhat Akhmediyarov opened his solo exhibition in uptown Almaty's fancy Aspan Gallery with overturned kazans—traditional cauldrons—hanging on threads. No one could pass through this room without causing these overturned objects to bump into each other, making a bell-like sound. Kazakhs traditionally overturn their kazans in times of great sorrow, such as when singing a commemorative song for the dead, *zhoktau*, which tears everyone's hearts. In his 2022 exhibition, Akhmediyarov was aiming to commemorate Qantar's victims by singing *zhoktau* through the overturned kazans (see Figure 7.2). In the gallery's other halls, Akhmediyarov exhibited a masterful series of portraits—of ordinary protestors and of armed riot police, all of their faces and body parts burnt on the textile base of the painting, with gunpowder used to convey the smell of the bullets, the smell of the regime-sanctioned violence. Not a single victim would be forgotten, Akhmediyarov was seeking to reassure the exhibition's visitors.

Through the gunpowder and portraits of Nazarbayev designed to resemble police-issued portraits based on witness descriptions, as well as the explosive and critical lyrics of the latest poets, civil society is searching for forms and language to move beyond Nazarbayev, not just to leave him behind but to liberate society from the trauma of his rule. This is perhaps why the term 'decolonising' has a more localised meaning in Kazakhstan. For many of my respondents in Kazakhstan's decolonial movement, the term is free of negative connotations of abuse or accusations and is instead a more positive term for liberating people from old hierarchies and traumas. Moving beyond Nazarbayev

AFTERWORD

Figure 7.1. Saule Suleimenova's *Qandy Qantar* (Bloody January) exhibit. Author's photo. Location: Dom 36, Almaty, July 2022.

also means liberating society of the labels, categories and norms established by this very Sovietised dictator; it is about searching for answers in historically traumatic events like December 1986 and openly addressing them, including Nazarbayev's role in ending the peaceful protest back then, in 2011 and again from 2019 to January 2022. To move beyond Nazarbayev is to form a distinct form of civicness, not just a form of civic nationalism that would again place the more complex sense of Kazakhstani-ness into a Procrustean bed of measurements when belonging cannot be measured statistically. To understand what it means to be Kazakhstani is to try to see the world and how people experience it through their eyes and their meaning-making processes; is to be empathetic and attentive to their narratives.

Writing a book on a question that torments my generation inevitably invites some self-reflection. Was I influenced by the central question of this book: What does it mean to be Kazakhstani? when I was growing up? Absolutely. This question was implicitly embedded in my everyday surroundings on my way to school and ran through

Figure 7.2. Askhat Akhmediyarov (right) with his *Qandy Qantar* installation. Kazakh decolonial poet Anuar Dyussenbinov (left) tries to record the sound that kazans make. Courtesy: author's photo. Location: Aspan Gallery, Almaty, July 2022.

the conversations at the dinner table. Most of my fellow Kazakhstanis had a similar experience of the country's independence period, and only more recently have some of us found a way to embed this question in the localised discussions on our decolonisation.

In our first-ever interview, famous Kazakh contemporary artist and public figure Almagul Menlibayeva told me that for her the end of the Soviet era was a very clear-cut affair. The old system collapsed, and she felt that she and the country then became independent. For many of my other respondents, the ending of one time and the passage to a different era of independence felt slightly different. I knew many people of my parents' generation who found it emotionally difficult to get rid of their Soviet passports. Most of them could not explain the feeling of needing to hold on to this last bit of sovietness. So, they kept the old red passports tucked inside their bedside cabinets together with their most important objects. Many of their compatriots did the same.

I never had a Soviet passport; nor do I have a distinct, personal understanding of what it felt like to live in Soviet times. I was too young when the country my grandparents and parents grew up in disappeared. Until the age of about sixteen, I also lacked a distinct political association with the new Kazakhstan. My national ID card—*udostoverenie lichnosti* in Russian or *kualik* in Kazakh—was issued on the wave of my uncle's campaign to get documents for all the 'youngsters' of the family as a way to mark our passage into adulthood. My uncle, a very charismatic man, had a lot of friends in the local bureaucratic agency that issued state documents and got me and my cousins our own appointments. This bureaucratic agency was perhaps the closest that ordinary people would come to their state.

At the time, the office that issued ID cards was located in a small room adjacent to the local police office,[15] with old Soviet furniture, a big mirror on the wall and a quickly moving queue. After several snaps of the camera, the clerk was meant to ask for basic information to fill in the blanks on the form—full name, date and place of birth, nationality. Since my uncle knew the people in the office, I was not asked any of these questions, and my parents filled all the blanks in for me. But until recently, any document would only be issued after an applicant had been asked whether they wanted to state their nationality. I always opted to keep mine blank, though the domestic ID (*udostoverenie lichnosti*) still required it. Yet, although the female clerk did not even ask me my nationality, my ID card stated that I was 'Kazakh'. Deep down inside, I thought that my last name, a very popular Kazakh name even before the stardom of the popular singer Dimash Kudaibergen, pre-empted this decision. The state somehow decided my ethnicity for me, continuing the old Soviet tradition of assigning children of multi-ethnic families the ethnicity of their father.

Ethnicity or language did not decide my everyday choices or bother me until I turned eighteen. Growing up, I travelled across different multi-lingual spaces—from my own home in the futuristic and unfinished new housing district where the Soviets had aimed to showcase the new 'Soviet dream', to my newly opened Kazakh-language school to my grandma's multicultural neighbourhood. As a bilingual child born to an ethnically mixed family, moving from one language to another felt incredibly natural to me, and for a very long time I found it hard to understand why it was difficult for others. Meanwhile, everything around me was rapidly changing—the streets where we walked each day quickly changed names, though many continue to call them by their old, Soviet names; the rusty-coloured currency with a bald Lenin swiftly changed to the colourful tenge with other, more familiar faces on them (among them Abai, whose poems I had failed to learn by heart in the first or second grade). Most importantly, the languages I was speaking with ease became highly politicised over the short period of the 1990s and remained a hot topic throughout my whole life.

Only when I graduated from school, passed my exams and started studying at the elite university in Almaty, where most of the students originated from different parts of my own country, and only there, in the fancy elevator of the former Soviet party school,[16] was I first confronted about my *true identity* when someone asked me if I was Kazakh or not. I responded by asking them what they meant. Identity is a contextual, ever-changing and hard-to-define concept, and I wondered whether there even is such a thing as a 'true identity'.

'Why did ethnicity matter?', I kept asking myself. I had no clear answers to these complex questions. My grandma spoke to me in

AFTERWORD

a dialect of what seemed like a combination of many Central Asian languages—a gift that kept on giving, enabling me to communicate with people anywhere, from the bazaar in Urumqi to a plaza in Samarkand. It was not Russian that connected me to all these different places; it was the language of my grandmother and the music she listened to while shedding tears (especially if it was in Uyghur or Uzbek, as I found out later). My family was multi-ethnic: sometimes we ate food with chopsticks not because it was fancy but because some of our extended family members ate with chopsticks their whole lives; sometimes we ate food by hand, and no one questioned why we ate by hand, chopsticks or with the Russian wooden spoon[17] that my grandma had in her kitchen. They say ethnicity starts with family and household traditions. My family tradition was not to discuss anyone's ethnicity and collectively sing songs in all the many languages we knew at our weekly family dinners.

In the places I grew up, ethnic identity was mostly taken for granted and never questioned. But if someone insisted, it was guessed from the last name, and people from mixed or 'metis' families (often mixed Russian and Kazakh, Korean and Russian, Korean and Kazakh, Kazakh and Tatar, Tatar and Dungan, or a combination of however many ethnic groups in one family) were cherished rather than singled out. Being *metis* was a sign of prestige and physical attractiveness—known colloquially as 'mixed blood'. But someone who was *metis* was rarely asked questions about their true identity. I grew up in an ethnically mixed household where we had to greet every other extended family member in a different language—Kazakh, Tatar, Uzbek or Uyghur, with Russian being the universal language connecting us all. I grew up with a highly contextual and flexible identity, in a space where shifting between languages was not a problem. So, my first real encounter with my state—apart from the bureau issuing IDs—was on my first day at the university, and this thought about identity and ethnicity, and categories of being someone attached to your skin, appearances, attitudes, values and language, did not leave me for years.

In this new environment of the university, where many of the students were from faraway places on the map of my homeland, I quickly learnt that questions of origin related not only to the cities where one came from and that questions of identity were always about ethnicity. *Kto ty po natsii?* or 'what's your nationality?' was a question someone could slip in as a joke during the small talk before class or while flirting at the school dance. For some, ethnicity served as a currency that helped them form friendship groups, but many chose their friends beyond ethnicity, often choosing partners for group projects from among the people with the highest GPA. So, grades were harder currency than ethnicity. But this ethnic currency played an important role in claiming a status in the local hierarchy of power. In the project of de-Nazarbayefication, we will all be faced with the question of how to proceed away from this division along ethnic lines and to move forward to a more inclusive and non-ethnic context. Perhaps giving up codified ethnic divisions is one way for Kazakhstani society and the state to finally get rid of its Nazarbayevite and Sovietised practices and terms.

Defining what it means to be Kazakhstani involves navigating contentious politics and social debates on the ground, as well as the complex web of imposed categories that contrast with lived experiences and the structures of formal and informal hierarchies, pressures and contextual meanings. This book is about these complexities and categories that Kazakhstani society has lived with for the past thirty years. Many of these categories were embedded historically in this land of 'more than 140 ethnic groups', and many were constructed during the thirty years of Nazarbayev's rule, from 1989 to 2019. I believe that time itself is an important actor in all these debates and processes. My attempt here is to expand and explain this snapshot of the 'independence' and post-independence years in a more sociological and *home*-based analysis. But in no way do I intend to make this perplexing complexity simple or straightforward. 'Kazakhstani' remains abundant, complex and diverse, even more so in the context of Russia's colonial war on Ukraine and ordinary Kazakhs' anxieties at the possibility of Russian troops crossing over our borders.

In this book, I continue the path of conceptualising the push-and-pull relationship between the state and ordinary citizens. In my work on postsoviet 'nationalising' regimes—states driven by a need to control and an obsession with nationalism—I wrote that

AFTERWORD

'the problem with nationalising regimes is that they produce a set of guiding and structural frameworks for political elites but not for the wider citizenry and their perceptions and imaginations of the nation and state'.[18] It is the perplexing problem of nationalising regimes that they tend to be encapsulated in their own visions of how to build states and nations. And when they think of ordinary citizens in these processes, they view them as 'masses' to whom categories of identifications can and must be prescribed. The 'state' in my data was often discussed from the position of powerful personalities— *vlast'* in Russian or, simply put, power. Elites themselves viewed the state as a living organism—a 'young republic' that requires taming and subjecting to the tight control of regime elites, as Nazarbayev wrote in one of his books:

> The young republic had to define the precise contours of statehood. Fully aware of the danger of losing time and further aggravating the crisis, presidential power enabled us to focus on resolving pressing problems and conducting the most urgent reforms as swiftly as possible instead of being sidetracked by protracted discussions and quests for compromises and half-measures.[19]

In this book, I wanted to take a different turn and speak of Kazakhstan's complex history through the words and narratives of ordinary citizens, ordinary Kazakhstanis, and tell the multiple stories of how they imagine and re-imagine themselves and the people around them, how they participate in this process of nation-building. I also wanted to highlight how their vision and their collective resilience was able to build true interethnic peace in the country and how the fruits of it belong to them, not Nazarbayev and his 'wise' policies. To centre the narrative on people and to focus on how they see and make sense of the world through languages—orusskii, Qazaq or Kishi Qazaq, through the contexts of everyday life and through their own values and civicness. I hope that the multiplicity, the pluriversality of these voices, something that truly defines Kazakhstaniness, wins over the overpowering narrative of Sovietised ethnicisation and the Nazarbayevite ambiguity of groupness. To be Kazakhstani is to accept the polyphonic nature of our multiversal identity and of the boundless knowledges and welcome embrace of our steppe.

NOTES

PREFACE

1. I am using the wider Eurasia concept, borrowing from ongoing discussions with decolonial activists and writers from non-Russian countries, such as those in Central Asia and the Baltic states. In using this term, I am aware that, within Russia itself, it has been hijacked by the likes of the neo-fascist and imperialist Aleksandr Dugin, who conceives of Eurasianism as an ideology in which Russia has a special imperial role to play in world affairs.
2. This concept has a long and tormented history connected to Alexander Solzhenitsyn's racist 1990 essay in which he called for Russia to annex Kazakhstan's northern territories and used the term 'underbelly' to define the whole region.
3. I have dedicated a lot of work to discussing why this monopoly over nation-building is persistent in Kazakhstan and other states that once formed part of the Soviet Union. More on that discussion can be found in my book *Toward Nationalizing Regimes* (see Kudaibergenova 2020).
4. Along with my Ukrainian friends and colleagues, I consider Russia's invasion to have started in March 2014 with the annexation of Crimea and then the long invasion of Eastern Ukraine. The dominant discourse often separates the 'full-scale invasion' of February 2022 from the start of the war in 2014.
5. Vova is short for Vladimir.
6. I also find the term 'post-Soviet' problematic when applied to the region because it does not take into account the experiences of the political communities that never managed to gain independence from

the Soviet Union or from Russia. To my colleagues in the North Asian regions of Siberia and non-Russian republics of Tuva and Buryatia, for example, 'postsoviet' means something completely different from what it means to the people of Uzbekistan or Kazakhstan or does not mean anything at all.
7. Tlostanova 2018, p. 120.
8. This was a very challenging fieldwork encounter for me to write out. The whole of Chapter 4 was also challenging to write, as it deals with difficult issues of discrimination and colonial hierarchisation.
9. This discussion session was part of a summer school on postsovietness that I co-organised with Bart de Brie at Tselinniy, the Centre for Contemporary Culture (Almaty), with the participation of three fantastic guests from Ukraine—Evheniia Moliar, Nikolay Karabinovych and Nikita Kadan (on Zoom). I am grateful to all the participants for their views, which gave me a lot of food for thought while writing this manuscript.
10. Among the exiled people with Russian passports who left Russia after the war and found themselves in Kazakhstan, Georgia, Armenia, Kyrgyzstan and Uzbekistan were many ethnic Russians but also members of other ethnicities. Many went to the Central Asian and Caucasian countries because they provided longer visa-free regimes. There were many reasons why these Russian citizens were in exile—some wanted to escape the September 2022 mobilisation, while others were opposed to the war and did not want to work in the country that had 'started the war', as they often told me. A minority of Russian relocants were former citizens of Kazakhstan or had some ties to Kazakhstan, such as extended family or parents who used to live in Kazakhstan before 1991 or 1995 when mass out-migration of Kazakhstani Russians took place (see Peyrouse 2007). I write more about these stories in Chapter 3.
11. 'Jeong' is a Korean concept my friend and colleague Olga Mun theorised in her writing. To *jeong* is to get through challenging tasks together.

INTRODUCTION

1. Brubaker 1998, p. 273.
2. See Suny 1993; Brubaker 1994; Esenova 1996, 2002; Bremmer and Taras 1996; Laitin 1998; Smith 1998; Schatz 2000; Masanov 2002; Surucu 2002; Dave 2007; Edgar 2007, 2019, 2022; Peyrouse 2007; Silova et al. 2014; Chinn and Kaiser 2019; Senggirbay 2019.

3. See Edgar 2022.
4. See Brubaker 1994, 2014; Laitin 1998; Zardykhan 2004; Peyrouse 2007; Dave 2007; Spehr and Kassenova 2012; Laruelle 2014, 2019.
5. See Suny 1993, 1999, 2001; Brubaker 1994, 2014; Tishkov 1996; Laruelle 2014, 2019, 2021.
6. See Nazpary 2002; Yessenova 2003.
7. Kazakh anthropologist Saulesh Yessenova's brilliant ethnography of rural–urban migration and work on the bazaar in 1990s Almaty remains one of the best examples of that era. See Yessenova 2009.
8. This remains a popular snack in Kazakhstan and Russia.
9. The term *mizernaia pensiya* for miniscule pension continues to feature in discussions of the postsocalist hardships in Kazakhstan and other postsocialist countries.
10. The school was understanding of the situation and allowed her to trade for a few months. But she was ultimately unable to sustain her business (she often told us how ashamed she felt because she was a teacher, not a cook) and eventually left the school.
11. The battle over the state language and the language law started as early as 1989. In the end, a consensus was reached whereby Kazakh would become the state language and Russian would be the language of 'interethnic communication' (see Fierman 1998). All state documents, including the constitution, are still printed and available in both languages, but the political elites slowly acquired a taste for speaking in Kazakh in their speeches. Very few of the highest-ranking politicians in Kazakhstan are non-ethnic Kazakhs, but many are Russophone Kazakhs—ethnic Kazakhs who do not speak their native language fluently and mainly communicate in Russian.
12. See Cummings 2002; Murphy 2006; Dave 2007; Mesquita 2016; Tutumlu 2019.
13. See Nazarbayev 1993, for example.
14. Also discussed by my brilliant colleagues in Tutumlu and Imyarova 2021.
15. In the early 1990s, these texts were met with enthusiasm because Nazarbayev was popular up until the reforms of 1993–4, when the regime became more authoritarian with the change of the constitution (1993) and the creation of a 'pocket parliament' made up of MPs extremely loyal to the president. It was later discovered that Nazarbayev had a team of skilled speech writers and ideologues (among them a talented sociologist Marat Tazhin, who probably introduced Nazarbayev to the concept of *anomie*).
16. I wrote about this dictatorial obsession with 'speaking to the people'

in my article, 'Compartmentalized Ideology', which discusses Nazarbayev's speeches from 1989 to 2016 (see Kudaibergenova 2019).

17. The incredibly polished academic language of the pamphlet clearly differentiates it from all the previous 'Communist-style' writings and speeches Nazarbayev authored from the mid-1980s to 1993. Most of his public texts were shadow written by a group of young technocratic elites, some of whom had studied sociology in the UK, such as Tazhin.
18. Nazarbayev 1993, p. 6.
19. See Jon Ungoed-Thomas, 'How the Kazakh Elite Put Its Wealth into UK Property', *The Observer*, 8 January 2022, https://www.theguardian.com/world/2022/jan/08/how-the-kazakh-elite-put-its-wealth-into-uk-property
20. This is perhaps one of the most vivid memories shared among the post-independence generation of Kazakhstanis. Due to the constant power outages and lack of basic amenities like heating, gas and water in 1993–6, people were forced to cook outside on open fires. I know of many stories of extended families who collected food products and cooked together to save money or provide for relatives who could not make ends meet; or stories of people who hunted for meat, went fishing in local rivers and lakes to put food on the table. My own relatives remember this period of the 'shock economy' in Kazakhstan as one of their worst nightmares. Some of my other interlocutors who shared similar memories growing up were surprised when I told them I had many happy memories of this period, in which I spent a lot of time with my extended family and learned to make handmade candles with my cousins and my grandma, who made it into a game for the kids.
21. This term often came up in discussions with political elites in Kazakhstan and elsewhere in the postsoviet states, who contrasted themselves with the 'ordinary folk' who had little say in the nation-bulding process (see Kudaibergenova 2020). I find this distinction problematic, as it suggests that ordinary people have no say in big political decisions. I strongly disagree with this stance, and in this book, I discuss how the ordinary people take an active role in shaping and navigating everyday identities and directly influencing the state identity they want to establish.
22. Hale and Onuch 2022.
23. See Dave 2007; Tutumlu and Imyarova 2021.
24. In my forthcoming work and in my ethnographies of dictatorial politics, I write extensively on what this other form of political culture

represents and how and why it remains meaningful to people inside and outside the dictator's inner circle. I detail how people manage to separate a dictator's frame from their own everyday practices and feelings of patriotism or belonging to the state.

25. See Brubaker 1999, pp. 55–71.
26. Brubaker 2004, p. 134.
27. For years, schoolchildren were taught a course called 'Self-Knowledge' (*samopoznanie* in Russian or *Ozin-ozi tanu* in Kazakh). The course was a mixture of ethics and morals. The course's author was Sara Nazarbayeva—President Nazarbayev's first wife (it was widely rumoured that the two were estranged, which Nazarbayev himself confirmed in his 2024 memoir by stating that he was in a civil marriage with another woman) who was active in the charity and education sector in the 1990s. The course was implemented in 184 schools in 2001 and made mandatory in primary schools in 2010; it has since been abandoned and taken out of the curricula. It is still unclear why such a course was introduced or what will be done to the thousands of textbooks and other teaching materials.
28. Kudaibergenova 2020, p. 9.
29. See Tutumlu and Imyarova 2021, p. 400.
30. In their 2018 analysis of online and state media from 2004 to 2015, as well as interviews with ordinary Kazakhstani citizens, Rees and Burkhanov remark that there was 'no consistent interpretation or popular understanding of these policies' or how they would affect people's daily lives (Rees and Burkhanov 2018, p. 441). I take this idea further to demonstrate how this everyday politics of identity matters in contesting what Kazakhstani means.
31. I have previously written about how the regime in Kazakhstan was able to frame the political opposition and nationalist groups and channel their discontent (Kudaibergenova 2016a); how the same regime used discourses of postcolonialism to frame political competition and their own agenda within and outside Kazakhstan (Kudaibergenova 2016b); and on the strategies involved in operating a personalistic nationalising regime in the non-democratic context of Kazakhstan compared to more democratic Latvia (Kudaibergenova 2020).
32. I briefly wrote about the collective feeling of 'home' for Central Asian scholars in 'When Your Field Is Also Your Home', OpenDemocracy, 7 October 2019, https://www.opendemocracy.net/en/odr/when-your-field-also-your-home-introducing-feminist-subjectivities-central-asia/
33. Before my postgraduate studies, I was actively engaged in creative

writing circles and wrote in Qazaq, Russian and occasionally in Spanish (when I studied in Spain). But since 2011–12, most of my writing (academic and creative) has been in English.

1. KAZAKHSTAN

   1. See Alima Bissenova 2017, for example.
   2. Many Kazakhstani opposition movements view 16 December as a commemoration date and day of mourning when they come to the central squares to remember the victims of the December 1986 protests (discussed in Chapter 2) and the victims of Zhanaozen 2011, which happened on 16 December 2011.
   3. I thank Dr Gaygysyz Joraev and Prof. Tim Williams, who invited me and many of my colleagues to an archaeological workshop on the archaeology of the Silk Roads in Almaty in May 2015. This vignette is from the fieldwork (often archaeological fieldwork, which I was allowed to observe).
   4. While the regime has sought to promote the idea that the artefact is a 'man', scientists are actually more supportive of the hypothesis that it is a woman.
   5. When the same book with a handprint was installed inside the Baiterek monument in Astana, it was revealed that the print is a copy of Nazarbayev's hand.
   6. An identical copy of the open book and its handprint was placed in the same site just days later, which led to a rumour that there were many of these open books. Kazakhstan is famous for monument theft. People usually steal bits and pieces of the central monuments, like the monument to the Asharshylyq victims in Astana, where a statue of a little boy or girl goes missing from time to time. It is believed that the thieves sell these parts of the monuments, as they are often made from bronze or other semi-precious materials.
   7. There are several reconstructions of the Scythian archaeological finds including the Golden Man full armour done by Krym Altynbekov.
   8. It is a very unusual museum. It has numerous halls dedicated to Kazakhstan's ancient history, but one of the biggest halls is dedicated to 'modern Kazakhstan' and effectively doubles as a shrine to Nazarbayev, with collections of his images, books and medals. Or at least it looked like that when I last visited in the summer of 2022, much to my surprise given the bloodshed of the 2022 Bloody January protests that had unfolded right across the street from the museum in Nazarbayev's now destroyed residency. Many unarmed protestors and

soldiers found refuge inside the National Museum during those days of heightened violence.
9. On the topic of *balbals*, see Kyzylbayeva 2016, for example.
10. These images were on national currency, in history textbooks, on the banners adorning official buildings and even in self-fashioned collections. Kulshat Medeuova has found *balbal* copies in private collections all over Kazakhstan. See Medeuova 2011, 2018, 2020.
11. See Mardasolov 2019.
12. By this statement, I do not intend to undermine the serious work and research that is done on these artefacts. The work of Kazakh philosopher Kulshat Medeuova and culturologist Zira Nauryzbayeva is exemplary in that regard. But I do want to specify how *balbals* became part of the regime's national obsession and how these artefacts are often taken out of context as mere souvenirs of Kazakh-ness.
13. See Diener 2005; Kuscu 2008; Cerny 2010.
14. Kindler 2018, p. 1. See also Cameron 2018; Pianciola 2001, 2004, 2018, 2022.
15. Kindler 2018, p. 2.
16. Kindler 2018, pp. 1–2.
17. See Diener 2005; Kuscu 2008; Cerny 2010; Pianciola 2022.
18. *Aul* has a broader meaning than just a 'village'. In the Qazaq language, it is a way of living, and many Qazaq philosophers and writers like Gerold Belger and Murat Auezov ascribe deeper philosophical meaning to the *aul*, actively separating its meaning from *derevnya* or village in Russian.
19. Like other Turkic languages in the Soviet Union, in the 1930s and 1940s the Kazakh language was transferred from the Arabic script into Latin and then into Cyrillic. This policy has divided Turkic-speaking communities in different parts of the world where these languages are still spoken. Many Kazakh repatriates who have returned to postsoviet Kazakhstan from China still use the Arabic script and find it difficult to adjust to Cyrillic. When I worked in the archives, I could read Qazaq in Latin script but not in Arabic (*tote*). Many of the documents were not even recorded when spoken in the Kazakh language simply because there were no translators or typing machines to record these moments. For example, some minutes of important meetings would have pages of text in Russian but would have gaps with the writing 'Speaks in Kazakh' and blank spaces until the discussion reverted to Russian. This erasure is an important part of the colonial history of Kazakhstan.
20. Kindler 2018, pp. 244–5.

21. See Dukeyev 2023; Shoshanova 2024.
22. See Fauve 2015.
23. Like many other children of the post-independence period, I learnt about the Stalinist crimes in Kazakhstan and Central Asia through different art exhibitions (the Zhoktau art exhibition, Saule Suleimenova's Residual Memory works and Aigerim Kapar's work and exhibitions on the subject).
24. I first wrote about this in my article 'Punk Shamanism' (see Kudaibergenova 2018).
25. Part of the painting was used as a cover for my first book, *Rewriting the Nation in Modern Kazakh Literature* (Kudaibergen 2017).
26. The KARLAG exhibition remained in place and attracted a lot of visitors. The museum has also hosted an exhibition by Askhat Akhmediyarov, who, along with his brother, Lukpan Akhmediyarov (a famous Kazakh journalist), is a fervent critic of the authoritarian regime in Kazakhstan. In 2016, the museum hosted the exhibition 'Time and Astana', curated by decolonial art curator Aigerim Kapar, which featured some excellent political art including Akhmediyarov's huge installation of a hammer and sickle he made and then burnt on the territory of a gulag near Astana on 31 May 2017. Unfortunately, Roza Abenova, the director of the National Museum's contemporary art section who supported many of these exhibitions, was forced to resign in 2017, which prompted a wave of public support and petitions opposing the decision.
27. Author's interview with Almagul Menlibayeva, December 2013.
28. See Kindler 2018, p. 1. See also Cameron 2018; Pianciola 2001, 2004, 2018, 2022.
29. Kindler 2018; Cameron 2018.
30. Kindler 2018, pp. 118–19.
31. Author's interview with Almagul Menlibayeva, Almaty, 15 June 2016.
32. In Russian: *gde mozhno druzhit s kem-to protiv kogo-to*.
33. Author's interview with Almagul Menlibayeva, Almaty, 15 June 2016.
34. Qazaq historian Aliya Bolatkhan's forthcoming work on ethnicities in exile is a testament to that. See also Kassymbekova 2013, 2017.
35. See Kassenova 2022, p. 29.
36. Kassenova 2022, p. 39.
37. Kassenova 2022, p. 76.
38. Kassenova 2022, p. 79.
39. In interviews, writers and artists of the late Soviet period often referred to kitchen discussions, when Soviet citizens organised home parties and discussed politics, becoming dissidents in their kitchens.

In Alma-Ata, there were various networks of 'kitchen dissidents' like the apartment of artists Rustam Khalfin and Lida Blinova, the circles around Olzhas Suleimenov, the networks of the Zhas Tulpar movement of Moscow- and Leningrad-educated Kazakh cultural elites, among them Murat Auezov, and many groups associated with semi-dissident writers like Satimzhan Sanbayev.

40. 'Kazakstan: Nazarbayev's Fading Personality Cult', IWPR, 11 February 2022, https://iwpr.net/global-voices/kazakstan-nazarbayevs-fading-personality-cult
41. Since the transcript of the meeting was recorded verbatim and Nazarbayev possibly spoke without a prepared speech, some of his wording is very interesting. Nazarbayev spoke only in Russian during the meeting. He used 'narod' (people) in this instance as a specific ethnic group defined as a *narod*, possibly referring to Kazakhs as a homogenous ethnic group (*Kazakh narod*) or Russians as a homogeneous ethnic group (*Russkii narod*). In the next instance, when he says 'ves' narod'—all people—he is referring to the whole population of Kazakhstan irrespective of their ethnic identification, but he still uses the same word, *narod* (people), rather than 'the population' (*naselenie*) or 'society' (*obshestvo*).
42. 'Transcript of the Meeting of the National Committee for State Policy under the President of the Republic of Kazakhstan on the Issue of Developing the Concept of State Policy with the Presence of Nursultan A. Nazarbayev', 15 June 1993, F5H, Op.1, Delo 1753, the Archive of the First President of Kazakhstan, Almaty. Translation mine.
43. Tutumlu and Imyarova ask this question right at the start of their paper (2021, p. 401).
44. Although the national-patriots had an opportunity to form a political party or an opposition movement on the wave of the language law discussions in 1988–9 and the early 1990s, their attempts to do so ultimately failed. By the early 2010s, when I was conducting my research in Kazakhstan, the so-called Kazakh national-patriots were active but not fully institutionalised. Many of them looked up to Nazarbayev and other politicians as patrons who could promote their nationalistic ideas.
45. Since about 1995, any discussions of nation-building have been held behind the closed door of the presidential administration; it is rumoured that Tazhin and his team masterminded ideological texts such as 'Kazakhstan-2030', the most famous state programme for development. The same team also produced all of Nazarbayev's annual

addresses to the nation, which were inaugurated in 1997 and specified the development path of the country for a given year.

46. In Russian: Assambleya Narodov Kazakhstana.
47. As Nazarbayev often referred to them in speeches given at closed meetings with members of his administration.
48. See Cummings 2006.
49. In the early 1990s, this region was predominantly Russophone.
50. 'Transcript of the Meeting of the National Committee for State Policy under the President of the Republic of Kazakhstan on the Issue of Developing the Concept of State Policy with the Presence of Nursultan A. Nazarbayev', 15 June 1993, F5H, Op.1, Delo 1753, Archive of the First President of Kazakhstan, Almaty.
51. Zugzwang is a position in chess whereby a player is obliged to move but is unable to do so without disadvantage.
52. The 2023 report of the Kazakhstani Committee on Statistics (https://stat.gov.kz) identified the Mangystau region, where Aktau and Zhanaozen are located, as the second poorest in the whole of the country when measured in terms of the number of people living below the poverty line. According to official statistics, 8 per cent of the region's population is unemployed; however, the official poverty and unemployment figures are masked by terms such as 'individual business-owner' or 'self-employed', which can mean that the person in question is barely surviving in precarious working conditions (for example as a taxi driver or market trader), but is still considered 'self-employed'.
53. He came not to speak to the striking and protesting workers but to take part in celebrations marking the fiftieth anniversary of oil being discovered in the region. The celebrations took place in the local Palace of Oil Workers. The protesting workers then called him over to speak to them, but the governor had little to say.
54. I use the term 'postsoviet politician' to indicate that he was part of the old Soviet-trained guard of the political elite.
55. https://rus.azattyq.org/a/school_children_strike_oil_workers_/24314806.html
56. Eyewitnesses and journalists reported that for months, around 1,000 to 1,200 oil workers came to the main square in Zhanaozen demanding better pay and working conditions. In late November, just weeks before the violence of 16 December 2011, around 1,200 workers were coming to the square each day despite the severe winter conditions. Most of these workers had not been paid for months, and some reportedly brought their children with them to the square.

57. Timur Kulibayev is married to Nursultan A. Nazarbayev's second daughter, Dinara Nazarbayeva. Together, the couple have a net worth of USD 4 billion, making them the leaders of the Kazakhstani *Forbes* ranking of the country's richest people.
58. His full comment, made on 29 September 2011 in Astana at the local discussion club 'Expert', is available in Russian at https://tengrinews.kz/kazakhstan_news/kulibaev-liderami-bastuyuschih-janaozene-neftyanikov-197979/
59. This term has negative connotations, and many experts have called for it to no longer be used, as it creates significant levels of discrimination; however, I use it here and elsewhere in its historical sense. When Kulibayev made his comment, the media accused him of *oralmanophobia* (see the roundtable discussion at Radio Free Europe on this theme - https://rus.azattyq.org/a/repatriate_diskrimination_kulibayev_janaozen_phobia_migration/24356665.html). I do concur with the critics of this term and use *qandas* when writing about the contemporary debates.
60. One of the Zhanaozen protestors among the so-called 'repatriates', Orazbay Tursynbayev, was quoted in a Radio Free Europe piece as saying that 'Timur Kulibayev divided Kazakhs into *oralmans* and … from his words it turns out that they [*qandas*, repatriates] are "second-rate people" (*lyudi vtorogo sorta*)', quote available in Russian at https://rus.azattyq.org/a/timur_kulibaev/24367270.html
61. One of Massimov's first political appointments (in 1991) was in the Ministry of Labour (Ministerstvo Truda), and from January 2007 to September 2012 he served his first term as prime minister. He then returned to his prime-ministerial position for a second term in April 2014, which lasted until 2016. Between the two terms, he occupied the high-ranking post of head of the presidential administration and was involved in many state-led programmes. During his second prime-ministerial term, he faced allegations of corruption involving the country's expensive preparations for EXPO-2017 in Astana. In September 2016, he became chairman of the National Security Committee. He was removed from this post following his arrest on 6 January 2022 on charges of 'treason' and organising a failed *coup d'état* against President Tokayev during the January 2022 protests. Massimov's trial was held in secret, behind closed doors, with no details available to the media or independent observers. In April 2023, it was announced he had been sentenced to eighteen years in prison; see 'Karim Massimov, Former Kazakh Intelligence Chief, Sentenced to 18 Years on Treason, Coup Charges', *The Diplomat*, 24

April 2023, https://thediplomat.com/2023/04/karim-massimov-former-kazakh-intelligence-chief-sentenced-to-18-years-on-treason-coup-charges/
62. On 17 November 2011, Kazakhstani media reposted parts of what looked like an official press release from the KazMunaiGas Exploration Production, the state company that owns 100 per cent of Ozenmunaigas and 50 per cent of Karazhanbasmunai in a joint venture, where most of the protesting oil workers were employed before the labour dispute. The press release read as follows: 'In May 2011 the organisers of illegal protest actions in PF "Ozenmunaigas" (OMG) and AO "Karazhanbasmunaibas" (KBM) did not engage in dialogue with the employer. The termination of work of part of the workforce was chosen as a measure to pressure the employer without observing the (re)conciliation procedures provided by the law.' Furthermore, the quoted press release stated that 'today there is no labour dispute in OMG nor in KBM and the activists of the illegal protest action who deliver their demands to the employers are no longer workers of these companies because they have been fired. The lawfulness of this decision has been confirmed by court decision [*Zakonnost' dannogo resheniya byla podtverzhdena resheniyami sudov*]'; quoted in https://tengrinews.kz/kazakhstan_news/primiritelnuyu-komissiyu-v-rd-kmg-ne-sozdavali-201787/
63. As one activist said in an interview published in Radio Free Europe's Kazakhstani section, around 200 people remained on the square every night; they took turns to 'warm up' in the cars. See https://rus.azattyq.org/a/oil_workers_strike_zhanaozen_aktau/24404828.html
64. Yntymaq Square in Akrau remains a highly symbolic place, where, on 1 January 2022, people started protesting, sparking the peaceful protests in Western Kazakhstan and the incredibly violent suppression of the protests in the southern part of the country.
65. I write about this in detail in my book *The Kazakh Spring* (see Kudaibergen 2024).
66. Elena Kostyuchenko, 'Zhanaozen', *Novaya Gazeta*, 21 December 2011, https://novayagazeta.ru/articles/2011/12/20/47465-zhanaozen
67. Marzhan cited in Kostyuchenko, 'Zhanaozen', *Novaya Gazeta*, 21 December 2011.
68. Mangilik El was a state programme that translates as Eternal Nation. It had little to no meaning apart from expressing the idea that Kazakhstan was an ancient nation.
69. Lillis 2022, p. 56.

70. Suny 2001, p. 27.
71. Verdery 1996, p. 62.
72. Gellner 2008, p. 6.
73. This idea is something that does not sit well with a number of pro-communist groups inside my own country and outside my discipline (sociology).
74. See Baigabatova et al. 2018; Sharipova et al. 2017; Rees and Burkhanov 2018.
75. See Zardykhan 2004; Peyrouse 2007; Jašina-Schäfer 2019, 2021; Kudaibergenova 2018.
76. See Masanov 2002; Surucu 2002; Karin and Chebotarev 2002; Cummings 2006; Dave 2007; Laruelle 2014; Rees and Williams 2017; Kudaibergenova 2020.
77. See Dadabaev 2017; also Brown 1990 and Smith 1989, among others.

2. THE DECEMBER 1986 PROTESTS IN ALMA-ATA

1. Zhenskii Pedagogicheskii Institute or Women's Pedagogical Institute; known locally by its Russian abbreviation ZhenPi.
2. Almaty residents distinguish between the upper and lower parts of the city. The upper part is the one leading towards the mountains (which are located in the city), while the lower side leads away from the mountains. Locals would often give directions around the city and its streets by referring to whether the destination was downtown, to the 'below' side or uptown, in the 'upper' side (e.g. *vverkh po Furmanova*— up on Furmanov Street).
3. Translated from Ponomarev and Dzhukeeva 1993, p. 224.
4. Following the December 1986 protests, many of Kunayev's closest aides were arrested and tried before being rehabilitated following the Soviet collapse. Kunayev was never arrested or tried for corruption. After the protests, Moscow-based elites launched a detailed 'audit' to check how many ethnic Kazakhs occupied higher positions in the governing institutions and searched and detailed the number of ethnic Kazakh students in the country's higher education institutions.
5. Kolbin arrived in Alma-Ata on 15 December 1986 along with G. Razumovsky, a high-ranking party official from Moscow who dealt with the 'cadres' issue in the Central Committee of the all-Union Communist Party. In his book, *Bez pravykh i levykh* (Without right and left), Nazarbayev remembers that he and other local elites only learned about the republic's new ruler when Kolbin emerged from his aeroplane.

6. In Soviet times, the city was named Alma-Ata; it was changed to its current name Almaty in 1993. In other chapters, I return to the current name of the city as Almaty.
7. Students in cities across Soviet Kazakhstan were also protesting on 17 December 1986, but since Alma-Ata was a major city and had the greatest numbers of protestors, the December 1986 protests are often called the 'Alma-Ata uprisings'. In this chapter, I focus on the historical documents that also describe Alma-Ata as the hotspot of the protests and the city where most of the casualties happened, even though most of the protestors came from different cities of Kazakhstan.
8. Mikhail Solomentsev worked as a second secretary of the Central Committee of the CPK (deputy to Kunayev at the time) for two years between 1962 and 1964. It was rumoured that he allegedly left his post after a scandal in his personal life. This is also mentioned by Nazarbayev in his 1991 book *Bez pravykh i levykh*: 'What was the use of Solomentsev who once left for Moscow to raise in ranks from his post as a second secretary of the Central Committee of the Communist Party of Kazakhstan almost with a scandal?' (Nazarbayev 1991, p. 181).
9. Solomentsev speech at the meeting of the Bureau of the Central Committee of the CPK on 23 December 1986 as quoted in the 'Report of the Commission of the Presidium of the Verkhovny Sovet of the Kazakh SSR on the December 1986 Events in Alma-Ata and Other Regions of Kazakhstan'. The head of the commission was the famous Kazakh writer Mukhtar Shakhanov. The commission also included deputies to the Kazakh SSR (during perestroika, these had been elected directly by the people), and such prominent politicians as Imangali Tasmagambetov, who later became one of Nazarbayev's closest allies. The report is available in full in Ponomarev and Dzhukeeva 1993. Solomentsev's speech is cited on p. 42.
10. Local KGB forces filmed the protestors. Some of the eyewitnesses remembered how young female protestors smiled at the camera thinking that it was a television camera and that they would be featured on the evening news as brave defenders of perestroika.
11. Kamalidenov was a leading Kazakh Communist politician. From 1985 to 1988, he was the first secretary of the Central Committee of the Communist Party of the Kazakh SSR, and prior to that he chaired the local security forces, the KGB. It was rumoured that he and Nazarbayev, at the time chairman of the Council of Ministers of the Kazakh SSR, were the main contenders for Kunayev's post as the

leader of the country. But on the wave of the corruption allegations in the Central Asian republics (the infamous 'cotton affair' in Uzbekistan, for example), Gorbachev decided against their appointment post-Kunayev and instead appointed Kolbin to the position, which he occupied until June 1989.
12. Ponomarev and Dzhukeeva 1993. Solomentsev's speech is cited on p. 42.
13. 'Report of the Commission of the Presidium of the Verkhovny Sovet of the Kazakh SSR on the December 1986 Events in Alma-Ata and Other Regions of Kazakhstan', in Ponomarev and Dzhukeeva 1993, p. 41.
14. It is still unclear who gave the order, as the local prosecutor general and the head of the local KGB reported that they had been given no directive to deal with the situation and that everything was directed from Moscow; from the findings of the report on the December 1986 events in Alma-Ata.
15. Quoted from Kunayev's testimony to the commission investigating the December 1986 events on 30 April 1990. His brief testimony is available in the original Russian in Ponomarev and Dzhukeeva 1993, pp. 140–1, and in his memoir.
16. Each Soviet republic had a first secretary of the Central Committee of the Communist Party (the leader of the republic) and second secretaries. The central elite in Moscow was also composed of the Central Committee of the Communist Party and Politburo, the highest political institutions in the whole of the USSR.
17. At a different point, other party elites went to speak to the protestors. Kunayev claims that this was Kamalidenov and Nazarbayev, both of whom also claim that they spoke to the protestors in their memoirs.
18. Kolbin himself refused to speak to the crowds and remained in the Communist Party headquarters in his office, frequently phoning Moscow.
19. Nazarbayev claimed that he joined the protestors and led them through the streets: 'I went with them [protestors], at the head of the column [*Ya poshel s nimi, vo glave kolonny*]'; quoted from Nazarbayev 1991, p. 180. However, none of the eyewitness accounts support that claim. Moreover, those who were inside the administrative building claim that Nazarbayev was also inside the building.
20. The Russian 'first'—*pervyi* or '01' (*nol' pervyi*)—was often used colloquially in Kazakhstan to refer to Nazarbayev himself during his presidency.
21. Nazarbayev 1991, pp. 179–80.

22. From Kunayev's testimony to the commission investigating the December 1986 events on 30 April 1990. See Ponomarev and Dzhukeeva 1993, pp. 140–1.
23. Ponomarev and Dzhukeeva 1993, p. 141. A year and a half later, Kolbin accused Kunayev of refusing to speak to the crowds.
24. The direct translation from the Russian saying is: 'We brewed this porridge, which means that we had to eat it up.'
25. Nazarbayev 1991, pp. 181–2.
26. *Anasha* is a form of locally grown cannabis. There is no evidence that large numbers of protestors were drug users, and the commission investigating the December 1986 protests established that no-one had been detained for possessing drugs or abusing alcohol. There were, however, numerous reports of trucks with free vodka and free food being distributed to the protestors; see Ponomarev and Dzhukeeva 1993 and reports of Alma-Ata residents.
27. See eyewitness reports and diaries in Ponomarev and Dzhukeeva 1993.
28. In the face of public opposition, some members of the old Communist elite were removed from the commission, which was re-organised to include representatives of independent organisations, such as the Latvian Bureau for Human Rights, as well as local members of the Kazakh intelligentsia (many of whom were non-Kazakhs).
29. Shakhanov himself became a target for a lot of hate mail and harassment, some of which came from KGB officers. In one letter, he was threatened with death: 'As soon as you find the corpses, you'll die.' See his interview in Utegenov and Zeinabin 1991, p. 52.
30. See the law enforcement officers' testimony to the December 1986 commission in Shakhanov 1990.
31. There were allegations that young female protestors were detained and then raped in the closed interrogation rooms of the old KGB and Soviet police after the December 1986 protests. None of the officers were arrested.
32. Mukhametzhanova wanted to leave the institute after the interrogation and live with her parents. More details about her are available at https://exclusive.kz/expertiza/obshhestvo/126811/. I would like to thank Kamila Smagulova for sharing the link and further information about Mukhametzhanova, who was also mentioned in the investigative documents compiled by the commission in 1990 and 1991.
33. Some of the videos are available in Asiya Baigozhina's 1990 documentary film 'December 1986: Chronicles of an Unannounced

Rally', which is available on YouTube with English subtitles: https://www.youtube.com/watch?v=Pwn97JcJuNs

34. After the protests, there was a lot of talk in the party about who 'allowed' so many students of 'Kazakh nationality' to get into the universities. For example, in Karaganda, First Secretary V. Lokotunin lamented that out of 20,000 students in the universities, 'more than a half is made up of faces [sic] of Kazakh nationality while only 14.6 per cent of them live [permanently by *propiska*] here [in Karaganda]'; cited in Utegenov and Zeinabin 1991, p. 46.
35. The table is cited from Zimovina 2017.
36. The commission investigating the protests concluded that around 8,500 protestors had been detained, so the figure of around or more than 10,000 protestors seems feasible.
37. Eyewitness interview in Baigozhina's film 'December 1986'.
38. Anonymous eyewitness reports.
39. From Kaplin's diaries of the events; see Ponomarev and Dzhukeeva 1993, p. 223.
40. See Ponomarev and Dzhukeeva 1993.
41. From Kaplin's diaries of the events; see Ponomarev and Dzhukeeva 1993, p. 223.
42. See the December 1986 commission in their report, Shakhanov 1990 and Utegenov and Zeinabin 1991.
43. From T. Imanbayev interview in Utegenov and Zeinabin 1991, p. 42.
44. This was confirmed by the cadets who were interviewed and by the investigative commission.
45. Cited in an interview with Ninel Fokina, one of the members of the December 1986 investigative commission and published in the *Ogni Alatau* newspaper on 4 October 1990; re-printed in Utegenov and Zeinabin 1991, p. 86.
46. Legally, this could be done with the official permission of the Ministry of Internal Affairs of USSR, but there were rumours that Gorbachev himself had allowed the forces to enter the rebellious city.
47. From the data collected by the investigative commission, cited in Utegenov and Zeinabin 1991, p. 25.
48. From the data collected by the investigative commission, cited in Utegenov and Zeinabin 1991, p. 28.
49. Cited in Utegenov and Zeinabin 1991, pp. 93–4.
50. Investigative commission interviews with V.A. Volkov, 16 October 1990, available in Ponomarev and Dzhukeeva 1993, pp. 158–9.
51. Eyewitness reports cited in Battaluly 2000. Uak Arken Battaluly was a forty-six-year-old lecturer at the Alma-Ata Architectural Institute

who was sentenced to seven years in Kolyma prison camp for his involvement in the December 1986 protests. He was rehabilitated in the 1990s. The book was published in 2000, but Battaluly could get only fifty physical copies as the security services confiscated the rest of the print run from the publishers. From his wife's interview to RFE Azattyq, available at https://rus.azattyq.org/a/arken_uak/1496648.html

52. Many other eyewitnesses also claimed that young women were targeted. The members of different Zheltoqsan movements (December 1986) later reported that some of the female protestors claimed they were now unable to bear children. The quotation is from eyewitness reports cited in Ponomarev and Dzhukeeva 1993.
53. Ponomarev and Dzhukeeva 1993.
54. From the memories of the detained protestors, see https://novaya.media/articles/2022/12/16/zheltoksan
55. Eyewitness report of Rakhmetov Talap, who lived on Baiseitova Street; available in Battaluly 2000.
56. Author's interview, Almaty, January 2011.
57. The street name still exists in contemporary Almaty and is translated as 'Street of Peace' (*ulitsya mira*).
58. From Tustukbayeva Gulnur, Bereke shop assistant testimony, quoted in Battaluly 2000.
59. This was one of the slogans of the protestors. In Russian, it reads as a metaphor—'kolba' from Russian translates as 'flask', which the protestors were using as a nickname for Kolbin.
60. Any mention of Nazarbayev being involved in any of the actions taken to counter the protests was censored after his appointment as the first secretary of the CPK in 1989. However, he remained in his position and was later able to climb up the career ladder.
61. Viktor Miroshnik, the head of the Kazakh KGB at the time, mentioned 'snowballs' (*snezhki*) and tree branches as the protestors' 'weapons' in his interview to the investigative commission.
62. Confidential interview, author's correspondence with the eyewitnesses.
63. Quoted in Ponomarev and Dzhukeeva 1993.
64. Nazarbayev 1991, p. 179.
65. Nazarbayev 1991, p. 179.
66. Rallies are still legally restricted in Kazakhstan. Rally organisers have to file a request at least a month before the rally itself indicating where it will take place, the number of people it will involve and the reasons for the rally to the official municipality. Many of these requests are

denied. Spontaneous protests, without special permission from the local authorities, are still prohibited.
67. The 91-metre Independence Monument is colloquially known as the 'Golden Man'. Erected in 1996 as one of the first major monuments to independence, this monument represented the deceased figure of the Scythian warrior found in an archaeological excavation outside Almaty in the 1970s. The deceased warrior was dressed up in the ritualistic costume made of pure gold, and this is where the name stems from.
68. See Brubaker 1996, 2014.

3. WHO ARE THE FOURTH *ZHUZ*?

1. Comment from the focus group (among Russians) in Almaty, 2014. *Otchet*.
2. The data from their surveys were only available to state officials and were not made public.
3. This secret report was issued in 1987 but only for the party leadership.
4. Tolstukhin 1987, p. 6,
5. Tolstukhin 1987, pp. 6–7.
6. Tolstukhin 1987.
7. The Virgin Lands campaign (*tselina*) was a project to boost agricultural production (wheat) in Northern Kazakhstan initiated by Nikita Khrushchev in 1953. The Soviet leadership viewed the Northern Kazakhstani and Siberian steppe as a 'barren space', and thus the campaign originated from the idea of cultivating this 'virgin' land. The project led to the mass migration of workers from the all-union republics and significantly changed the composition of the Kazakhstani population by bringing in many Russians, Ukrainians and Germans to Northern Kazakhstan. Unfortunately, this colonial project continues to be used by far-right Russian groups to claim that Northern Kazakhstan's territory belongs to Russia.
8. Tolstukhin 1987, p. 19.
9. Tolstukhin 1987, p. 21.
10. Tolstukhin 1987, pp. 32–3.
11. Tolstukhin 1987, p. 33.
12. Political-sociological report, 'The Making of Perestroika and the Problems of Enhancing Interethnic Relations in Kazakhstan', fond 708, op. no. 135b, 30 January 1987 and until 12 June 1987, 'A Special Report to Kolbin', p. 15.
13. See Fierman 1998, pp.171–86; Dave 2007.

14. See Fierman 1998, pp. 171–86.
15. Author's interview with Kazakh national-patriots in Almaty, August 2013. Their names have been kept anonymous.
16. He was very happy to learn that I did go to a Kazakh-language primary school and could speak to him in Kazakh. I did not tell him that I mainly used my everyday Kazakh to communicate with my maternal grandmother who refused to identify with any ethnic group and only spoke Russian when it was necessary and preferred a type of Kazakhified dialect in her communication with her grandchildren. That is to say that my real knowledge of Kazakh stemmed not from my schooling, which I often found very Sovietized, but from my interpersonal relations with someone who would not be deemed as Kazakh by the state or the national-patriots themselves.
17. Author's interview with a Kazakh opposition leader, Almaty, 12 September 2012.
18. Author's interview with Kazakhophone activist, Almaty, 15 July 2023.
19. Skalozubov's Batyl Bol initiative, launched in the summer of 2022, became an instant success in Kazakhstan. His full interview in Russian is available at https://rus.azattyq.org/a/32068650.html
20. Poll results available in Russian at https://demos.kz/opros-tret-kazahstancev-stala-huzhe-otnositsja-k-rossii-posle-nachala-vojny/
21. Data for the end of 2023.
22. This is a discriminatory Soviet term usually used in sense of 'faces of Caucasian nationality' in contrast to Russians, who were considered 'Europeans' in the Caucasian states and Central Asia. I use a more open-ended term, *litsa opredelennoi natsional'nosti*—'faces of a specific nationality' (i.e. ethnicity and/or any other group identity) to situate the debate over Otherness.
23. See 'Putin Calls Ukrainian Statehood a Fiction: History Suggests Otherwise', *New York Times*, 21 February 2022, https://www.nytimes.com/2022/02/21/world/europe/putin-ukraine.html#:~:text=Putin%20declared%20Ukraine%20an%20invention,the%20newly%20created%20Soviet%20state
24. See Farangis Najibullah, 'Putin Downplays Kazakh Independence, Sparks Angry Reaction', RFE/RL, 3 September 2014, https://www.rferl.org/a/kazakhstan-putin-history-reaction-nation/26565141.html
25. Hirsh 2005, p. 12.
26. Hirsh 2005, p. 14.
27. The most derogative and racist colloquial terms in Russia for Central Asian and Caucasian migrants relate to racist and degrading

connotations of colour (blackness is often ascribed to these ethnic groups in all sorts of variations), locality (to the region of origin— *Kavkazets*, Central Asian) and backwardness. In these racist terms, there are localised N-words in Russian that describe the colonial Other from Central Asia and the Caucasian states as 'uncivilised', 'barbarian', 'uncultured'. There are even specific terms used solely for Central Asians, such as 'churka'—a highly offensive, racist term. In her article on the changing uses of the term *churka* in Russia, Barinova identifies how the use of this term is specifically connected to the figure of ethnicised Central Asian migrants seen as the 'enemy' of Russians. See Barinova 2013.

28. See Ó Beacháin and Kevlihan 2013, pp. 337–56; Kesici 2011, p. 31.
29. Tutumlu and Imyarova 2021 provide an excellent analysis of the similarities between Nazarbayev's nation-building policies and his focus on multi-ethnicity and Brezhnev-era slogans and policies.
30. I detail this in Kudaibergenova 2020.
31. On the history of LAD and its secessionist claims, see Peyrouse 2007. Currently the LAD movement claims to have up to 50,000 members in twenty-four of their regional offices all over Kazakhstan.
32. 'Otchet po rezultatu sotsiologicheskogo issledovaniya na temu: analiz vospiryatiya mezhetnicheskoi politiki gosudarstva russkoiazychnym naseleniyem i predstavitelyami russkogo ethnosa (na osnove katchestvennykh dannykh)' [Report on the results of the sociological study on ethnic Russian respondents' perception of the state interethnic policies], Almaty, 2014, p. 15.
33. *Otchet*, p. 14.
34. In Russian: 'Gruppa anonymnykh russkih.'
35. *Otchet*, p. 14.
36. Respondent, village in Almaty region, *Otchet*, p. 13.
37. Respondent, the city of Almaty, *Otchet*, p. 7.
38. Respondent, Pavlodar city (Northern Kazakhstan), *Otchet*, p. 16.
39. The 2014 survey of the Russian population in Kazakhstan is particularly useful because it was carried out right after the annexation of Crimea and the start of the war (with the Russian state's involvement) in Eastern Ukraine. I juxtapose its findings with existing data after 2022 at the end of the chapter.
40. Respondent, Almaty, *Otchet*, p. 17.
41. Respondent, Pavlodar city (Northern Kazakhstan), *Otchet*, p. 18.
42. Respondent, Semey city (Eastern Kazakhstan), *Otchet*, p. 20.
43. Respondent, Oral city, *Otchet*, p. 20.
44. Respondent, Karaganda city, *Otchet*, p. 9.

45. Respondent, Kokshetau city (Northern Kazakhstan), *Otchet*, p. 23.
46. Respondent, Oral city, *Otchet*, p. 11.
47. Respondent, Pavlodar city (Northern Kazakhstan), *Otchet*, p. 7.
48. Focus group excerpt from Almaty, *Otchet*, p. 10.
49. Respondent, Karaganda city, *Otchet*, p. 23.
50. Respondent, Oskemen city, *Otchet*, p. 23.
51. Respondent, Oskemen city, *Otchet*, p. 24
52. Respondent, village in Pavlodar region (Northern Kazakhstan), *Otchet*, p. 25.
53. Respondent, Oral city, *Otchet*, p. 25.
54. Respondent, village in Aqmola region (Northern Kazakhstan), *Otchet*, p. 25.
55. Respondent, Semey city (Eastern Kazakhstan), *Otchet*, p. 25.
56. The vast majority of the respondents in the 2014 study of Kazakhstani Russians' attitudes to ethnic relations in their own country and in other states in the near abroad supported the idea that what happened in Ukraine was fuelled by Ukrainian nationalism and what in some respondents' view was the Ukrainians' treatment of Russians in Ukraine.
57. Author's narrative interview with anonymous ethnic Russian, Almaty region, August 2023.
58. I cite the question asked but do not use the term 'special operation' in my own analysis.
59. Data from Tlegen Kuandykov, 'Russia–Ukraine War: Perceptions in Central Asia', Central Asia Barometer, 21 April 2023, https://ca-barometer.org/assets/files/froala/64f96d89f2ba614021af71e8ccf8acafa6c8a0f4.pdf
60. I first interviewed Kay during my doctoral fieldwork in Kazakhstan in 2012–13. I kept in touch with her over the following ten years, including the time of the Bloody January 2022 protests and Russia's full-scale invasion of Ukraine in February 2022. Kay often brought back colourful stories from her frequent trips to Russia and often laughed about the strange habits of 'Russians from Russia' (*russkie iz Rossii*).
61. Diversifying their savings in different currencies became a norm for many Kazakhstanis, especially after 'Black Tuesday' in February 2014—an unexpected devaluation of the Kazakh tenge—but keeping savings in Russian roubles was not as widespread.
62. At least that used to be the case before the 2022 war.
63. Author's interviews with Kay in 2013–14.
64. Kay never called Russia's war her own and never used the expression

nasha voina when talking about the Russo-Ukrainian war. But she also ridiculed the term 'special operation' and often laughed when mentioning it. But she often said 'their war' without clearly identifying whom she meant by 'them', that is, whether the Russians or the Ukrainians.
65. Author's interview with Kay, Almaty, July 2023.
66. Author's fieldnotes, Almaty, July 2023.
67. I use this word here in its direct transliteration from Russian completely aware of its racist connotations as it is often used against racialised 'non-Russian [*nerusskie*] migrants in Russia'.
68. In July and August 2023, I conducted a short fieldwork in Almaty to find potential respondents among the Russian citizens who came to Kazakhstan to stay for a longer time than the 183 days that were permitted according to Kazakh legislation. I used a snowballing technique to meet more potential Kazakhstani residents among those who moved away from Russia in 2022 and settled in Kazakhstan. My initial sample was around thirty to forty people, most of whom stated that they felt as though they had been welcomed in Kazakhstan. Local media focused on similar studies and reported more or less similar results: see https://www.dw.com/ru/novyj-dom-novoe-delo-kak-relokanty-iz-rossii-zivut-v-kazahstane/a-67132259
69. Author's fieldnotes, Almaty, July 2023.
70. Author's fieldnotes, Almaty, July 2023.
71. Ukrainian president Volodymyr Zelensky also featured on the show in his younger days.
72. Author's fieldnotes, Almaty, July 2023.
73. Author's fieldnotes, Almaty, July 2023.
74. This surge in the numbers of those seeking to learn the language was partly driven by a desire for local knowledge: there were no dictionaries that explained what *Rukhani Kenguru* was (a collection of bilingual poems by Kazakh decolonial poet Anuar Dyussenbinov), nor enough explanations of the word 'oyatu' (political awakening, calls for political activism), and certain 'it' places were not on the usual digital maps.
75. Author's fieldnotes, Almaty, July 2023.

4. *MANKURTS* VERSUS *MAMBETS* (THE 'M'-WORD)

1. See Russia-based media reports: https://topcor.ru/23567-nastojaschij-majdan-u-kazahstana-mozhet-byt-esche-vperedi.html, Moskovskaya Gazeta https://mskgazeta.ru/politika/kazahskij-bunt-otsrochil-uhod-

putina--9476.html. Krizis V called 'mambets' something like Russian 'vatniki' (derogatory term): https://vkrizis.ru/world/kazahskij-mambet-i-gorod-tragediya-raskola/. See also Rabkor.ru https://rabkor.ru/columns/editorial-columns/2022/01/09/hypocrisy_and_malice/. Russian *Novye Izvestiya* even had it in their headline - https://newizv.ru/news/2022-01-12/mambety-protiv-agashek-i-almatosov-v-chem-prichina-sotsialnoy-zlosti-v-kazahstane-341888

2. I consider this word and its use a slur and try to use the shortened M-word where possible. I hope that further publications and analysis of this unfortunate word will be able to reconcile the discriminatory, derogatory and colonial legacy of this word.
3. Kudaibergenova and Laruelle 2022, p. 15.
4. Bissenova 2017, pp. 642–67.
5. Arystanbek 2023, pp. 301–20.
6. Arystanbek 2023, p. 316.
7. Bissenova 2017, p. 643.
8. Bissenova 2017.
9. Kabdrakhmanov 2006.
10. Author's interview with anonymous, April 2022.
11. *Otchet*, p. 25.
12. Mukanova and Steenberg 2021, p. 89.
13. Mukanova and Steenberg 2021, p. 90.
14. https://masa.media/ru/site/pochemu-mambet-eto-oskorblenie
15. Alexander 2018, pp. 204–20.
16. Yessenova 2003, pp. 76–7.
17. About the bazaar as a site of anthropological research, she writes, 'the ambiguous temporality and "in-betweenness" of the bazaar, the place where the epochs and the worlds—urban and rural—met, is emblematic of a protracted *liminal* phase in which recent migrants are caught together with the rest of the society, all involved in the same passage from state socialism to the market economy, which for the former villagers is associated with their displacement and migration' (Yessenova 2003, p. 130).
18. Yessenova 2003, p. 129.
19. See Turaeva 2022, p. 103478; Hatcher and Thieme 2016, pp. 2175–91.
20. There were many sanatoriums in Soviet Alma-Ata that were located on the outskirts of the city, in the mountains and some even inside the city.
21. This phrase was often used in 2021–22 in online Kazakhophone discussions in Kazakhstan. Many movements advocating for the

inclusion of the Kazakh language in marketing campaigns and simple daily services like Kazakh-language menus in restaurants emerged out of this need to cater to predominantly Kazakhophone speakers.

22. Author's interview, Almaty, August 2012.
23. Author's interview, Almaty, August 2012.
24. A Kazakh word for 'sure' or 'of course'.
25. Author's interview, Almaty, July 2023.
26. The band's name focuses on 1991—the year of Kazakhstan's independence. All four band members are bilingual, although they sing predominantly in Kazakh and are known for bringing new words and new concepts from Kazakh language into public use.
27. The group started as a YouTube sketch show and then moved into the production of music videos and songs that criticised the authoritarianism and corruption of Kazakhstan. Their highly acclaimed video '5K' (5000 KZT is a label for the widespread bribe-giving culture) criticised the Kazakh regime for its failures in addressing the COVID-19 pandemic and widespread corruption. They combine their rap lyrics with Russian and Kazakh verses.
28. In art, the works of Saule Suleimenova, Almagul Menlibayeva, Kuanysh Bazargaliev, Askhat Akhmediyarov, Creolex Zentrum, Medina Bazargali, Suinbike Suleimenova, Aiganym Mukhametzhan, art curator Aigerim Kapar and her art institution Artcom; in writing, the work of Assem Zhapisheva (not just her journalistic work but her creative writing and film scripts), Elmira Kakabayeva, Zoya Falkova, Zarina Mukanova, Tilek Yryspbek, Pavel Bannikov and Anuar Dyussenbin, to name a few among this wave who have been influential in the decolonial movement of Kazakhstan.
29. Smagulova 2008, pp. 440–75.
30. The summer weather in Astana is highly unpredictable—it can be quite chilly and rainy even in August, while the winter temperatures go as low as minus 40 degrees C.
31. For a discussion of some of these decolonial voices in Kazakhstan, see Tlostanova 2018.
32. Name changed for confidentiality. Author's communication and field notes.
33. Author's interview, August 2012.
34. Thanks to the popularity of K-pop and Korean soap operas.
35. Partly due to the deepening of Turkish–Kazakh business relations.
36. For discussions on the Islamisation of Kazakhstan, see Junisbai, Junisbai and Zhussupov 2017, pp. 1–25; Schwab 2015, pp. 51–70; Bigozhin 2022, pp. 22–35.

37. 'Orys' is Russian in Kazakh.
38. Gerold Belger, https://online.zakon.kz/Document/?doc_id=31184067
39. See the Esimde Central Asian memory initiative's website for further discussion of *mankurtisation*: https://ru.esimde.org/archives/4057
40. Information courtesy of Aiganym Mukhametzhan.
41. Artist's text provided by Aiganym Mukhametzhan.
42. Yessenova 2003, p. 9.

5. 'WE ARE THE ORDINARY PEOPLE'

1. Prices for the highly popular commodity jumped from KZT 85–90 per litre (around USD 0.19) to KZT 120 per litre (around 0.26). This adds up when travelling long distances.
2. See Bruce Pannier, 'Protests Erupt in Kazakhstan after Gas Prices Double on New Year's Day', RFE/RL, 4 January 2022, https://www.rferl.org/a/kazakhstan-fuel-protests-protests/31639462.html
3. Sorbello 2021, pp. 16–17.
4. Under Nazarbayev, all local, regional and city governors were appointed by the president. His successor, Tokayev, conceded to the demands of the opposition and has allowed some governors to be elected. But to this day, key regional governors and city mayors are still appointed by the president.
5. Kazakh journalists like Timur Nusimbekov and Daniyar Moldakhmetov were on the streets with the protestors in Almaty. Their reports of the first days of January 2022 are available at https://adamdar.ca/post/noch/278 and https://eurasianet.org/kazakhstan-notes-from-a-protest
6. The names of the victims are available on the prosecutor general's official webpage: https://www.gov.kz/memleket/entities/prokuror/press/news/details/413195?lang=ru
7. Major ethnic conflicts are unusual in Kazakhstan, and every eruption of ethnic tension creates lasting legacies of trauma and requires a prolonged period of reconciliation. The January 2022 protests were very different in the structure of the violence—the protestors predominantly channelled their rage against the political regime rather than any other societal groups, including ethnic minorities.
8. I write about this in more detail in Kudaibergen 2024.
9. These processes echoed similar developments in some major Russian cities where a protest culture also developed.
10. From Zhanbolat Mamay's speech at his court hearing in late March

2023. In April 2023, Mamay was convicted of organising mass riots and received a suspended sentence of six years in prison, see Mihra Rittmann, 'Opposition Figure Convicted in Kazakhstan', Human Rights Watch, 12 April 2023, https://www.hrw.org/news/2023/04/12/opposition-figure-convicted-kazakhstan. He denied the allegations.

11. In June 2022, Sagintayev was appointed to the Eurasian Economic Committee. This decision was made in late May 2022 in Moscow. Sagintayev served as mayor of Almaty from June 2019, a post to which he was directly appointed by President Tokayev. Before that, Sagintayev served for two and a half years as prime minister. He was heavily criticised for mismanaging the Almaty crisis, but President Tokayev claimed that Sagintayev had found himself 'in a difficult situation' for which he was not to blame (*'vinit' ego ya by ne stal'*). From Tokayev's interview with Khabar state television, quotations available at: https://informburo.kz/novosti/tokaev-o-smene-akima-almaty-a-vy-sami-hoteli-by-chtoby-on-ostalsya

12. See 'Kazakhstan: Killings, Excessive Use of Force in Almaty', Human Rights Watch, 26 January 2022, https://www.hrw.org/news/2022/01/26/kazakhstan-killings-excessive-use-force-almaty; see also Zhandayeva and Rosenberg 2022.

13. Author's fieldnotes and personal communication.

14. Kudaibergenova 2022, pp. 271–6.

15. State TV channels like Khabar focused heavily on this when reporting on the January protests to create a sense of disorganised and violent mobs while downplaying the political nature of the protests.

16. Author's correspondence, 11 January 2022.

17. The official line from the state prosecutor announced in early January 2023 was that the protests were organised as a failed *coup d'état* and that it was 'curated' by the security services, see https://rus.azattyq.org/a/32209427.html

18. The decision to rename the Kazakh capital, Astana, to Nur-Sultan in honour of its founder—Nursultan Nazarbayev—was made unilaterally by his successor, Tokayev, and ratified by the Senate in March 2019 amid mass protests against the renaming. Along with the capital, the regime also renamed one of the central streets in Almaty after Nazarbayev and erected monuments to the dictator across the country. During the January protests, crowds of angry protestors destroyed every plaque that bore Nazarbayev's name and toppled his monument in the southern city of Taldyqorgan—an image that became a symbol of the protests. In March 2022, the name of the

capital city was returned to its old name, Astana. None of the toppled monuments was replaced; their empty plinths remain as a reminder of the protests.
19. Author's interview with eyewitnesses, Almaty, July 2023.
20. Author's interview with eyewitnesses, Almaty, January 2022, personal communication.
21. See the report on prosecutor general's investigation statements: https://rus.azattyq.org/a/kazakhstan-bloody-january-official-version/32210613.html
22. See 'Kyrgyz Musician Says He Was Severely Beaten in Kazakh Custody, Suffered Multiple Injuries', Human Rights Watch, 24 January 2022, https://www.rferl.org/a/kazakhstan-kyrgyz-musician-severely-beaten/31668455.html
23. Almost 38 per cent of the respondents in a Demoscope poll believed that the January protests were 'a provocation organized by some political forces to seize power in the country'; 27.7 per cent believed they were initially peaceful but 'escalated into riots and looting in places'; and 14.6 per cent that they were 'an attack by terrorists who were trying to destabilize the situation in the country'. For the full poll results, see 'What People in Kazakhstan Think of the January Events', Demoscope, 7 February 2023, https://demos.kz/what-people-in-kazakhstan-think-of-the-january-events/?lang=en
24. On 6 January 2022, President Tokayev asked for a deployment of troops from CSTO member states (Russia, Belarus, Tajikistan, Armenia and Kyrgyzstan) to help stabilise the situation in Kazakhstan. The CSTO was formed in 1992, and the deployment of troops to Kazakhstan marked the first time that its troops had intervened in a localised conflict. The CSTO withdrew its troops on 19–20 January 2022, just a month before Russia's full-fledged invasion of Ukraine.
25. Author's correspondence, 15 January 2022.
26. Translated from Kazakh.
27. Author's communication with an eyewitness, July 2023.
28. Author's communication with an eyewitness, July 2023.
29. Author's fieldwork and communication with eyewitnesses, July–August 2023.
30. 'What People in Kazakhstan Think of the January Events', Demoscope, 7 February 2023, https://demos.kz/what-people-in-kazakhstan-think-of-the-january-events/?lang=en
31. Activist Berik Abishev was later injured and had five surgeries. There were several crowdfunding campaigns to collect money for his family

and his medical treatment. He could not speak for a very long time and only slowly started recovering.
32. '"We don't even cry anymore":Torture, Ill-treatment and Impunity in Kazakhstan in Connection with the "Bloody January" Events', IPHR, n.d., https://www.iphronline.org/wp-content/uploads/2023/01/Kazakhstan-January-Report-ENG.pdf
33. '"We don't even cry anymore"', p. 14.

6. THE LONG POST-JANUARY

1. Author's personal communication.
2. See Petr Trosenko, '"I was passing by!": A Second Day of Detentions in Almaty', RFE/RL, 10 June 2019, https://www.rferl.org/a/kazakhstan-almaty-dozens-of-people-detained/29991569.html
3. I write about this in a more detailed ethnographic account in my book *The Kazakh Spring* (2024), which focuses on the protests in Kazakhstan from the spring of 2019 until Bloody January 2022.
4. This phrase was often repeated to the female activists detained or harassed by the police, as they told me in our interviews and conversations during my fieldwork for *The Kazakh Spring* (2024).
5. The investigation into the death of the family and subsequent trial of Daniyar Egembayev, an army serviceman, concluded there had been an 'abuse of power'. Egembayev was sentenced to seven years in prison for the killing. See more on the trial: https://rus.azattyq.org/a/32475726.html and 'Military Man Sentenced to Seven Years for Shooting His Family during the January Events in Taldykorgan', KazTAG, 26 June 2023, https://kaztag.kz/en/news/military-man-sentenced-to-seven-years-for-shooting-his-family-during-the-january-events-in-taldykorg
6. Manshuk Asautai, 'Kazakh Court Acquits Defendant in High-Profile Trial Related to Killing of 4-Year-Old during 2022 Unrest', RFE/RL, 15 November 2023, https://www.rferl.org/a/kazakhstan-killing-4-year-old-defendant-acquitted-2022-unrest/32685985.html
7. The story of Baurzhan Seidomarov, who died in Taraz during the Bloody January protests and was accused of terrorism, shocked Kazakhstan. His family fought against these allegations, see: https://rus.azattyq.org/a/kazakhstan-taraz-bloody-january-victim-baurzhan-seidomarov/32190135.html
8. Author's communication, July 2023.
9. Author's communication, July 2023.
10. PaperLab 2023 opinion poll with random sample of 1,000 mobile

phone respondents all over Kazakhstan. See Aldiyar Auyezbek and Serik Beissembayev, 'The Perception of the January Events in the Kazakhstani Society', Paperlab, 2023, https://paperlab.kz/perceptions-of-the-jan-events-in-the-kaz-society

11. Quoted in Galiya Khassenkhanova, 'January Events Were Attempted Coup, Says Kazakh Prosecutor General', Astana Times, 5 January 2023, https://astanatimes.com/2023/01/january-events-were-attempted-coup-says-kazakh-prosecutor-general/

12. BBC News, 'Kazakhstan unrest: Troops ordered to fire without warning', 7 January 2022, https://www.bbc.co.uk/news/world-asia-59907235

13. Assel Tutumlu, 'The Unraveling of Kazakhstan's Social Contract', The Diplomat, 1 January 2023, https://thediplomat.com/2022/12/the-unraveling-of-kazakhstans-social-contract/

14. Interview with an anonymous respondent, July 2023.

15. From Kazakh journalist Daniyar Moldabekov's essay 'Dignity', available in Russian at: https://adamdar.ca/post/dostoinstvo/279. Moldabekov was a key eyewitness of the protests in Almaty. His book about the protests was due to be released in January 2024; however, soon after the announcement that the book could be pre-ordered, the publication was delayed due to censorship, see https://rus.azattyq.org/a/kazakhstan-almaty-bloody-january-daniyar-moldabekov-interview/32798494.html

16. See Hannah Chapman and Raushan Zhandayeva, 'Attitudes toward Russia's War on Ukraine in Kazakhstan and Kyrgyzstan', PONARS Eurasia, 12 December 2023, https://www.ponarseurasia.org/attitudes-toward-russias-war-on-ukraine-in-kazakhstan-and-kyrgyzstan/

17. See Demiscope's three waves of surveys tracking Kazakhstanis' attitudes to the war in Ukraine https://demos.kz/otnoshenie-kazahstancev-k-vojne-v-ukraine-2/ [AQ: transliteration]

AFTERWORD

1. Quoting from the Bashtan Bashta's 'O'decolon' podcast, available in Russian on YouTube: https://www.youtube.com/watch?v=aZLfBxTCoZw&t=324s

2. Tlostanova 2018, p. 128.

3. Nazarbayev's multi-million state programme Rukhani Zhangyru is a case in point. Even after years and millions poured into the programme, people were unclear what it was aiming to achieve.

Decolonial poet Anuar Dyussenbinov even wrote a poem with the telling name 'Rukhani Kangaroo' to ridicule the meaninglessness of late Nazarbayevite-era politics.
4. See Report on 'The Role of Nazarbayev in building independent Kazakhstan' based on surveys and opinion polls, 2013 and the 2014 Report on the 'Analysis of the state inter-ethnic politics policies perceptions in Russian-speaking population and members of the ethnic Russian communities' (2014).
5. Tutumlu and Imyarova 2023, p. 4.
6. Tutumlu and Imyarova 2023, pp. 14–15, quote from Smagul, 2020B in text.
7. Tutumlu and Imyarova 2023, p. 9.
8. Stalin 1942, p. 51.
9. Data from the Ministry of Education on the language of instruction in secondary schools.
10. See Kudaibergenova and Laruelle 2022; Kudaibergen 2024.
11. This concept is also known colloquially as *kormushka*—the Russian word for a feeder.
12. See details of Bolashak-educated ex-minister of national economy Kuandyk Bishembayev's sentencing in a major corruption case in 2018: Catherine Putz, 'Former Kazakh Economy Minister Sentenced to 10 Years on Corruption Charges', *The Diplomat*, 15 March 2018, https://thediplomat.com/2018/03/former-kazakh-economy-minister-sentenced-to-10-years-on-corruption-charges/
13. Viktoriya Kim, 'Guilty Verdict in High-Profile Kazakhstan Domestic Violence and Murder Case', Human Rights Watch, 13 May 2024, https://www.hrw.org/news/2024/05/13/guilty-verdict-high-profile-kazakhstan-domestic-violence-and-murder-case
14. The 2020 song and poem are about social problems and the alleged corruption of the post-independence Kazakhstani regime. My translation from the Russian.
15. These bureaucratic institutions grew into bigger structures now known as TSON—the Centre for Serving People (Tsentr obsluzhivaniya naseleniya), and most of their services are now available online.
16. The term 'party school' comes from the Soviet *partshkola*—literally the school for Communist Party members and higher-ranking officials who attended 'upgrading' courses in Marxist–Leninist ideology. In 1992, President Nazarbayev transferred the building and the campus of the former Soviet 'party school' to a Western-type business school that a decade later became a full-fledged university

with undergraduate and graduate degrees taught entirely in English by a mixed faculty of foreign and local staff.
17. A source of squabbles with my cousins, all of whom competed for the wooden spoon in the belief that it made all food, especially porridge, extra-delicious.
18. Kudaibergenova 2020, p. 175.
19. Nazarbayev 2008, p. 8.

BIBLIOGRAPHY

Alexander, C., 2018. 'Homeless in the Homeland: Housing Protests in Kazakhstan', *Critique of Anthropology*, 38(2), pp. 204–20.
Arystanbek, A., 2023. '"Can you beat your wife, yes or no?" A Study of Hegemonic Femininity in Kazakhstan's Online Discourses', *East European Politics*, 39(2), pp. 301–20.
Baigabatova, N., Tolamissov, A., Rakhipova, S., Ashimova, D., Khuangan, O. and Smagulov, K., 2018. 'Ethnocultural Identity of Kazakhs of Mongolia in Everyday Life', *Codrul Cosminului*, 24(1), pp. 79–96.
Barinova, A.O., 2013. 'Language Representation in Collective Image of the Migrant in Russian Society' [Языковая репрезентация собирательного образа мигранта в российском обществе], *Вопросы психолингвистики*, 18, pp. 174–81.
Battaluly, U.A., 2000. *Materialy genocida organizovannogo N.A. Nazarbayevym protiv kazakhskogo naroda v 1986 godu* [Materials of genocide organised by N.A. Nazarbayev against Kazakh people in 1986], Alma-Ata: n.p.
Bekus, N. and Medeuova, K., 2011. 'Smena epoch kak smena stolits: Astana kak global'nyi tsentr' [Change of epochs like a change of capitals: Astana as a global centre], D-Space, Eurasian National University, Astana.
Bigozhin, U., 2022. 'Becoming Muslim in Soviet and Post-Soviet Kazakhstan', *Ketmen*, 1, pp. 22–35.
Bissenova, A., 2017. 'The Fortress and the Frontier: Mobility, Culture, and Class in Almaty and Astana', *Europe-Asia Studies*, 69(4), pp. 642–67.
Bremmer, I. and Taras, R. (eds), 1996. *New States, New Politics: Building the Post-Soviet Nations*, Cambridge: Cambridge University Press.
Brown, B., 1990. 'The Public Role in Perestroika in Central Asia', *Central Asian Survey*, 9(1), pp. 87–96.
Brubaker, R., 1994. 'Nationhood and the National Question in the Soviet

Union and Post-Soviet Eurasia: An Institutionalist Account', *Theory and Society*, 23, pp. 47–78.
Brubaker, R., 1998. 'Myths and Misconceptions in the Study of Nationalism', in J. Hall (ed.) *The State of the Nation*, Cambridge: Cambridge University Press, pp. 233–65.
Brubaker, R., 1999. 'The Manichean Myth: Rethinking the Distinction between "Civic" and "Ethnic" Nationalism', in H. Kriesi, K. Armingeon, H. Siegrist and A. Wimmer (eds) *Nation and National Identity: The European Experience in Perspective*, West Lafayette, IN: Purdue University Press, pp. 55–71.
Brubaker, R., 2006. *Ethnicity without Groups*, Cambridge, MA: Harvard University Press.
Brubaker, R., 2014. 'Nationalizing States Revisited: Projects and Processes of Nationalization in Post-Soviet States', in J. Jackson and L. Molokotos-Liederman (eds) *Nationalism, Ethnicity and Boundaries*, London: Routledge, pp. 165–91.
Cameron, S., 2018. *The Hungry Steppe: Famine, Violence, and the Making of Soviet Kazakhstan*, Ithaca, NY: Cornell University Press.
Cerny, A., 2010. 'Going Where the Grass Is Greener: China Kazaks and the Oralman Immigration Policy in Kazakhstan', *Pastoralism*, 1(2), pp. 218–47.
Chapman, H. and Zhandayeva, R., 2023. 'Attitudes toward Russia's War in Ukraine in Kazakhstan and Kyrgyzstan', PONARS Policy Memo no. 877, December.
Cheskin, A. and Kachuyevski, A. (eds), 2021. *The Russian-Speaking Populations in the Post-Soviet Space: Language, Politics and Identity*, London: Routledge.
Chinn, J. and Kaiser, R., 2019. *Russians as the New Minority: Ethnicity and Nationalism in the Soviet Successor States*, London: Routledge.
Cummings, S.N., 2002. *Kazakhstan: Power and the Elite*, London: I.B. Tauris.
Cummings, S.N., 2006. 'Legitimation and Identification in Kazakhstan', *Nationalism and Ethnic Politics*, 12(2), pp. 177–204.
Dadabaev, T., 2017. 'Evaluations of Perestroika in Post-Soviet Central Asia: Public Views in Contemporary Uzbekistan, Kazakhstan and Kyrgyzstan', in T. Dadabaev and H. Komatsu (eds) *Kazakhstan, Kyrgyzstan, and Uzbekistan: Life and Politics during the Soviet Era*, New York: Palgrave Macmillan, pp. 103–39.
Dave, B., 2007. *Kazakhstan: Ethnicity, Language and Power*, London: Routledge.
Diener, A.C., 2005. 'Kazakhstan's Kin State Diaspora: Settlement Planning and the Oralman Dilemma', *Europe-Asia Studies*, 57(2), pp. 327–48.

Dukeyev, B., 2023. 'Representation of the Kazakhstani Famine (1931–33) in Secondary School History Textbooks, 1992–2021', *Central Asian Survey*, 42(2), pp. 383–401.

Edgar, A.L., 2007. 'Marriage, Modernity, and the "Friendship of Nations": Interethnic Intimacy in Post-war Central Asia in Comparative Perspective', *Central Asian Survey*, 26(4), pp. 581–99.

Edgar, A., 2019. 'What to Name the Children? Oral Histories of Ethnically Mixed Families in Soviet Kazakhstan and Tajikistan', *Kritika: Explorations in Russian and Eurasian History*, 20(2), pp. 269–90.

Edgar, A., 2022. *Intermarriage and the Friendship of Peoples: Ethnic Mixing in Soviet Central Asia*, Ithaca, NY: Cornell University Press.

Esenova, S., 1996. 'The Outflow of Minorities from the Post-Soviet State: The Case of Kazakhstan', *Nationalities Papers*, 24(4), pp. 691–707.

Esenova, S., 2002. 'Soviet Nationality, Identity, and Ethnicity in Central Asia: Historic Narratives and Kazakh Ethnic Identity', *Journal of Muslim Minority Affairs*, 22(1), pp. 11–38.

Fauve, A., 2015. 'A Tale of Two Statues in Astana: The Fuzzy Process of Nationalistic City Making', *Nationalities Papers*, 43(3), pp. 383–98.

Fierman, W., 1998. 'Language and Identity in Kazakhstan: Formulations in Policy Documents 1987–1997', *Communist and Post-communist Studies*, 31(2), pp. 171–86.

Gellner, E., 2008. *Nations and Nationalism*, Ithaca, NY: Cornell University Press.

Hale, H.E. and Onuch, O., 2022. *The Zelensky Effect*, London: Hurst.

Hatcher, C. and Thieme, S., 2016. 'Institutional Transition: Internal Migration, the Propiska, and Post-socialist Urban Change in Bishkek, Kyrgyzstan', *Urban Studies*, 53(10), pp. 2175–91.

Hirsch, F. 2005. *Empire of Nations: Ethnographic Knowledge and the Making of the Soviet Union*, Ithaca, NY: Cornell University Press.

Hobsbawm, E.J., 1992. *Nations and Nationalism since 1780: Programme, Myth, Reality*, Cambridge: Cambridge University Press.

Jašina-Schäfer, A., 2019. 'Everyday Experiences of Place in the Kazakhstani Borderland: Russian Speakers between Kazakhstan, Russia, and the Globe', *Nationalities Papers*, 47(1), pp. 38–54.

Jašina-Schäfer, A., 2021. *Everyday Belonging in the Post-Soviet Borderlands: Russian Speakers in Estonia and Kazakhstan*, Lanham, MD: Rowman & Littlefield.

Junisbai, B., Junisbai, A. and Zhussupov, B., 2017. 'Two Countries, Five Years: Islam in Kazakhstan and Kyrgyzstan through the Lens of Public Opinion Surveys', *Central Asian Affairs*, 4(1), pp. 1–25.

Kabdrakhmanov, K. 2006. 'Mambetizm kak odin iz neizbezhnyh putei natsionalnogo kulturnogo razvitiya' [Mambetism as one of the inevitable ways of national cultural development], Online.Zakon.kz.

Karin, E. and Chebotarev, A., 2002. 'The Policy of Kazakhization in State and Government Institutions in Kazakhstan', IDE, Middle East Studies Series no. 51, 'The Nationalities Question in Post-Soviet Kazakhstan'.

Kassenova, T., 2022. *Atomic Steppe: How Kazakhstan Gave Up the Bomb*, Stanford: Stanford University Press.

Kassymbekova, B., 2013. 'Humans as Territory: Forced Resettlement and the Making of Soviet Tajikistan, 1920–38', in M. Reeves (ed.) *Movement, Power and Place in Central Asia and Beyond*, London: Routledge, pp. 43–64.

Kassymbekova, B., 2017. 'Understanding Stalinism in, from and of Central Asia: Beyond Failure, Peripherality and Otherness', *Central Asian Survey*, 36(1), pp. 1–18.

Kassymbekova, B. and Marat, E. 2022. 'Time to Question Russia's Imperial Innocence', PONARS Policy Memo no. 771, April.

Kesici, O., 2011. 'The Dilemma in the Nation-Building Process: The Kazakh or Kazakhstani Nation', *Journal on Ethnopolitics and Minority Issues in Europe*, 10(1), p. 31.

Kindler, R., 2018. *Stalin's Nomads: Power and Famine in Kazakhstan*, Pittsburgh, PA: University of Pittsburgh Press.

Kudaibergen, D.T., 2017. *Rewriting the Nation in Modern Kazakh Literature*, Lanham, MD: Lexington Books.

Kudaibergen, D.T., 2024. *The Kazakh Spring: Digital Activism and the Challenge to Dictatorship*, Cambridge: Cambridge University Press.

Kudaibergenova, D.T., 2016a. 'The Archaeology of Nationalizing Regimes in the Post-Soviet Space: Narratives, Elites, and Minorities', *Problems of Post-communism*, 64(6): pp. 342–55.

Kudaibergenova, D.T., 2016b. 'The Use and Abuse of Postcolonial Discourses in Post-independent Kazakhstan', *Europe-Asia Studies*, 68(5), pp. 917–35.

Kudaibergenova, D.T., 2018. 'Punk Shamanism, Revolt and Break-up of Traditional Linkage: The Waves of Cultural Production in Post-Soviet Kazakhstan', *European Journal of Cultural Studies*, 21(4), pp. 435–451.

Kudaibergenova, D.T., 2019. 'Compartmentalized Ideology and Nation-Building in Non-democratic States', *Communist and Post-communist Studies*, 52(3), pp. 247–57.

Kudaibergenova, D.T., 2020. *Toward Nationalizing Regimes: Conceptualizing Power and Identity in the Post-Soviet Realm*, Pittsburgh, PA: University of Pittsburgh Press.

Kudaibergenova, D.T., 2022. 'Art and Protest in Kazakhstan', *Current History*, 121(837), pp. 271–6.

Kudaibergenova, D.T. and Laruelle, M., 2022. 'Making Sense of the January 2022 Protests in Kazakhstan: Failing Legitimacy, Culture of Protests, and Elite Readjustments', *Post-Soviet Affairs*, 38(6): pp. 441–59.

Kuscu, I., 2008. 'Kazakhstan's Oralman Project: A Remedy for Ambiguous Identity?', PhD diss., Indiana University.

Kyzylbayev, A.T., 2016. 'Stone Figures: Great Monuments in the Steppe' [Каменные изваяния–величественные памятники в степи], *Редакционная коллегия*, p. 188.

Laitin, D.D., 1998. *Identity in Formation: The Russian-Speaking Populations in the Near Abroad*, Ithaca, NY: Cornell University Press.

Laruelle, M., 2014. 'The Three Discursive Paradigms of State Identity in Kazakhstan', in M.Y. Omelicheva (ed.) *Nationalism and Identity Construction in Central Asia: Dimensions, Dynamics, and Directions*, Lanham, MD: Lexington Books, pp. 1–20.

Laruelle, M., 2021. *Central Peripheries: Nationhood in Central Asia*, London: UCL Press.

Laruelle, M., Royce, D. and Beyssembayev, S., 2019. 'Untangling the Puzzle of "Russia's Influence" in Kazakhstan', *Eurasian Geography and Economics*, 60(2), pp. 211–43.

Lewis, D., 2016. 'Blogging Zhanaozen: Hegemonic Discourse and Authoritarian Resilience in Kazakhstan', *Central Asian Survey*, 35(3), pp. 421–38.

Lillis, J., 2022. *Dark Shadows: Inside the Secret World of Kazakhstan*, London: Bloomsbury.

Marsadolov, L.S., 2019. 'Eastern Balbals and Western Commemorative [Acts] as Important Components of Organising Sacred Space in Pazyryk in Altai' [Восточные балбалы и западные поминальники как важные составные части организации сакрального пространства в Пазырыке на Алтае], *Сохранение и изучение культурного наследия Алтайского края*, 25, pp. 155–62.

Masanov, N., 2002. 'Perceptions of Ethnic and All-National Identity in Kazakhstan', *The Nationalities Question in Post-Soviet Kazakhstan*, 51(7), pp. 47–85.

Medeuova, K.A., 2020. 'Prolonged "Sovietness" and Transformation of Collective Memory: Soviet and Post-Soviet Memorial Complexes in Kazakhstan' [Затянувшаяся 'советскость' и трансформации коллективной памяти: советские и постсоветские мемориальные комплексы в Казахстане], *Новое литературное обозрение*, 1, pp. 256–74.

Medeuova, K.A. and Sandybayeva, U.M., 2018. 'Sacred Geography in Kazakhstan: Commemorative Politics of the State and Local Practices in Public Spaces' [Сакральная география в Казахстане: коммеморативная политика государства и локальные практики в публичных пространствах.] *Мир Большого Алтая*, 4(3), pp. 436–45.

Mesquita, M., 2016. 'Kazakhstan's Presidential Transition and the Evolution of Elite Networks', *Demokratizatsiya: The Journal of Post-Soviet Democratization*, 24(3), pp. 371–97.

Moldabekov, D., 2022. 'Dostoinstvo' [Dignity], 11 January, https://adamdar.ca/post/dostoinstvo/279

Mukanova, Z. and Steenberg, R., 2021. 'Returnees, Blood Relatives or Backwards? Foreign Politics, Stigma and Coloniality in the Debate on How to Call Ethnic Kazakh Immigrants to Kazakhstan', AUGU.

Murphy, J., 2006. 'Illusory Transition? Elite Reconstitution in Kazakhstan, 1989–2002', *Europe-Asia Studies*, 58(4), pp. 523–54.

Nazarbayev, N., 1991. *Bez pravykh i levykh* [Without right and left], Moscow: Molodaya Gvardiya.

Nazarbayev, N., 1993. *Ideinaia konsolidatsiia obshchestva kak uslovie progressa Kazakhstana* [The ideational consolidation of society as a condition of progress in Kazakhstan], Almaty: Foundation for Political Research, Kazakhstan XXI Century.

Nazarbayev, N., 2008. *The Kazakhstan Way*, London: Stacey International.

Nazpary, J., 2002. *Post-Soviet Chaos: Violence and Dispossession in Kazakhstan*, London: Pluto Press.

Ó Beacháin, D. and Kevlihan, R., 2013. 'Threading a Needle: Kazakhstan between Civic and Ethno-nationalist State-Building', *Nations and Nationalism*, 19(2), pp. 337–56.

Peyrouse, S., 2007. 'Nationhood and the Minority Question in Central Asia: The Russians in Kazakhstan', *Europe-Asia Studies*, 59(3), pp. 481–501.

Pianciola, N., 2001. 'The Collectivization Famine in Kazakhstan, 1931–1933', *Harvard Ukrainian Studies*, 25(3/4), pp. 237–51.

Pianciola, N., 2004. 'Famine in the Steppe: The Collectivization of Agriculture and the Kazak Herdsmen 1928–1934', *Cahiers du monde russe*, 45(1–2), pp. 137–92.

Pianciola, N., 2018. 'Ukraine and Kazakhstan: Comparing the Famines', *Contemporary European History*, 27(3), pp. 440–4.

Pianciola, N., 2022. 'Sacrificing the Qazaqs: The Stalinist Hierarchy of Consumption and the Great Famine of 1931–33 in Kazakhstan', *Journal of Central Asian History*, 1(2), pp. 225–72.

BIBLIOGRAPHY

Ponomarev, V. and Dzhukeeva, S. 1993. *Dokymenty i materialy o sobytiyah 1986 goda v Kazakhstane*, Moscow: Panorama.

Rees, K.M. and Williams, N.W., 2017. 'Explaining Kazakhstani Identity: Supraethnic Identity, Ethnicity, Language, and Citizenship', *Nationalities Papers*, 45(5), pp. 815–39.

Rees, K. and Burkhanov, A., 2018. 'Constituting the Kazakhstani Nation: Rhetorical Transformation of National Belonging', *Nationalism and Ethnic Politics*, 24(4), pp. 433–55.

Satpayev, D. and Umbetaliyeva, T., 2015. 'The protests in Zhanaozen and the Kazakh Oil Sector: Conflicting Interests in a Rentier State', *Journal of Eurasian Studies*, 6(2), pp. 122–9.

Schatz, E., 2000. 'The Politics of Multiple Identities: Lineage and Ethnicity in Kazakhstan', *Europe-Asia Studies*, 52(3), pp. 489–506.

Schwab, W., 2015. 'Islam, Fun, and Social Capital in Kazakhstan', *Central Asian Affairs*, 2(1), pp. 51–70.

Senggirbay, M., 2019. 'Ethnic Identity of Kazakhstani Russians: The Dynamics of Change and the Place of Russia as a Kin State', *Journal of Nationalism, Memory & Language Politics*, 13(1), pp. 67–89.

Shakhanov, M., 1990. 'Zheltoqsan Report', Alma-Ata: n.p.

Sharipova, D., Burkhanov, A. and Alpeissova, A., 2017. 'The Determinants of Civic and Ethnic Nationalisms in Kazakhstan: Evidence from the Grass-Roots Level', *Nationalism and Ethnic Politics*, 23(2), pp. 203–26.

Shoshanova, S., 2024. 'The Asharshylyq in Contemporary and Public Art of Kazakhstan: The Politics of Commemorating the Kazakh Famine of the 1930s', *History & Memory*, 36(1), pp. 45–82.

Silova, I., Yaqub, M.M. and Palandjian, G., 2014. 'Pedagogies of Space: (Re)mapping National Territories, Borders, and Identities in Post-Soviet Textbooks', in J.H. Williams (ed.) *(Re)Constructing Memory: School Textbooks and the Imagination of the Nation*, Leiden: Brill, pp. 103–28.

Smagulova, J., 2008. 'Language Policies of Kazakhization and Their Influence on Language Attitudes and Use', *International Journal of Bilingual Education and Bilingualism*, 11(3–4), pp. 440–75.

Smith, G., 1989. 'Gorbachev's Greatest Challenge: Perestroika and the National Question', *Political Geography Quarterly*, 8(1), pp. 7–20.

Smith, G., 1998. *Nation-Building in the Post-Soviet Borderlands: The Politics of National Identities*, Cambridge: Cambridge University Press.

Sorbello, P., 2021. 'Industrial Relations in Kazakhstan's Oil Sector (1991–2019)', PhD diss., University of Glasgow.

Spehr, S. and Kassenova, N., 2012. 'Kazakhstan: Constructing Identity in a Post-Soviet Society', *Asian Ethnicity*, 13(2), pp. 135–51.

Stalin, J., 1942. *On the National Question*, London: Lawrence & Wishart.

Suny, R.G., 1993. *The Revenge of the Past: Nationalism, Revolution, and the Collapse of the Soviet Union*, Stanford: Stanford University Press.

Suny, R.G., 1999. 'Provisional Stabilities: The Politics of Identities in Post-Soviet Eurasia', *International Security*, 24(3), pp. 139–78.

Suny, R.G., 2001. 'The Empire Strikes Out: Imperial Russia, "National" Identity, and Theories of Empire', in R.G. Suny and T. Martin (eds) *A State of Nations: Empire and Nation-Making in the Age of Lenin and Stalin*, Oxford: Oxford University Press, pp. 23–66.

Suny, R.G. and Martin, T. (eds), 2001. *A State of Nations: Empire and Nation-Making in the Age of Lenin and Stalin*, Oxford: Oxford University Press.

Surucu, C., 2002. 'Modernity, Nationalism, Resistance: Identity Politics in Post-Soviet Kazakhstan', *Central Asian Survey*, 21(4), pp. 385–402.

Tishkov, V., 1996. *Ethnicity, Nationalism and Conflict in and after the Soviet Union: The Mind Aflame*, London: Sage.

Tlostanova, M., 2018. *What Does It Mean to Be Post-Soviet? Decolonial Art from the Ruins of the Soviet Empire*, Durham, NC: Duke University Press.

Tolstukhin, D., 1987. 'Obshetvennoe mnenie naselenia KazSSR' [Public opinions of the KazSSR population], Archive of the First President of Kazakhstan Holdings, Almaty, Kazakhstan.

Turaeva, R., 2022. 'Propiska Regime Regulating Mobility and Migration in Post-Soviet Cities', *Cities*, 121, p. 103478.

Tutumlu, A., 2019. 'Governmentalization of the Kazakhstani State: Between Governmentality and Neopatrimonial Capitalism', *Theorizing Central Asian Politics: The State, Ideology and Power*, Cham: Palgrave Macmillan, pp. 43–64.

Tutumlu, A. and Imyarova, Z., 2021. 'The Kazakhstani Soviet Not? Reading Nazarbayev's Kazakhstani-ness through Brezhnev's Soviet People', *Central Asian Survey*, 40(3), pp. 400–19.

Tutumlu, A and Imyarova, Z., 2023. 'Pogroms in Post-Nazarbayev's Kazakhstan', Oxus Society for Central Asian Affairs.

Utegenov, T. and Zeinabin, T., 1991. *Alma-Ata, 1986, dekabr': Kniga-khronika* [Alma-Ata 1986 December chronology], Alma-Ata: Kollegiia Audarma.

Verdery, K., 1996. *What Was Socialism, and What Comes Next?*, Princeton: Princeton University Press.

Yessenova, S., 2003. 'The Politics and Poetics of the Nation: Urban Narratives of Kazakh Identity', PhD diss., McGill University.

Yessenova, S., 2009. *The Politics and Poetics of the Nation: Urban Narratives of Kazakh Identity*, LAP Lambert Academic Publishing: n.p.

Zardykhan, Z., 2004. 'Russians in Kazakhstan and Demographic Change: Imperial Legacy and the Kazakh Way of Nation Building', *Asian Ethnicity*, 5(1), pp. 61–79.

Zhandayeva, R. and Rosenberg, R., 2022. 'Kazakhstan's Bloody January: Digital Repression on the "New Silk Road"', Toda Peace Institute, Policy Brief no. 140.

Zimovina, E. 2017. 'Ethnic Aspect of Social-Demographic Processes on the Eve and during the Perestroika Period', *Vestnik Moskovskogo universiteta*, 2(21), pp. 77–109.

INDEX

Abai Kunanbaiuly, 131, 166, 194
Abdybayev Zarpen, 77
Activist platforms, 171
Aiganym Mukhametzhan, 140
Aigerim Tleuzhan, 165, 166
Aikorkem Meldekhan, 169
Airport attack, 170
Ak Orda, 22, 33, 144, 161, 172
Akezhan Kazhegeldin, 45
Akhmet Baitursynov, 32
Akimat, 51, 148, 149, 156, 165
Aktau, 49–51, 143–145, 171
Aleksandr Solzhenitsyn, 117
Alexey Skalozubov, 94
Alikhan Bokeikhanov, 32
Alima Bissenova, 123
Alma-Ata protests, 16, 34, 40, 59–64, 67, 69, 73–75, 77–78, 80–81, 83, 87–89, 153, 207, 211–215, 222
Almagul Menlibayeva, 31, 32, 36, 193, 206, 223
Almaty, 14, 16, 19, 21–23, 28, 31, 34, 36, 37, 44, 51, 56, 76, 79, 85, 100, 101, 112, 115–116, 119, 123, 124, 127, 128, 130, 131, 145, 148–153, 155–156, 159, 160, 163, 165, 168–173, 175–176, 186, 190–192, 194, 200, 201, 204, 206–208, 211, 212, 216–221, 223–228
Altyn Adam, 21
Ana tili, 121
Anglophone, 138
Anomie, 7, 201
Anti-nuclear, 39, 40, 43, 66
Anti-regime, 49, 58, 159
Anuar Dyussenbinov, 192, 221, 229
Apparatchik, 6, 44, 53, 79
Aqtaban Shubyryndy, 153
Archaeological, 21, 22, 24, 204, 217
Argyn tribe, 93
Arman Zhuman, 170
Asharshylyq 13, 20, 21, 24, 25–29, 31, 125, 153, 204
Askhat Akhmediyarov, 190, 192, 206, 223
Aspan Gallery, 190, 192
Asphalt Kazakhs, 121
Assel Tutumlu, 174, 183, 228
Assem Zhapisheva, 18, 181, 223
Assembly of the People of Kazakhstan (ANK), 44, 105

INDEX

Astana, 19, 29, 32, 38, 52, 123, 132, 144, 172, 186, 188, 204, 206, 209, 223, 225, 226
Atyrau, 14, 93, 147, 158, 159
Auezov theatre, 147
Aul, 26, 27, 30, 31, 38, 129, 140, 141, 205
Authoritarian, 6, 8, 12, 13, 16, 32, 44, 47, 98, 116, 141, 144, 147, 154, 159, 160, 169, 172, 175, 178, 184, 185, 187, 189, 201, 206, 223
Avtozak, 168
Az IYa, 40, 134

Bakhytzhan Sagintayev, 147
Bakhytzhan Toregozhina, 54
Baku, 81
Balbals, 23, 24, 205
Baltic states, 105, 117, 199
Barakholka, 128
Barrack psychology, 84
Bekbosynov, A, 74
Bekbotayev's cradle, 32
Belarus, 169, 226
Berik Asylov, 173
Beszhan Toleubekuly, 167
Bilingual, 11, 18, 46, 48, 116, 131, 194, 221, 223
Bisenbayev, 75
Bishimbayev trial, 189
Blizzard, 63, 71, 74, 76, 80, 81, 85
Bloody January 2022 protests, 17, 20, 58, 85, 130, 145, 155, 164, 169, 173, 174, 177, 182, 185, 191, 204, 220, 227
Borat Sagdiyev, 11
Brezhnev Square, 61–63, 70, 75, 76, 86, 87, 156, 163

Catherine Alexander, 127

Central Asian, 14, 15, 60, 97, 107, 112, 114, 120, 140, 177, 195, 200, 203, 213, 219, 224
Central Kazakhstan, 34
Chechen traditions, 108
Chingiz Aitmatov, 120
Citizens' rights, 178
Citizenship, 11, 102, 115
Civic culture, 9, 146, 155
Civic identity, 8, 9, 12, 101, 146, 155, 159
Civic nationalism, 9, 191
Civic–ethnic divide, 9
Civic-minded activists, 159
Civicness, 9, 17, 154, 160, 163, 179, 182, 191, 197
Civil society, 154, 189, 190
Coalition against Torture, 158
Collective farms, 35
Collectivisation, 20, 31, 34, 35
Colonial division 124, 130, 141
Colonial past 131, 140
Colonial war, 17, 196
Colonialism, 10, 16, 69, 78, 81, 86, 98, 120, 131, 203
Communism, 55, 121, 138
Communist, 6, 12, 55, 70, 134, 135, 136, 202, 211, 212, 214
Communist Party of Kazakhstan (CPK), 6, 9, 59, 62, 63, 64, 70, 81, 82, 84, 165, 212
Communist Party of the USSR, 61
Contemporary Kazakhstan, 16, 23, 94, 116, 131
Crimea, 29, 32, 114, 117, 118, 138, 199, 219
Cult of personality 182, 187
Cultural diversity, 106
Cultural elites, 5, 117, 207
cultural heritage, 38
Cyrillic, 27, 55, 205

INDEX

Daniyar Moldabekov, 175, 228
December 1986 protests, 16, 20, 21, 40, 43, 53, 57, 59–86 *see* Alma-Ata protests
Decolonial, 15, 17, 55, 56, 58, 116, 117, 122, 134, 140, 141, 181, 185, 186, 190, 192, 199, 206, 221, 223, 229
Decolonisation, 131, 140, 181, 191
Decolonising, 138, 181, 182, 189, 190
Democratic Choice of Kazakhstan, 45, 188
Democratisation, 11, 17, 80, 86, 94, 146, 150, 151
Demoscope, 154
de-Nazarbayefication, 18, 181, 189, 196
Dictatorship, 7, 8, 10, 11, 41, 43, 102, 146, 149, 169, 189, 190
Digital ethnography, 12
Dikiy Arman, 172
Dimash Kudaibergen, 194
Dinmukhamed Kunayev, 59, 60, 63, 64, 65, 88, 211, 212, 213, 214
Discourses, 16, 20, 203
Discrimination, 10, 17, 95, 97, 123, 126, 128, 138, 140, 182, 200, 209
Divide and rule, 3, 12, 187
Dmitry Tolstukhin, 87, 90, 217
Domestic violence, 14, 15, 122, 161, 178, 179, 189, 229
Donbas, 18, 42
druzhba narodov, 90
druzhinniki, 62, 68
Dungans, 183, 184

Eastern Kazakhstan, 38, 47, 99, 109, 219, 220

Eduard Limonov, 117
Ekibastuz, 17, 161
Elbasy, 46, 183
Elena Kostyuchenko, 52, 210
Erbolat Dosayev, 176
Ermukhamet Shilibayev, 165
Ernest Gellner, 54
Esimde, 140, 224
Ethnic backgrounds, 110, 187
Ethnic cleavages, 58
Ethnic colouring, 17
Ethnic conflict, 3, 4, 42, 78, 96, 98, 101, 106, 160, 182, 184, 224
Ethnic connotations, 124
Ethnic cultural centres, 99
Ethnic currency, 196
Ethnic differences, 12
Ethnic discrimination, 97
Ethnic diversity, 160, 82
Ethnic divisions, 3, 9, 17, 60, 90, 91, 97
Ethnic groups, 3, 4, 10, 11, 55, 57, 58, 86, 96–99, 102, 103, 106, 124, 132, 182, 184, 195, 196, 207, 218, 219
Ethnic hierarchies, 97
Ethnic identity, 12, 92, 101, 195
Ethnic Kazakhs, 1, 3, 20, 24, 43, 48, 50, 60, 61, 66, 69, 77, 78, 83, 86, 87, 88, 89, 91, 92, 93, 95, 96, 98, 110, 115, 124, 125, 126, 130, 132, 146, 183, 201, 211
Ethnic majority, 146
Ethnic minorities, 3, 92, 98, 100, 146, 182, 183, 224
Ethnic questions, 5
Ethnic recognitions, 55
Ethnic Russians, 13, 44, 58, 66, 77, 78, 86, 87, 88, 91, 92, 93,

243

INDEX

95, 96, 99, 100, 101, 105, 108, 109, 125, 137, 200
Ethnicity, 3, 17, 20, 110, 160, 196
Ethnocultural group, 9
Ethnocultural makeup, 10
Ethnographic study, 128
Ethno-Kazakh, 44
Ethnonationalism, 55
Ethnonationalist, 15, 43, 78, 98, 146
Ethnonationalist conflicts, 98
Ethno-nationalist groups, 98
Euromaidan, 104
External policing, 13

Famine *see* Asharshylyq
Fifth paragraph, 4, 27, 96
Fillip Goloshekin, 36, 66
Flamingo dance, 186
Floods, 14, 15
Food shortages, 176
FOURTH ZHUZ, 87–118, 217
Francine Hirsh, 97
Francophone, 138

G. Elemisov, 75
Gendered violence, 189
Generation 'P', 188
Genghis Khan, 22
Gennady Kolbin, 60, 61, 63, 64, 65, 67, 68, 69, 71, 73, 74, 78, 79, 80, 81, 82, 83, 84, 91, 92, 211, 213, 214, 216, 217
Gen-Z Kazakhstanis, 130
Gerold Belger, 139, 205, 224
Glasnost, 68
Globalised economy, 129
Golden Horde, 91
Golden Square, 37
Gorbachev, 6, 59, 60, 68, 70, 78, 79, 89, 213, 215

gosudarstvo Kazakhstan, 43
Governance, 17, 49, 94, 98, 160, 161, 178, 188
Gramota, 135
Gulagisation, 29
Gulags, 28, 30, 32, 36, 37, 38, 40, 157

Hierarchical relations, 186
History of the Kazakh SSR, 91
Holodomor, 25, 26, 31
Human palm, 21
Human trauma, 28
Hybrid identities, 10, 119, 132

Identities, 3, 10, 11, 15, 17, 51, 56, 57, 58, 86, 93, 95, 96, 98, 100, 101, 110, 117, 118, 119, 132, 189, 202
ideological stability, 188
Ilyas Esenberlin, 91
Imangali Tasmagambetov, 83, 212
Imperial collapse, 4, 120, 132
Inequality, 16, 144, 147, 148, 178, 182, 184
Institute of Cossackness, 99
Interethnic affairs, 101
Interethnic balance, 68
Interethnic communication, 89, 93, 201
Interethnic conflict, 3, 4, 42, 78, 96, 98, 101, 182, 184
Interethnic divisions, 90
Interethnic harmony, 47, 89, 182
Interethnic policies, 102, 126, 219
Interethnic relations, 17, 80, 87, 89, 105, 217
Interethnic stability, 42, 44, 102, 104, 182, `183
Inter-ethnic tensions, 160
Interethnic violence, 62

INDEX

International Partnership for Human Rights, 158
Internationalism, 36, 37, 47, 77, 78, 90
Irina Kairatovna, 131
Issyk, 21, 22, 24, 25, 31
Issyk museum, 23

Joseph Stalin, 11, 25, 27, 28, 29, 30, 32, 33, 35, 36, 37, 38, 40, 134, 157, 184, 229
Journalistic investigations, 173
Juldyz Smagulova, 132

Kabden Essengari, 39
Kairat Ryskulbekov, 67
Kalas Nurpeisov, 165
Kamalidenov
Kanat Kabdrakhmanov, 123
Karaganda, 32, 33, 36, 38, 44, 102, 104, 215, 219, 220
Karakemer, 183
Karazhanbasmunai, 49, 210
Karim Massimov, 50, 151, 154, 209, 210
KARLAG, 32, 36, 206
Kashgar, 4
Kassym-Jomart Tokayev, 18, 41, 52, 93, 145, 147, 150, 51, 152, 154, 163, 165, 170, 171, 172, 174, 183, 187, 209, 224, 225, 226
Kazakh accent, 113
Kazakh activism, 94
Kazakh Communist Party, 61, 62, 63, 64
Kazakh Constitution, 21
Kazakh decolonisation, 131
Kazakh Dream, 6
Kazakh flag, 14, 32
Kazakh history, 30, 41, 85, 91, 116

Kazakh intellectuals, 32
Kazakh literature, 113, 206
Kazakh language, 5, 16, 28, 43, 45, 53, 56, 61, 93, 95, 96, 106, 116, 117, 125, 131, 132, 138, 139, 181, 205, 223
Kazakh-language rallies, 144
Kazakh-language speaking clubs, 189
Kazakh nationalism, 47, 87, 91
Kazakh nationalists, 43, 48, 62, 87
Kazakh national-patriots, 20, 28, 45, 55, 86, 94, 207, 218
Kazakh oil booms, 127
Kakh parliament, 189
Kazakh population, 61, 88, 89, 128
Kazakh Russian, 139
Kazakh society, 81, 92, 93, 94, 120, 140, 177, 185
Kazakh song, 30, 61
Kazakh statehood, 29
Kazakh steppe, 12, 23, 28, 35
Kazakh tradition, 23
Kazakh translations, 129
Kazakh values, 28, 123
Kazakh woman, 5, 52, 76, 134, 135
Kazakh workers, 128
Kazakh Writers' Union, 36
Kazakhness, 16, 56, 106, 123, 131, 139
Kazakhophone, 55, 94, 125, 129, 131, 138, 185, 218, 222, 223
Kazakh-speaking communities, 10, 89, 129
Kazakh-speaking groups, 17
Kazakhstan 2030, 48
Kazakhstan International Bureau for Human Rights, 158
Kazakhstani cities, 112, 116, 127, 175, 182

245

INDEX

Kazakhstani citizens, 39, 48, 53, 155, 159, 178, 203
Kazakhstani diaspora, 179
Kazakhstani identity, 10, 20, 103, 141, 179
Kazakhstani public, 60, 184
Kazakhstani Qazaqs, 57
Kazakhstani Russian, 57, 86, 92, 93, 95, 96, 101, 107, 113, 117, 200, 220
Kazakhstani society, 9, 11, 16, 18, 20, 58, 86, 141, 146, 178, 189, 196, 228
Kazakhstaniness, 197
Kerei, 29
KGB, 16, 62, 63, 66, 67, 68, 69, 71, 74, 77, 79, 81, 83, 91, 212, 213, 214, 216
Kimdik, 20, 54, 56, 57
Kishi Qazaq, 117, 197
KNB, 183
Komsomol, 80, 83, 134, 135, 136
Kordai, 183, 184
korennoi almatinets, 69, 131
korennoi zhitel, 130
Krymbek Kusherbayev, 50
kualik, 193
Kuandyk Bishimbayev, 12, 188, 229
Kudaibergen(ova), 26, 27, 30, 194, 199, 202, 203, 206, 210, 211, 219, 222, 224, 225, 229, 230
Kulak, 27
Kulshat Medeuova, 132, 205
Kurgans, 22
KVN, 113
Kyrgyzstan, 93, 120, 150, 171, 183, 200, 226, 228
Kyzyl Orda, 19, 131, 147

labour disputes, 49
Lenin(ist), 61, 64, 68, 70, 72, 74, 78, 80, 133, 134, 135, 137, 176, 194, 229
Leonid Brezhnev, 66, 148, 219
Llinguistic discrimination, 10, 95
Linguistic distinctions, 117
Linguistic divisions, 94
Linguistic hierarchies, 129
Linguistic switching, 185
Literacy, 7
LPG prices, 144, 145, 177, 178
Luhansk People's Republics, 18
Lyazzat Asanova, 67, 74, 81

Madina Baideldinovna, 122, 134, 136
Madina Tlostanova, 56, 181, 186, 200, 223, 228
Mambets, 11, 119, 121, 123, 124, 126, 138, 139, 140, 141, 178, 221, 222
Mangilik El, 45, 52, 188, 210
Mangystau region, 145
Mankurt Dreams, 140
Mankurtisation, 140
Mankurtizer, 140
Mankurts, 11, 17, 119, 121, 128, 129, 130, 138, 139, 140, 141, 221
Marlene Laruelle, 122
Marshrutka, 24, 101
Masa, 126
Mashas, 1
Mass migration, 127, 217
Mass mobilisation, 108, 109, 112
Mass protests, 9, 17, 53, 111, 119, 143, 145, 150, 153, 157, 171, 225
Memes, 187
Mendybayev, 80
metis, 195
mezhnatsional'noe, 42

INDEX

Migrants, 24, 112, 114, 116, 128, 218, 219, 221, 222
Mikhail Gorbachev, 59, 60, 68, 70, 78, 79, 80, 213, 215
Mikhail Solomentsev, 61, 63, 80, 83, 89, 212, 213
Minsk, 138
Mirzoyan, 66
Mixed Kazakhs, 17
Mixed linguistic reality, 185
Modernisation, 12
Moldanazar, 131
Moldir Kabylova, 188
mono-Kazakh speakers, 129
Monument, 21, 24, 25, 28, 29, 46, 52, 53, 71, 82, 84, 132, 133, 151, 152, 154, 157, 163, 164, 165, 176, 204, 217, 225, 226
Morozov, 65
Moscow 15, 83, 106, 107, 132, 138
Moscow elites, 9, 59, 70, 80, 213
Moscow leadership 17, 35, 62, 63, 68, 69, 71, 87, 89, 90, 91, 211, 212
Mukhtar Shakhanov, 44, 67, 72, 74, 83, 85, 94, 212, 214, 215
Multicultural neighbourhood, 194
Multiculturalism, 87, 106
Multi-ethnic, 1, 7, 38, 45, 78, 98, 106, 132, 160, 182, 184, 187, 194, 195
Multilingual, 13, 14, 15, 56, 106, 139
multiversal identity, 197
Murat Auezov, 40, 205, 207
Murat Kalmataev, 82
Museum, 21, 22, 23, 24, 28, 31, 32, 33, 38, 82, 133, 136, 163, 204, 205, 206
muzhitskii dozhd, 112

M.word, 119, 120, 122, 125, 140, 141, 222
Myrzhaqyp Dulatov 32

N. Bereshev, 73
nasha voin, 111, 112, 221
Natalya Sokolova, 49
National anthem, 145
National identity, 1, 3, 4, 8, 9, 10, 16, 19, 20, 21, 45, 55, 145, 151, 187, 188, 189
National imagination, 145
National Museum, 23, 32, 33, 205, 206
National trauma, 16
Nationalism, 9, 12, 13, 20, 36, 44, 47, 57, 87, 91, 104, 121, 191, 196, 220
National-patriots, 20, 28, 44, 45, 55, 86, 94, 139, 207, 218
Nation-building, 9, 10, 11, 13, 20, 21, 43, 45, 47, 48, 53, 55, 68, 84, 85, 86, 98, 106, 181, 197, 199, 207, 219
Nation-state, 15, 44, 48, 54
navedem poryadok, 65
NursultanNazarbayev, 3, 6, 7, 8, 9, 10, 12, 13, 16, 18, 19, 20, 21, 23, 29, 32, 38, 41, 42, 43, 44, 45, 46, 47, 48, 49, 50, 52, 53, 58, 60, 62, 64, 65, 70, 71, 74, 80, 81, 82, 83, 84, 92, 93, 96, 98, 102, 104, 106, 118, 124, 125, 131, 134, 135, 146, 147, 149, 151, 152, 154, 157, 164, 168, 171, 172, 173, 174, 181, 182, 183, 184, 185, 186, 187, 188, 189, 190, 191, 196, 197, 201, 202, 203, 204, 207, 208, 209, 211, 212, 213, 214, 216, 219, 224, 225, 228, 229, 230

INDEX

Nazarbayevite slogans, 182
Neftyaniki, 50
nepolnotsennii Kazakh, 139
Nevada-Semipalatinsk, 38, 40, 41, 42, 43, 66
New Kazakhstan, 8, 52, 116, 141, 170, 172, 193
NKVD, 32
Nomadic geography, 24
Nomadic societies, 12
Nomads, 20, 25, 30, 31, 34, 35, 36, 109
non-Kazakh, 45, 48, 56, 94, 95, 108, 214
non-Russian, 86, 94, 97, 107, 125, 126, 199, 200, 221
non-urbanite communities, 128
Northern Kazakhstan, 101, 107, 109, 117, 157, 217, 219, 220
Northerners, 96
Novosibirsk, 72, 109
Nuclear testing, 20, 21, 39, 41 see Semipalatinsk Polygon
Nuray, 169
Nurlan Dalibayev, 165
Nurlan Nogayev, 145
Nur-Otan, 151, 185, 187
Nur-Sultan, 19, 225

OGPU, 36
oil sector, 144
Oksikbai, 26
Oleg Miroshkhin, 64
Olzhas Baidildinov, 144
Olzhas Khudaibergenov, 188
Olzhas Suleimenov, 40, 41, 42, 66, 134, 207
Online campaign, 178
Operation Blizzard, 73, 74, 76, 80, 81, 85

Opinion polls, 95, 99, 173, 177, 182, 229
Opposition, 13, 28, 44, 45, 46, 49, 50, 51, 65, 78, 84, 85, 94, 146, 147, 154, 159, 173, 203, 204, 207, 214, 218, 224, 225
Oral city, 99, 102, 105, 112, 219, 220
Oralman, 50, 115, 124, 125, 126, 129, 209
Ordinary citizens, 6, 12, 51, 143, 144, 179, 182, 185, 196, 197
Ordinary Kazakhstanis, 16, 171, 172, 197
Orusskii, 117, 197
Oskemen city, 99, 105, 113, 158, 220
overturned kazans, 190
Oyan, Qazaqstan, movement 85, 86, 146, 147, 166, 181
Ozenmunaigas, 49, 51, 52, 210

Paolo Sorbello, 144
Parallel communities' paradigm, 185
Parliamentary elections, 172
Pavlodar, 14, 92, 93, 101, 103, 105, 219, 220
Perestroika, 57, 64, 68, 69, 70, 80, 83, 90, 91, 212, 217
pink flamingos, 186
pogrom, 183, 184
Police brutality, 15, 150, 174
Police mistreatment, 173
Police torture chambers, 16
Policymakers, 187
Politburo, 6, 61, 63, 80, 89, 90, 213
Political decision-makers, 16
political elite, 6, 10, 11, 12, 18, 43, 55, 70, 98, 189, 197, 201, 202, 208

INDEX

Political engagement, 146
Political parties, 144
political transformation, 145
Polygon, 13, 38, 39, 40, 91 *see* Semipalatinsk
Polylingual group, 138
Population, 6, 9, 25, 28, 39, 43, 60, 61, 69, 78, 88, 89, 90, 93, 96, 97, 99, 114, 122, 125, 127, 128, 131, 171, 207, 208, 217, 219, 229
Post-independence Kazakhstan, 8, 13, 20, 120, 133, 135, 136, 229
Post-independence period, 83, 85, 86, 119, 135, 159, 206
Post-January identity, 154
Post-national society, 55
post-Nazarbayev era, 42, 188, 189
post-postsoviet identity 187
Postsoviet, 1, 5, 8, 9, 15, 17, 18, 37, 50, 54, 55, 56, 67, 92, 95, 97, 98, 101, 105, 117, 120, 122, 131, 133, 135, 138, 141, 163, 181, 182, 187, 188, 189, 196, 200, 202, 205, 208
Post-traumatic future, 178
post-war Kazakhstan, 100
Ppotential secessionism, 47
Power dynamics, 10
Presidential administration, 9, 33, 45, 207, 209
Presidential power, 197
Propiska, 60, 89, 127, 215
pro-Russian, 44
protest culture, 145
pro-Ukraine, 175, 176
Public response 17
Puppet bureaucrats, 187

qandas, 50, 124, 125, 209
Qandy Qantar (Bloody January), 17, 53, 54, 58, 153, 155, 156, 159, 165, 170, 171, 172, 174, 190, 191, 192
Qazaq, 5, 8, 11, 13, 14, 16, 20, 52, 55, 56, 57, 58, 85, 86, 94, 9, 111, 116, 117, 121, 125, 129, 130, 131, 139, 140, 185, 197, 205, 206,
Qazaqstan, 52, 85, 86, 146, 147, 152, 166, 170, 171, 181

Rabskoe chvanstvo, 123
Racism, 38, 182
Rally, 14, 15, 28, 40, 49, 56, 60, 62, 65, 69, 70, 80, 84, 116, 143, 144, 146, 147, 159, 164, 166, 167, 170, 171, 172, 175, 176, 179, 215, 216
Red propaganda, 55
Red Terror, 41
Regime elites, 185, 197
Regime–society relations, 12, 131, 154
Remaining in January, 178
Remembrance Day, 29, 30, 33
Repatriation programme, 125
Republican Slavic Movement(LAD), 99
Riga, 81
Rigid groupness, 96
Riot police, 71, 72, 77, 78, 79, 81, 148, 190
Rukhani Zhangyru, 45, 188, 228
Russian culture, 139
Rural economy, 128
Rural population, 122, 127
Russian aggression, 176
Russian colonialism, 98, 120
Russian communities, 47, 99, 229
Russian identity, 92
Russian imperialism, 18, 42

249

INDEX

Russian imperialists, 117
Russian invasion, 16, 95
Russian language, 89, 90, 93, 108, 116, 117, 139
Russian oppression, 40
Russian propaganda, 18, 104, 108, 112, 114, 177
Russian roubles, 109, 110, 220
Russian–Kazakh divisions, 117
Russian–Kazakh relations, 57
Russianness, 92, 101, 108, 111, 117, 118
Russians, 9, 10, 13, 34, 44, 48, 52, 57, 58, 76, 77, 78, 86, 87, 88, 90, 91, 92, 93, 94, 95, 96, 97, 98, 99, 100, 101, 102, 103, 104, 105, 106, 107, 108, 109, 111, 112, 113, 114, 116, 117, 118, 121, 122, 125, 126, 137, 182, 184, 200, 207, 217, 218, 219, 220, 221
Russification, 10, 12, 34, 43, 89, 119, 121, 126, 138
Russo-English speech, 57
Russo-Kazakh border, 112
Russo-Kazakh culture, 41
Russo-Kazakh divide, 21, 96
Russo-Kazakh relations, 87
Russophone, 11, 61, 93, 94, 101, 125, 129, 131, 138, 177, 201, 208

Sabira Mukhamedzhanova, 67, 74
Sabit Mukanov, 36
acha Baron Cohen, 11
Sagimbayeva G, 76
Salamat Mukashev, 64
Saltanat Nukenova, 14, 15, 58, 161, 178, 188, 189
Samrat, 190
Samruk-Kazyna, 50

Sary-Arka park, 176
Sarzhal, 39
Saule Suleimenova, 190, 191, 206, 223
Saulesh Yessenova, 127, 128, 141, 201, 222
Security Council, 183
Seitkulov family, 169
Self-determination, 61, 68
Self-discrimination, 140
Self-identification, 34, 57, 99, 118
Semey, 13, 102, 105, 113, 219, 220
Semipalatinsk, 20, 21, 38, 39, 40, 41, 42, 43, 66, 113, 115
settler colonialism, 10, 69, 78, 81, 86
shala, 17, 55, 121, 130, 139
Shaman, 122
Shanyraq, 127
Shestidesyatniki, movement, 41
Shetpe, 52
Shu, 141
Shymkent, 115
Slav nationality, 113
Slavic organisations, 47
Slavs, 10, 113, 114
Slovo o Polku Igoreve, 40
Slur, 97, 119, 120, 122, 128, 140, 141, 182, 222
Social and economic inequality, 144
Social dynamics, 10
Social engagements, 161
Social media chats, 171
Social movements, 13, 44, 98
Social order, 149
Societal identity, 57
Socio-cultural environment, 55
Socio-economic crises, 160
Socio-lingual communities, 90, 100

INDEX

SOS Taldykol, 186
South Kazakhstan, 135
Southerners, 96
Soviet citizens, 5, 206
Soviet colonisation, 37, 43, 119, 125, 131, 134, 141
Soviet cosmopolitanism, 121
Soviet elite, 80, 117
Soviet era, 27, 36, 156, 193
Soviet future, 134
Soviet internationalism, 47, 77
Soviet Kazakhstan, 6, 16, 40, 53, 59, 74, 86, 89, 91, 93, 205, 212
Soviet legacy, 17, 132, 133, 134, 136, 181
Soviet nationality, 55, 58, 62, 68
Soviet passport, 127, 136, 137, 193
Soviet period, 1, 8, 20, 26, 29, 37, 47, 66, 96, 101, 128, 134, 138, 166, 188, 206
Soviet politics, 60
Soviet rouble, 1, 135
Soviet rule, 17, 26, 55, 126, 133
Soviet Union, 4, 5, 6, 7, 11, 19, 25, 27, 36, 37, 38, 41, 43, 48, 53, 83, 89, 90, 91, 96, 97, 98, 132, 134, 135, 136, 137, 138, 177, 199, 200, 205
Sovietness, 5, 37, 121, 132, 133, 137, 138, 164, 184, 187, 193, 200
Soviets, 3, 27, 29, 35, 36, 37, 38, 40, 55, 58, 96, 98, 134, 187, 194
Stalinist atrocities, 30, 40
Stalinist communication, 28
Stalinist crimes, 29, 206
Stalinist language reforms, 27
Stalinist projects, 11
Stalinist repression, 36
Stalinnik, 37
State identity 9, 11, 202
State programme, 6, 45, 48, 132, 170, 188, 190, 207, 210, 228
State propaganda, 150, 160, 172, 173
State violence, 159
State-building, 6
Statehood, 15, 20, 29, 138, 197, 218
State–society relations, 174
Stazhirovka, 188
Steppe, 12, 15, 19, 22, 23, 26, 28, 30, 31, 34, 35, 36, 39, 91, 157, 197, 217
Stigmatisation, 125, 126
suinbike Suleimenova, 190, 223

Taldykol lakes, 186
Taldyqorgan, 145, 152, 157, 158, 160, 169, 172, 225
Taraz, 145, 227
Tatar, 2, 10, 31, 35, 69, 99, 110, 115, 121, 195
Tbilisi, 63, 81
Techeniya, 43
Tekeli, 25
Telegram chats, 112, 171
Tengri shamanistic rituals, 24
Tilek Yrysbek, 126
Timur Kulibayev, 50, 209
Tleuzhan Imanbayev, 75, 76, 215
Togzhan Kassenova, 39
Tolstukhin Committee, 87
Tolstukhin report, 90
Tomsk, 109
Torture, 16, 32, 35, 54, 67, 74, 81, 129, 140, 150, 155, 158, 159, 169, 178, 227
Trauma, 16, 20, 21, 26, 28, 29, 31, 33, 34, 35, 39, 43, 54, 57,

58, 81, 85, 86, 92, 141, 151, 153, 155, 156, 159
165, 174, 175, 178, 189, 190, 191, 224
Tribal conglomerates, 117
Trilingual, 10, 18, 56
trilingual Kazakhstani

Ukraine, 16, 18, 25, 29, 31, 42, 94, 95, 96, 104, 105, 107, 108, 109, 110, 111, 112, 114, 116, 117, 118, 131, 134, 140, 174, 175, 176, 177, 196, 199, 200, 218, 219, 220, 226, 228
Ukrainian, 2, 31, 69, 99, 100, 101, 102, 107, 108, 110, 111, 116, 175, 176, 199, 217, 218, 220, 221
Uralsk, 99, 112 *see* Oral
Urban culture, 128
urban dwellers, 127
urban Kazakhs, 34, 123, 128, 139
urban migrants, 128
urban migration, 61, 122, 123, 127, 201
Ust-Kamenogorsk, 67, 158
Ust-Kamenogorsk Pedagogical Institute, 67
Uyghur, 2, 31, 160, 195

Vigilantes, 62, 68, 71, 72, 78
Vikram Ruzakhunov, 150
Viktor Miroshnik, 68, 83, 216
Vilnius, 81
Vladimir Putin, 32, 96, 108, 112, 114, 115, 116, 117, 175, 176, 177, 218, 222
Violence, 14, 15, 28, 32, 35, 38, 48, 49, 51, 53, 54, 56, 57, 62, 67, 70, 71, 72, 73, 76, 80, 83, 86, 87, 121, 122, 145, 148, 149, 150, 152 153, 154, 155, 156, 158, 159, 160, 161, 169, 170, 172, 173, 174, 175, 178, 179, 183, 186, 189, 190, 205, 208, 224, 229
violent suppression, 86, 171, 21
Virgin Lands campaign, 11, 115, 132, 217
voyenniy bilet, 136
vremennaya propiska, 127

Wagner Group, 108
Wake Up, Kazakhstan, 85
Western Kazakhstan, 49, 143, 144, 145, 146, 147, 158, 171, 210
Wild capitalism, 5
World Organisation against Torture, 158

Yevgeny Prigozhin, 108
Yntymaq Square, 51, 171, 210
Yurt, 22
Yuzhnye, 101

Zagranitsa, 107
Zakash Kamalidenov, 60
Zarina Mukanova, 126, 223
Zemfira, 1, 2
Zhana Qazaqstan 52, 170, 171
Zhan-Aidar Karmenov, 165 144
Zhanaozen protests, 13, 15, 17, 20, 46, 48, 49, 50, 51, 52, 53, 85, 131, 143, 144, 145, 153, 159, 171, 172
Zhanaozen massacre, 53, 159, 172
Zhanbolat Mamay, 147, 154, 224
Zhanibek, 29
Zhas Tulpar, 41, 207
Zheltoqsan protests, 16, 17, 51, 52, 53, 74, 81, 82, 83, 85, 91, 153, 216

INDEX

Zheltoqsanovscy, 81
Zhenskii Pedagogicheskii Institute, 59, 211
Zhetysu, 92
Zhoktau, 30, 190, 206
Zhuzes, 117
Zolotoi Kvadrat, 37
Zugzwang, 48, 49, 208
Zulfiya Imyarova, 183